Becoming
Wordsworthian

A Performative Aesthetics

ELIZABETH A. FAY

The University of Massachusetts Press

Amherst

Becoming

Wordsworthian

Library of Congress Cataloging-in-Publication Data

Fay, Elizabeth A., 1957–
    Becoming Wordsworthian : a performative
aesthetics / Elizabeth A. Fay.
        p.   cm.
    Includes bibliographical references (p.   ) and
index.
    ISBN 0-87023-960-0 (alk. paper)
    1. Wordsworth, William, 1770–1850 —
Aesthetics.   2. Brothers and sisters — England —
History — 19th century.   3. Poets, English — 19th
century — Family relationships.   4. Authorship —
Collaboration — History — 19th century.
5. Wordsworth, Dorothy, 1771–1855 — Aesthetics.
6. Poetry — Authorship — History — 19th
century.   7. Masculinity (Psychology) in
literature.   8. Aesthetics, British — 19th
century.   9. Authorship — Sex differences.
10. Self in literature.   I. Title.
PR5892.A34F39   1995
821'.7 — dc20   94-37565
                                                          CIP

British Library Cataloguing in Publication data
are available.

This book is published with the support and cooperation
of the University of Massachusetts Boston.

Contents

Acknowledgments

⁓

For permission granted for use of manuscripts, and for photographs of pages of Dorothy Wordsworth's "Commonplace Book," DCMS 120 from the Dove Cottage Library, I want to thank the Trustees of the Wordsworth Trust. For their aid in helping me find rare volumes, I want to thank the librarians at the American Antiquarian Society in Worcester, Massachusetts, and the Special Collections of the Margaret Clapp Library of Wellesley College, and especially Jeff Cowton at the Dove Cottage Library.

I owe intellectual debts to many people, but particularly Jerome McGann, Susan Horton, Orrin Way, Peter Manning, Charles Meyer, and Eleanor Fox-Fay. Similarly, I want to acknowledge Alan Liu, Allen Reddick, and Bruce Graver for their helpful input. And I owe a great debt of gratitude to Paul Wright in his capacities as both editor and colleague.

I also want to acknowledge the Romantic Literature and Culture Seminar of the Center for Literary and Cultural Studies at Harvard University for their helpful responses to a section of Chapter 5 in February 1992, and *European Romantic Review* for permission to use "Wordsworth, Women, and Romantic Love: A Question of Nation," *ERR* 3, no. 2 (Winter 1992): 133–46.

Introduction

⁀

*B*ecoming Wordsworthian argues that the Wordsworthian imagination *necessitates the performative.* The performative is not "performance," the artful and artificed role playing often associated
with Byron; nor is it the awareness of the self as a social, and socially symbolic, entity, as for Mme. de Staël or Mary (Wollstone-
craft/Godwin) Shelley. The sense of the term as it will be used
here is also in contradistinction to the linguistic "performative,"
where the agency of the word act creates reality, although this
linguistic function is clearly operative in certain of William
Wordsworth's poetic forms.[1] Indeed, *Becoming Wordsworthian* is
less concerned with Wordsworthian poems — the Lucy poems,
for instance — that call into being their own constitutive reality.
Rather, I will be concerned here with the imaginative impetus
that compels the creation of such poems, as well as others, so
that they appear descriptive rather than performative, remembered rather than enacted, naturalized rather than socialized.

I

"Performative," when it is taken in the sense of the compelling imagination, redresses the issues of constitutive versus descriptive formations by calling into play the sociality of the creative act. To the extent that Wordsworthian genius is socially impacted, it must be understood as doubly gendered, and collaboratively *engendered*. To the extent that this is true, the performative then lies within the romantic sincerity of the Wordsworthian speaker-poet, indeed, within the sincerity of *both* William and Dorothy Wordsworth. Neither of these two artists intentionally acted parts, but both enact interdependently mythic (rather than social or fashionable) roles or scripts because they felt them to be sincere, which is to say affecting.

"Affect" is a term that carries heavy resonance in the Wordsworthian oeuvre, but the affective disposition weighs most heavily with the enacting subject rather than the reader or even textual object of the Wordsworth poem. Most importantly, the affects are what construe "sibling love," that emplotted emotional matrix derived from sentimental fiction that grounds the poetic project which, for the Wordsworths, is the making both of poetic texts *and* of the poetic life. What is affective, what is emplotted, and what is sincere are thus not antithetical but imbricated concepts. The notion of a "Wordsworthian performance" or, even worse, of a performative imperative within what I will term the Wordsworthian aesthetic directly confronts the conventional topos of Wordsworth's romantic sincerity. At the same time it challenges our received notions of who "Wordsworth" is and the very stability by which he presents himself in his poetry. Sincerity connotes immediacy, lack of artifice, a stable selfhood, and a devotion to truth. It divides high art from popular art forms by diverting the self-consciousness of mockery and farce to a self-consciousness of being. Put another way, romantic sincerity is also an aestheticization of the self which takes that aesthetic distillation seriously—so seriously that we do not question its motivations even when, as for many readers of *The Excursion*, we are not comfortable with its intensity and self-absorption.

To apply a more Brechtian awareness of self-enactment to one of the major figures of the romantic period is not to impose anachronistic considerations in order to complicate a simple scenario. Rather, it is to call forth the cultural complexity in which the young William Wordsworth discovered himself poetically and composed himself in order to meet the exigencies of the day. More importantly, such a move allows us to resituate Wordsworth the man against the poet "Wordsworth." *Becoming Words-worthian* argues that the poet, as opposed to the man, is more than William Wordsworth and more than "a man speaking to men." He is at once a performance of himself and two enacting selves: William and Dorothy Wordsworth combined. To claim this is to speak within the larger context of current romanticist scholarship, specifically the debate concerning the role of women writers within romanticism, the relation of sentimental literature and literature of sensibility to High Romanticism, and the ways in which the backlash against a particular movement is carried out on the body of women writers' works. Thus, in the Victorian backlash against eighteenth-century sensibility, key groups associated with feminine intellectual and artistic endeavor such as the Bluestockings and the Della Cruscans, along with their texts, have been lost in subsequent accounts of the period. In forgetting these figures, we can then only consider major writers who seem to have sprung full-blown from their native ground in the terms of genius and originality that such writers have themselves promoted. That is, readers remember William Wordsworth as he has written about his blessed childhood as Nature's priest, even while they forget which authors he was reading as he began to form his mature self.

The Della Cruscans offer an example of the strong impact of sensibility on Georgian culture and poetics, and on the gendering problematic that so complicates the issues of this study. A small circle of literati formed in Florence by Robert Merry under the auspices of Hester Thrale Piozzi, it was initially dominated by men. When in 1787 Merry sent poems mysteriously signed "Della Crusca" to the magazine, *The World,* during his slow return to London, the readerly and poetic response was intensely female; despite the formative influence of this movement on male canonical poets such as Byron and Shelley, the Della Cruscans were feminized and remembered as decorative and superficial poets, a passing fashion. Similarly, English women poets heavily invested in sensibility provided important influences to poets who perceived themselves to be speaking in the public forum and for the nation. Charlotte Smith, whose work will play a part in Chapter 1, belongs to this category of intensely popular poets who proved seminal to self-styled prophetic poets such as Wordsworth.

To speak of poetic cults or popular women writers leaves out perhaps the most formative influence on the mature poet Wordsworth, Dorothy Wordsworth. I engage the culture of sensibility here as the strong ground of Wordsworthian aesthetics in order to rework the reception of Wordsworth's masculinist project. But more importantly, it resituates Dorothy Wordsworth within the exclusionary terrain of High Romanticism as a partner in her brother's poetic project. Although current research on women writers in the romantic period determinedly mines cultural history in order to dig forgotten women poets out of the archives, it was necessary to develop a different approach for *Becoming Wordsworthian* since Dorothy Wordsworth's literary output is small and, with certain exceptions, unpublished. The approach I developed, in which the performative is taken as an ongoing moment of "becoming," reconstructs the poetic moment of William and Dorothy's collaborative experience, and of their textual as well as their self-composition. Such a reconstruction must take into account the fictive landscape as constituted by a literature of sensibility and by the pastoral Lake District which the Wordsworths together perceived themselves as inhabiting.

My method is thus more related to the recent feminist work of reconstructing histories of romantic, Georgian, or sentimental cultures to recontain both lost and standard canonical writers. Yet, because Dorothy Wordsworth's relation to these literary cultures is figuratively allied only through her relation to William and her (un)acknowledged impact on his poetry, it is difficult to treat her extant texts in the same terms as the published work of popular women poets such as Mary Robinson, Charlotte Smith, or Felicia Hemans. Therefore, the scholars I respond to most strongly are necessarily those who champion a Wordsworthianism founded on the poetic genius of William and the failed talent of Dorothy; that is, scholars who advocate the story as W. Wordsworth, Coleridge, De Quincey, and Arnold have chosen to tell it. Among these, Margaret Homans and Alan Liu have provided the most authoritative and insightful work on the subject of Dorothy Wordsworth's artistry and presence in the Wordsworthian landscape, and their early work in particular underlies this project.

In addition, other scholars working in this vein have, by an association of symptomatic ideas, treated Dorothy Wordsworth as the failed poet Dorothy, a sentimental heroine whose physical and artistic infertility results anticlimactically in a diseased and disastrous old age. Still other scholars, however, even while accepting standard narratives concerning William's and Dorothy's relationships to the making and unmaking of genius, have begun to question W. Wordsworth's and other canonical poets' statements about originality, authority, and ideology.[2] In such queries lies the space for asking yet further questions about the aesthetic framework by which the poet "Wordsworth" could come into being.

Marlon B. Ross, in *The Contours of Masculine Desire* (1989), and Anne K. Mellor, in *Romanticism and Gender* (1993), have asked such questions and cleared just such a space. Their work represents the debate between the possibilities of a "male" and a "female" literary romanticism, in which the determination of which one precedes and implicates the other is still very much in flux. Therein, however, we find the grounds to consider a halfway space in which both gender and literary gendering is interdeterminate, collaborative, and inconclusive. The archeology and redistribution of formerly lost or forgotten women poets of the period force a differential gloss against ongoing scholarly assertions of British romanticism as an epical achievement characterized by its audible *agon,* poetic origination, and a masculinist or Frankensteinian dissemination of culture. It remains to be seen how these men and women poets will eventually be read in terms of each others' presence on the cultural scene. But for William and Dorothy Wordsworth, we have already at hand the material data by which to reassess their literary relation in regard to the process of redistribution. Further, their case insists on a discrimination of that redistribution so as to be read as two-in-one rather than one against or in spite of the other, as with literary pairings such as Lord Byron and Mme. de Staël, Charlotte Brontë and Robert Southey, Charlotte Dacre and Percy Shelley, or even William Wordsworth and Joanna Baillie ("who, by the bye," he writes to his wife in 1812, "is no Witch in Poetry" [Darlington, 177]). Finally, the collaborative model will be determinate here not only for analyzing Dorothy Wordsworth's privately circulated texts but for revisiting William Wordsworth's marketed texts in terms of that private circulation.

What I have just suggested is that "Wordsworth" is a poet who demands a third strategy of reading because the two strategies available for romantic texts — that which assumes an originary poet genius and that which posits a gendered literary warfare — are inadequate. This third strategy understands "Wordsworth," as I have said, to be a consensual being composed of William and Dorothy; therefore, the reader of Wordsworth's (published) poetry must be fully constrained by the private circulation of texts that interrogate its "becoming." This critical strategy should come into play any time writers demonstrate their awareness of debt to family members who also write, whether we are reading the Lambs, the Shelleys, the Brontës, the Rossettis, or the Brownings.

If the material data for reassessment are in place, a methodology clearly is not, particularly since the Wordsworths are not a normative literary pair in the sense that their output is as collaborative as is their poetic vision. Therefore, I have resorted to a number of terms coined specifically for this material, such as "the performative," "Wordsworthian aesthetics," "the address-to-women," "the feminized sublime," "nest," "the Wordsworthian Life," and "mapping." The first two terms derive from my thinking about Julia Kristeva's semiotic theory; I take Kristeva's key concepts of subjectivity and the creative impulse through the linguistic moment but turn them from essentially static terms of embodiment into the performative — that is, rhythm as an enacting drive and a lyric drive.

To use Kristeva at all is a departure from Wordsworth studies, and to use Kristeva to produce a mythopoetic reading within a frame of cultural studies is a departure from psychoanalytic and psycholinguistic criticisms. I want to stress that *Becoming Wordsworthian* is *not* psychoanalytic in impulse and that Kristeva's value for this study is the richness of her insight into patriarchal culture and, more specifically, into the nature of what she calls the "subject-on-trial." Poetic language, she argues, "posits its own process as an undecidable process between sense and nonsense, between *language* and *rhythm*," and for this reason the speaking subject, in conflict with its unconscious, must be "a questionable *subject-in-process*" (*Desire*, 135; emphasis hers). All other coinages derive from this base of the subject's relation to the signs of himself or herself extruded onto the landscape, whether that terrain be geophysical, cultural, or literary and aesthetic. These terrains are interspersed and treated as one and the same world view in works such as William Wordsworth's *The Prelude* and its predecessor poem, "Home at Grasmere," and such as Dorothy Wordsworth's *Grasmere Journals* and the poems of her later life. "Mapping" is the way in which their complexities can be grasped as "natural" and essential ones. *Becoming Wordsworthian* maintains as much as possible this collusion, which I call the "Wordsworthian Life," of the subjective and objective aspects of the Wordsworths' collaborative imaginary while attempting to denaturalize its processes and premises. The "address-to-women" is the lyric form that inscribes the collaborative artistic endeavor on which the Wordsworths embark when they decide to live together.

Finally, in setting up a study of the performative as a romantic instance that is compatible with and essential to romantic sincerity, it is crucial for us to distinguish between the sentimental novel and the literature of sensibility in terms relevant to the adolescent and orphaned Dorothy Wordsworth's tenuous relation to the world. Within this framework, the terms will surely have shifted somewhat from their eighteenth-century inflections. The sentimental novel, like *Clarissa* and *Paul et Virginie,* demands the death of the heroine in return for another's redemption. In both its determinate morality and its emotional extravagance, it depends on the psychologized world of romance and is thus affiliated with the even more exploitative gothic. Because the heroine's sexuality inheres impossibly with her purity, it becomes overwhelmingly desirable to the decadent masculine authority of the villain. The sentimental, both in the promises it makes and in the distorted world it portrays, partakes of the same tendencies that will produce the dark, transgressive side of romanticism that we find in works such as Byron's *The Giaour.* Literature of sensibility does not share this surreal, paranoid world; nor is it invested in the realism of the domestic novel. It is instead pastoral, atemporal, mythic; its psychology is that of eighteenth-century philosophical sympathy, its principle is the associative. It is characterized by "romantic" or "sentimental" friendship, and as Austen reveals in *Sense and Sensibility,* the affective disorder of sensibility is melancholy.

The performative that *Becoming Wordsworthian* examines takes place within the realm of sensibility and not that of sentiment (although the young Dorothy Wordsworth imagined herself into this space) and not realism (although we tend to attribute via sincerity this space to the adult William). Sensibility provides our organizing schema so that we can foreground the specifically masculine romantic act of composing the self *as if* originary within the nexus of the domestic and literary circle. Sensibility comprises the consensual status of William and Dorothy Wordsworth's life together; self-origination provides the allegory by which William claims poethood; self-composition is the romantic performance of Wordsworthian "becoming."

I claim this against the normative understanding of "William Wordsworth" as a self-representation that is internally and externally consistent; like his poet-speaker he is eternally in the present now, though with a prehistory of elation and sensual melancholia that determines the disturbingly eidetic "spots of time." He is also the social being who holds himself apart.[3] But, in fact, W. Wordsworth's rhetorical ploys to express his recursive cognitive and writing processes (alternations of memory, vision, and the writing moment) are extremely self-conscious and call into doubt the moment of self-making. The very naturalness of his mythopoetics will cease to be aesthetically acceptable under these conditions of trial without some preexisting support to shore it up. The atemporality of pastoral nature is not enough, and W. Wordsworth is very aware of the trials that time imposes on the individual, on the growth of his imagination, aptitude, understanding, and place in the world. For him, the Poet who is completed by his sibling companion, the poet of pastoral lyric and vision, is always threatened by the specter of the solitary Poet who walks pastoral paths in spiritual crisis, but he is also always — through his ties to the sister-maiden — within safety.

However, when without retreat (without a sustaining companion or "second self"), the subject is everywhere on trial and, somewhat like Milton's Lucifer, carries his solitude and his voice with him. Dorothy Wordsworth, too, knows this solitude, particularly as a weariness that descends when William has left her behind to keep house. In the crisis of these periods she, too, experiences deep self-doubt about her literary powers, the exercise of which nevertheless continually renews William's affection for her, and the stoppage of which threatens that mutual regard. I view this self-doubt and solitude as the process of endlessly becoming who one *is:* the subject in question. It is a subject of the threatening dreamscape.

The dreamscape that invokes a necessary otherness, a compelling completion missing from Enlightenment cityscapes and republican civic spheres, becomes sited for both Wordsworths in the mothering pastoral land of Cumbria. William is both author *and* figure in this scape, and when he is solitary in the land without his complementary self, he confronts the oppositional other who is not Dorothy but the Reaper, herself solitary and harvesting we know not what seeds from what organic growth ("The Solitary Reaper"). The Reaper or rural maiden (speaking in her own "strange" tongue) and the Poet speak *at* but not to each other through the dreamlike, liminal thetic, and in this space Nature is heard. (See Chapter 1 for a discussion of thetic space.) Indeed, Nature is heard when the poet has "traced the stream" of poetic language from "the very place of birth/In its blind cavern, whence is faintly heard/The sound of waters" (*Prelude* XIII.172–75),[4] a place strangely connected with what the alienating and naturalized figure of the solitary young harvester carries in her very person. The way to get at that "place of birth" is through the company of the sister, inhabiter of the threshold. This is William's particular version of the dream, and it informs his creation of the address-to-women. Dorothy Wordsworth is interested in repressing, not seeking, the trial of thetic conflict and prefers real scenes to dreamscapes, but she values the pastoral daydream for itself, over and above town or city life. She also rejects the alienating rural maiden, whose presence records a site of liberal guilt over the gentry's harvesting of peasants from the land, and chooses to inhabit a maiden role more closely aligned with poetic composition than with the poetic inspiration William's addresses insist on.

Thus the poems that articulate the weight and the nature of the Wordsworths' interrelation are addresses by each sibling to a maiden who is hailed by the poet-speaker. For William, whose addresses to the maiden come early in his poetic career, the speaker typically desires that the maiden walk with him in nature ("Then come, my Sister! come, I pray"), in the hope that something intangible will be accomplished by this shared activity ("Some silent laws our hearts will make," "We from to-day, my Friend, will date/Our living calendar" ["To My Sister"]). William Wordsworth's regularization of the looser eighteenth-century address to a woman (interestingly, a favorite of women poets) creates a form as discrete as the Coleridgean conversation poem, whose coordinates M. H. Abrams isolated and labeled the "greater romantic lyric" ("Structure and Style"). Abrams's designation of "greater" valorizes this psychologized form against the "lesser" nature lyric.[5] But it is this lesser lyric that W.

Wordsworth champions, a double plot of pastoral simplicity and contemplative intricacy. Wordsworth's address-to-women, in a manner Mar-
vell had not foreseen with his shepherdess, creates dialogue across the gap
of Coleridge's monologic "conversation" and despair. Dorothy Wordsworth also writes addresses to women, although later in life and after she
can no longer inhabit the maiden position herself; her poems simultaneously reinforce the address-to-women formulas and redress them to a
more habitable and personal version.

The address-to-women, however, has a lengthier history than this; its
roots lie in the courtly love lyric, a verse form and theme with which
Wordsworth was well acquainted through Shakespeare and the love ballads republished by antiquaries, and from his translation from the French
of "The Birth of Love" (1795). Equally important was Ariosto, who he
helped Dorothy to read and who he later translated in part, as well as the
Italian verse he studied at Cambridge.[6] The courtly love tradition itself
exemplifies social fiction on a larger scale, which the Wordsworths practiced more particularly; it is, in this sense, fully performative and thus
offers a historical grounding for the Wordsworthian Life.

The poet-lover, usually discoursing in the lady's absence, reveals the
state of his soul and the depth of his desire. He can do so because in a very
real sense he does not need her; he himself contains her in his translation
of her person into an ideal ego that feeds his imagination more vividly
than is possible for the woman herself to accomplish.[7] This ideal ego (the
idealization of the ego's object), or an emblematic vision of it (Beatrice
centered in the rose petals), subsumes the fleshly lady, writing her out of
presence. In loving the woman through his ideal ego, the lover loves
himself; when he sings of his love to himself, he attempts to see how she
would see him and so places her in his ego ideal (the place of internalized
social censure), from where he imagines her seeing him at his finest.[8]

What William Wordsworth saw as incapacitating in the courtly love
attitude was the power the lady could hold over the speaker if his humility
retreated into ego loss. The love lyric's power, on the other hand, was that
it turned affect into discourse, masking sexual relations — even negating
them — with words.[9] Dialogue as poetry only occurs once there is a syntag-
matic ease in the address that the addressee receives easily. That is, she is
not made absent by being displaced with the speaker's emotion and pain,

so that she is constituted as the subject and not the object of the address.[10] D. Wordsworth literally becomes the Maiden as she reads the poems that address her, but in addition each woman reader — from the Hutchinson sisters to Isabella Fenwick — is invited to stand synecdochally in her place and become the sister.

The maiden, or Dorothy figure, is both unattached to any other man and dependent on the brother-speaker. She is not objectified as courtly beloved (Dante's Beatrice) or as a natural woman (William's Lucy); instead, she is partly self and partly other, and as such her character can be recognized in other women who share some or all of her sisterly characteristics. Her own posture is ambiguated by her participation in a situation orchestrated by the Wordsworthian speaker to position himself powerfully against her. In empowering his voice she allows her own sublimation, but the very structure of the address speaks against a simple objectification of the woman. Both sublimation and subjectivity vary within the relational triangles of poet-reader-text and speaker-addressee-hero; ratios are balanced and disturbed in moving from one to the next, but the homogeneity reigns overall as a semblance of pastoral.

The discussion of the address-to-women, as one of the most important aspects of the performative drive, Wordsworthian aesthetics, and pastoral Life, recurs throughout *Becoming Wordsworthian*. Equally important is the discussion that begins in Chapter 1 which works out the mapping of the Wordsworths' imaginary geography. Missing the kind of Eastern and oriental sectors that Byron's or De Quincey's imaginary employs, it confines its parameters instead to a historical and aesthetic intersection on the geographical site such that the mapping takes on those kinds of multidimensional complexities that plagued Napoleon's cartographers. How do we think about, and then how do we represent, the kinds of intersections that arise when temporal and spatial trajectories array themselves in and against the aesthetic? And further, how does this kind of terrain embed the performative as a mode of becoming?

Wordsworth resolves this dilemma in numerous ways, including the suspension of time in the pastoral landscape; this is the subject of Chapter 2. The valleyscape mined in this chapter involves a less severe yet more dramatic resolution of the problem through what I will discuss as the pastoral sublime, most recognizable as the drama of the female figure in the landscape: "The Solitary Reaper" or "Lucy Gray." The pastoral sublime, itself an oxymoronic term, performs the same fusion of apposite entities as do other Wordsworthian endeavors, such as the *Lyrical Ballads*. As a concept, it is indeed performative because it allows the subject-on-trial to play out mythopoetic roles within a multiply determined rather than overdetermined space. When the setting frees up the script in this fashion, the performative is naturalized, unconstrained by the artifice of an overdetermined aesthetic space. The pastoral is itself a space of domestication and therefore, according to Wordsworth's own philosophic deliberations, beauty. Nonetheless, and despite Burkean pronouncements as to the terrain appropriate to particular emotions and experiences, the domestic is also capable of situating sublime transport. It is in this sense that we will understand the pastoral as a transgressive space.

These notions — that there is an intersection, even temporal cohabitation, of the sublime with the pastoral and the domestic — run contrary to everything we have read or known about British romantic thought and literature. Chapter 3 offers the terms of an alternative, indeed, performative reading by examining specifically how Dorothy Wordsworth wrote herself into being and into the aesthetic map, within and against the confines discussed in the previous chapter.

Chapter 4 undoes the resolutions of Chapter 3 by examining another, apposite, aspect of world making: the sheer aesthetic space of the sublime. However, the discussion of more traditional evaluations in this chapter reveals that even these assumptions must be questioned in the context of the performative and a Wordsworthian aesthetics. This subject is particularly important to this study because the sublime, with its religio-philosophical background, forces the issue of Dorothy Wordsworth's collaborative contribution to the poems by which "Wordsworth" is most regarded in romantic studies. Is she herself merely the ground on which William strives for sublimation, or does she play a more active and critical role in construing a Wordsworthian sublime that accommodates her presence at all?

Chapter 5 concludes by repeating the intervention of Chapter 3 in order to reroute the disturbing differential of the romantic sublime, even as a Wordsworthian construct, in terms of the woman's subjective trial and alternative routes of poetic discovery.

ONE

The Wordsworthian Performative

August 31, 1800 — . . . At 11 o'clock Coleridge
came, when I was walking in the still clear
moonshine in the garden. He came over
Helvellyn. Wm. was gone to bed. . . . We
sate and chatted till 1/2-past three, W. in
his dressing gown. Coleridge read us a
part of Christabel. *Talked much about*
the mountains, etc. etc. . . . Losh's opinion
of Southey — the first of poets.

Grasmere Journals

Geoffrey Hartman, to whom we always return to understand Wordsworth's verse, wrote of the "selfhood Wordsworth knew," its relation to Nature and the death of Nature, its relation to his special mission and the death of his mission (Hartman, 338). In just such a way, we know the self called Wordsworth through the eyes and sensibility of older critics whose judgment we trust: Coleridge, with his descriptions of masculine poethood; Mill, with his Wordsworthian curative for the sick soul; Arnold, with his cure for a Philistine culture. And we have based contemporary criticism on similarly mystical foundations, including Hartman's exploration of mission, Abrams's vision of Wordsworth's "program for poetry," and de Man's understanding of Wordsworth's sublime imagination in *Blindness and Insight*. We comprehend Wordsworth to be first of all a strong poet in the Bloomian sense, a Miltonic successor sensible of both his inheritance and his seed. He is thus a visionary, just as he and Coleridge claim; a teacher, as he and Arnold claim; and Nature's priest, as he and Mill claim. It must be noted that like all transmitted beliefs, these are so little self-evident that students must be taught them over and against their own observations.

Within the parameters of these critical beliefs, we also accept that Wordsworth was the strong partner and Coleridge the weak, albeit Coleridge's imagination and genius were rich enough to fertilize that strong ground. On a lesser level and to a lesser extent, we accept that Dorothy Wordsworth had some part in the production of Wordsworth's poetry although, as anthologies and scholarly books have made clear, we view her greatest contributions to be that of note-taker and amanuensis for her brilliant brother. We tend to think, parametrically, of William and Dorothy Wordsworth as separate and unequal beings with distinct and non-overlapping voices and imaginations. We allow that Dorothy Wordsworth wrote in her journals with a poetic voice but tend to conclude that she was unable to grasp the largeness of William's imaginative meditations or to follow his poetic sublimity. She seems, like Mary Shelley, to have been a silent companion to the fervent poetical, political, and philosophical conversations between men despite the testimony of her journal entries, as in this chapter's epigraph.[1]

Similarly, we do not allow ourselves to consider that influence could go the other way: that Dorothy's imagination and poetic voice could at all have influenced her brother, her elder by one year. W. Wordsworth's voice seems to us distinct, hardly touched even by Coleridge's enthusiasms despite the claims the younger poet makes in his *Biographia Literaria*. Coleridge is clear as to which voices touch him, from Bowles and Southey to Bürger, and we accept this account while we acknowledge the genius of his transformative borrowings. We also give credit to the notion that Wordsworth and Coleridge cross-fertilized each other's imaginations even when we cannot trace distinct borrowings or distinguish which lines each wrote for the other, as Wordsworth claims to have done for "The Ancient Mariner." But when Wordsworth says he was inordinately influenced by a voice other than Coleridge's or Milton's, his footnotes to Charlotte Smith for example, we tend to ignore the hint. The traces he leaves of Dorothy's impress we similarly overlook.

Becoming Wordsworthian challenges these standard readings of Wordsworth by arguing that William's aesthetics and visions depended heavily and integrally on Dorothy's own visual and poetic compatibilities. Whereas William Wordsworth looked inward to see the order of things, Dorothy looked outward to see how things escape order. That is, the Wordsworthian world view was a product of both their imaginations working together, not her subservience to him or, the opposite, his exploitation of her abilities but a team collaboration to which William affixed the name "Wordsworth" and claimed for his own. It can be argued that Coleridge attempted to borrow the same rights for himself, since his notebooks for the early years of friendship include references to and echoes of Dorothy's thoughts and words. But however much Coleridge himself collaborated with Wordsworth over genre mediation (the conversation poem) or long-term project goals (*The Recluse*), William never *achieved* what Coleridge envisioned. Although he took from Coleridge the impetus to change and enlarge the Wordsworthian world view at various times, its foundations had already been set. Charting this world view as situated and intersected with the inflections of Dorothy's voice, vision, and interpretive skill will occupy much of this study, because it provokes and institutes the Wordsworthian aesthetic. Its terrain is not so much the dells and heights of the Lake District as it is the mythic or fictive ground that composes what I will be calling the Wordsworthian Life.

Ten years after their marriage, when William was visiting his brother while Mary Wordsworth was visiting hers, she wrote to him about the difficulty of finding one's way: "We were ill off not having provided ourselves with a good Map [on the return from Usk]. . . . If we had had a traveller like you with us we should have done better — but Tom is too shy to make himself acquainted with a Country he is a stranger in" (Darlington, 252). Unlike Mary's shy brother, Dorothy and William are both willing to be "acquainted with a Country" and to do so "in any other way than by [one's] *own observations.*" Mary's emphasis marks what she sees as William's superiority as a user of maps, his interpretive schema by which observation, inquiry, and utterance resolve into correct readings of the landscape. This is a theme he himself makes much of in poems like "Resolution and Independence" (referred to hereafter by the title given it in the Wordsworths' circle, "The Leech-gatherer") and "Home at Grasmere." This chapter will explore the implications of mapping the aesthetic terrain and the necessities of provoking the spatial settings in which to engage the performative. This is the performative as the Wordsworthian Life which William and Dorothy created and inscribed together and which is written into being through the aesthetic terrain of their daily self-imagining, and mapped by way of William's philosophizing and psychologizing imagination. One of these implications, that of the psyche in pursuit of the aesthetic space — that sense of self which Julia Kristeva terms "the subject-on-trial" — will organize the subsequent sections of the discussion, which will pursue the subjective traveler as not only William but Dorothy.

ᕫ *Mapping*

The conception of a geographical imaginative that is both autobiographical and mythic — the Wordsworthian Life — is necessarily, or at least should be, that of the stately rhythms out of which biography is compiled. It is this publicly accessible life that is lionized and adumbrated in the years of the poet's fame. But the private vision underlying the public is that of a fictive bohemian existence, out of which William and Dorothy created their Wordsworthianness and in which only one of their brothers felt close enough temperamentally to participate. Being Wordsworthian was not a birthright but a state, one to which spiritual "brothers" such as Coleridge were openly welcomed and adopted. But such a state must entwine the public and private lives, the ways of being in the world, so that acting and being (acting the role of the self) are the same. The fictions under which such role acting becomes possible, positive, and desirable make available a phenomenon I will call performative aesthetics. And it is the private aspects of such a Life in which the performative — which can seem so public to us — creates the possibility of poetic creation. It is only on this ground that we can begin to see that poetry as collaborative and emergent, that is to say, self-productive.

William Wordsworth was aware of Dorothy's agency and depended on it as much as she depended on his. The "as much" in this claim is qualifiable but not always quantifiable; therefore, the following chapters will trace the passage of roles played and the interaction/interactivity of these roles without declaring the poet-visionary or the sister-maiden as the dominant one. Rather, the dictates of the material direct us to take these roles as interactive in the most collaborative sense, regardless of whose name is put on the final product. In addition, the determination of the final project as merely literary is as questionable as is the name put on it. Both textuality and "Wordsworth" must take a double valence in this study: The textual is both the literary text and the lived or performative text, both of which come together in Wordsworthian Life; "Wordsworth," when inscribed on a poem, may mean the poet Wordsworth or "my sister" whose poem is included in the brother's volume. But this last doubling does not cut deep enough: "Wordsworth" in the sense this study will engage it means both brother and sister together at once.

I treat the Wordsworthian relation as kinship in the sense of collaboration, a siblinghood invested in romantic theories about the shared experience of childhood, theories that seem to contradict but are actually compatible with utopian notions of spiritual fraternity. The more conventional story that has been told about the male genius and his sister companion is that of producer and helper. But the dark overtones of romantic and revolutionary years can yield a less innocent relation, and one which has been hinted at in the Wordsworths' case. Certainly, by analogy with the sexual economies of Byron's and Shelley's households, incest can be taken as a parlayer of intimate space and shared enthusiasms. In this light, William's poems to Dorothy and Dorothy's language of love as expressed in her journals take on private meanings. I argue against this possibility in the Wordsworth household, not least because the fictional basis of the Wordsworthian Life relied on sentimental friendship. On the other hand, collaboration is more readily taken as a sharing between men, as in the shared labor of Wordsworth and Coleridge. In this context, even the married Coleridge's desire for Wordsworth's sister-in-law, Sara, is not read as incestuous. I therefore tell this story in such a way as to resituate siblinghood as twinship, or twinned souls. Indeed, William is quite explicit about his feeling that he and Dorothy need share no words in order to communicate; Dorothy is quite explicit that William has always been her best-loved, her most intimate brother. To examine twinship as a poetic paradigm requires some regridding of our own literary charts. It requires that we recognize the relation between a life and the fictional stories that influence how one lives one's life; it requires a differentiation between a life lived and a Life, a construction of one's life that revises both the past and the present moment according to fictions of the self. In short, it requires an awareness of role performativity, an aestheticized version of Hegelian Becoming, that is to say, an intense and sincere experiencing of the moment.

Wordsworthian scholars do not like to regard William Wordsworth as invested in roles beyond that of seer and sage because the concept of role playing seems deliberately at odds with Wordsworth's insistent sincerity. However, in the sense that I intend "performativity," it is not antithetical to sincerity but explains its necessity. Wordsworthian romanticism, in fact, is much less invested in a single story than critics have traditionally liked to believe. Rather, it is invested in particular kinds of telling, in revisiting the scenes of telling, and in the effect of performative telling. Although many of Wordsworth's important poems feature tale-tellers as characters, *Becoming Wordsworthian* will focus less on those actors than on the poet who himself acts, tells, and listens — and on the kinds of life stories that impregnate his imagination, life stories that Dorothy Wordsworth was particularly good at observing and recording.

I am looking, therefore, not for a single story to unpack from its grammatical wrappings but for the tale-telling as itself a way of living or self-making. The charting of this locutionary terrain is peculiarly invested with romantic myths, yet even here I am not seeking something as grounded as the cultural imagination or as memorable as the Wanderer or Leech-gatherer. I am interested, rather, in the map itself, for it is in the strictest of Wordsworthian senses a stageable map, a performative directive. There is, however, no performance per se because this is a traveler's map, a charting of imaginative grounds by which one can enact a particular aesthetic state of being or coming into being. Dorothy Wordsworth's "Commonplace Book," DCMS 120, which will be discussed further in the final chapter, contains a large number of her poems copied in, for safekeeping, album-style; but it also charts out, graphically and iconographically, a traveler's log. It calls attention to its function with a bookseller's advertisement for the life of Saint Paul pasted to its front endpaper, and Paul's presence as the patron saint of travelers oversees and protects the imaginative journey within. Mapping, the notebook reveals, is itself a poetic process; it is also one that can seem barely tangible to the critical eye, especially when those aspects enumerated publicly by one party are well known enough to drown out another party's contributions.

Alan Liu theorizes that the phenomenal world of Wordsworthian Grasmere comprises a self-completing universe,[2] spatially laid out within a "dome of labor" onto which Liu maps a traveler's or tourist's orientation:

> Poetic Composition (William) stands at the north point; Housework (Dorothy) at the south; and Textual Work and Walking in Nature at the west and east, respectively, so as to define a horizontal line between the hemispheres of William and Dorothy. ["On the Autobiographical Present," 117]

Liu's schema provides one of the most interesting readings of Wordsworthian life. The dome is a "structure of interactive completion," a collaborative effort entering into all phases. But Liu reads completion through desire, so that "expecting" to participate in the west–east axis allows Dorothy to find "fulfillment" in housework, which is "onerous by itself." Thus Dorothy's actions read each other at the same time that they share in an intersubjectivity with William achieved through the "individual's trust in total communion" (118).

Such a model helpfully traces the architectural thinking implicit and explicit in cottage activity, yet the prohibitions Liu locates within the dome work to efface rather than reveal crucial aspects of Dorothy Wordsworth's Grasmere days. Liu finds four major activities which structure both daily life and the journal itself: the making of William's poetry; textuality as the reading and writing of letters, journals, books, and the copying of manuscripts and revisions; housework; walking/gardening in nature. In fact, Dorothy Wordsworth's version of the myth encompasses more than these four William-related activities. While Liu admits to leaving conversation and social visits out of his model, he also leaves out the daily activity of Dorothy's own writing, its process and concerns. What has been marginalized here, then, are those aspects of Wordsworthian life that are strictly Dorothy's: community and community-making activities, and her own production of art. Liu's William-based mythic structure joins with other critical attempts to account for Dorothy's place in the Wordsworthian project and its mapping: The project is William's alone, and

Dorothy's activities can be seen only as William himself inscribes them, that is, as complementary and not collaborative.

Liu's study is an innovative reading of the pastoral myth that appears in D. Wordsworth's journals, but his reliance on terms such as "intersubjective sharing" (118) veils the traditional stance hidden behind his discussion, for what he (and other critics) means here is "fusion." Fusion implies loss of the self in the other, and as a romantic ideal it would seem a normative way to read Dorothy's desire. However, the difficulty with imposing architecture on relation is that it stabilizes and encloses that relation, reducing performative being to complementary support, a bracing of the primary subject; in short, Liu's rendering is in the style of William Wordsworth's romantic fusion. Dorothy Wordsworth's ideal of being, on the other hand, involves a dynamic relation between selves, an interaction that preserves communal participation and sharing. Only recently have studies begun to appear that represent the Wordsworthian project as dual, with Dorothy a strong participant in its making,[3] but Liu's exegesis provides a strong point of departure for charting the Wordsworthian terrain precisely because, even in the midst of Dorothy's writing, it looks through William's eyes alone.

There is good reason for this, since the public mapping out of the self's relation to society and nature demands the publication of aesthetic and political principles. In constructing his schematic map, Wordsworth became particularly good at adapting principles from different systems of thought to a larger conceptual structure in order to provide himself with the principles he needed to make sense of the world. Like his friend Coleridge, he had a synthetic imagination, but it was also an imagination that retained distinct ideas while making room for others by reworking the relations between them. From his childhood with and without Dorothy Wordsworth, William had come to think about his world according to the terms of sensibility and poetic melancholy, terms available to the heroic mode as well as the domestic for a construction of one's self in the world. In particular, a Humean aestheticization of morals underwrites the high value assigned a self-drama of melancholy; Wordsworth learned the merit of this cultural code from his adored Hawkshead schoolmaster, William Taylor. His earliest published poems exemplify those attitudes made popular by the sentimental poetry of Thomas Gray, Anna Seward,

Charlotte Smith,[4] and Helen Maria Williams. But they also reveal the trace of another influence on his thought congenial to the melancholic and sympathetic disposition: picturesque nature and the Rousseauistic social contract. The former predisposed Wordsworth toward the landscapes of rural Britain; the latter led him to the political turmoil of London and then of Paris.

These two dispositions were not mutually exclusive in W. Wordsworth's imagination. Even after his encounter with the highly charged political world of London during Burke's 1791 parliamentary falling-out with Fox, Wordsworth's response was not to dispel melancholic self-drama but to embrace it as idealized social concern. If Wordsworth was more swayed by the Jacobin pamphleteering that seconded his own recent French experience, he seems at least to have found Burke's chivalrous and self-dramatizing metaphors in the *Reflections* worth remembering. However, more agreeable publications were poetic effusions like Helen Maria Williams's 1792 "To Dr. Moore . . . [on the French Revolution]," or Charlotte Smith's melioration of dissonance and drama in *The Emigrants: A Poem* (1792). The latter work was written after Wordsworth had already introduced himself to her on the eve of his second trip to Paris in 1791 and had obtained letters of introduction from her to Helen Maria Williams (the British translator of the sentimental *Paul et Virginie*), who was residing in Paris.[5] Although Wordsworth will soon position himself against both Rousseau and Burke in his struggle for a national as well as personal voice, he will never overturn the lasting influence Smith's melancholic sonnets and sentimental novels have on his aesthetic ground. This claim of poetic influence is worth fuller attention than it will be given here, in lieu of which there will be an ongoing attention to the multiply gendered ground of Wordsworthian aesthetics and to the ways in which feminine strives with masculine in Wordsworth's territorial imagination.

In the face of the more obvious and masculinist influence of writers like Rousseau, Burke, and Coleridge, Wordsworth's familiarity with Smith's emotive self-dramatization provides an interesting backdrop to the substantial role Dorothy will shortly come to play in the creation of the poet "Wordsworth." Much later William continues to acknowledge his debt to Smith, writing in a textual note to his "Stanzas suggested in a steamboat off Saint Bees' Heads, on the coast of Cumberland," that he had adopted the form of his poem from "St. Monica" by Charlotte Smith, "a lady to whom English verse is under greater obligations than are likely to be either acknowledged or remembered. She wrote little, and that little un-ambitiously, but with true feeling for rural nature, at a time when nature was not much regarded by English Poets" (Hutchinson and de Selin-court, 724 n.). Smith, who wrote copiously rather than little, is so much the master of the "naturally" melancholic pose that Wordsworth recalls her output as small because he had read it as an expression of self, an atti-tude inherent in sentimental literature. It is also an attitude Wordsworth cultivated for himself in his works and in his life work. Dorothy Words-worth records in her journal for Christmas Eve, 1802, that "—beloved William is turning over the leaves of Charlotte Smith's sonnets, but he keeps his hand to his poor chest pushing aside his breastplate." Words-worth is being both melancholic (Mary and Dorothy are quite well, she notes) and poetical: Previously occupied in translating Ariosto, he is now sitting by Dorothy who had been "repeating some of his sonnets to him, listening to his own repeating, reading some of Milton's and the Allegro and Penseroso."

Smith occupies, along with Milton and Wordsworth himself, a senti-mental and authorizing presence in Wordsworth's aesthetic landscape. And through her associations with Helen Maria Williams, Smith also provided an early bridge from sentimentalism to the Rousseauistic atti-tudes that provide a continental model for the melancholic pose. Rous-seau's *Emile* was particularly popular with the radicals who frequented the booksellers in Saint Paul's Churchyard. During his second visit to France, however, Wordsworth experiences his most intense encounter with politi-cal and private passion; smitten with Annette Vallon and Michel Beaupuy both, he fathers a daughter out of wedlock and virtually engages to be an officer for the Girondists. Two extreme experiences are the result of ex-treme conditions, high sympathy, and sublime desires. On returning to England to supplement his funds, William finds his enthusiasms abated but is devastated a few months later by Britain's declaration of war against the nation he would have died for. Either England must be renounced or a new way of seeing the world must be found.

James Chandler argues that Wordsworth's responses to this enormous personal and national dilemma can be traced to two years pivotal to

Wordsworth's political and poetic development: 1793, when "Descriptive Sketches" and "An Evening Walk" were published, and 1798, when he published *Lyrical Ballads* with Coleridge. Significantly, both are key years in the progress of the French Revolution: The first was positive despite the execution of Louis XVI and his queen, and the second pessimistic, with Britain's second coalition formed against Napoleon. Between them lie two opposed ways of thinking about the world that will come to represent the two axes of Wordsworth's conceptual map. The first is Rousseauistic: Prior to 1793 Wordsworth had been initiated into a literary project influenced by Rousseau's writings on the relation of man to nature; we should also add Smith to this axial delineation. The year 1798 marks the expression of Wordsworth's philosophical shift from sensibility to reflect Burke on the constitution of human culture by custom and use. The 1798 valuing of mind over sense, and of habit over innovative experience, does not dismiss these earlier terms for Wordsworth; the seemingly radical Rousseau is made to accommodate the nominally liberal Burke,[6] while Smith finds home ground at the crossover. Thus the 1797 "Margaret" is fitted into the later *Excursion,* and the 1798 autobiographical blank verse "On Man, Nature, & Society" will later become the epical *Prelude.* The two phases of thought come to coexist, mapped over one another in Wordsworth, as placement and displacement, self and supplement self, valley and world. And where they meet comes to represent a point of departure, a threshold into the noumenal or sublime.

It is not anomalous that Wordsworth perceives the world here from a doubled position, 1793 and 1798 fitted onto each other as a grid; other romantic poets did as well. Coleridge's "Rime of the Ancient Mariner" displays a double-mapped narrative structure that superimposes a seventeenth-century gloss (published in the 1817 version) on the reenvisioned Bürger-style ballad (written in 1798). And later Byron will write his double-plotted masterpiece, *Don Juan,* with a narrator's plot located in 1818–24 and a narrative or hero's plot that begins in 1787 and is projected to end in 1793 on the guillotine of the French revolutionaries.[7]

Wordsworth's 1799 *Prelude* is the most obvious example of the productiveness of such a doubling for him during this turbulent period, and his subsequent revisions and complications of this text reveal the generative advantage of seeing from a nonsingular, nonunified perspective. I am arguing that William Wordsworth's poetics depends upon a way of seeing that specifically contradicts the speaker position that his nineteenth-century readers and twentieth-century scholars have so celebrated. Our received understanding of how to read Wordsworth's poetry is as a monologic and univocal discourse in which a strong, unified vision is revealed in order that it be absorbed through the reading process. Scholars have commented upon Wordsworth's recursive quality, particularly in his quest poems such as the 1805 *Prelude,* but for the most part continue to agree as to the singleness of his voice. I want to extend the significance of the doubleness Chandler has pointed to in Wordsworth's formative period by contending that there is an even more significant doubling in these years, that between his sister and his self.

☙ Determining the Aesthetic Terrain

Of her four brothers, Dorothy chose to keep house for the one with the least resources, the most precarious future. Prior to choosing to live with William, Dorothy writes to her best friend that

> I confess you are right in supposing me partial to William. Probably when I next see Kit, I shall love him as well. . . . His disposition is of the same cast as William's, and his inclinations have taken the same turn, but he is much more likely to make his fortune. . . . [William] reads Italian, Spanish, French, Greek, Latin, and English, but never opens a mathematical book. . . . his pleasures are chiefly of the imagination, he is never so happy as in a beautiful country. [*EY,* DW to JP, 6 June 1791][8]

Christopher Wordsworth "is no despicable Poet," but he is able to "draw his mind from . . . fascinating studies to others less alluring" (*EY,* DW to JP, 16 February 1793). Dorothy has already made up *her* mind, and turning away from the younger brother she dreams of sharing house with William. And the drama of the dream is telling. When the news of William's illegitimate daughter reached their uncle's family (where Dorothy was living) and was followed by his strange silence during what she later knew was his near nervous breakdown, Dorothy herself broke down. But the severe fatigue and depression that she suffered were as much emotional and provoked as they were manifestly physical. As she waited to hear from William she wrote to her friend Jane Pollard with what her biographers call "the language of sensibility," but which is also self-dramatizing, pouring out "all the passionate feelings which were pent up in everyday life: how she would 'palpitate with rapture when I once more throw myself into your [Jane's] arms," yet "'[y]ou can have no idea of my impatience to see this dear Brother' . . . 'long, long Months. I measure them with a Lover's scale'" (Gittings and Manton, 41–42). All through this emotional play she is plotting for her future with William and dreaming of keeping his house for him.

William, too, dreamed of life with Dorothy, particularly wishing for her presence during his first walking tour of the continent. Even in his first published poem, "An Evening Walk" (1793), he imagines writing to her in order to project his voice into a receptive and hearing space, and he imagines her response.[9] This discursively interactive intercourse takes the form of what I have called here the address-to-women, a lyric form that occurs frequently in the Wordsworths' poetry but rarely in any other poet's work, or at least not with the peculiar delineations William develops. W. Wordsworth develops this poetic form early in his career, deriving it initially from the eighteenth-century practice of addressing poems to specific persons but imposing formal constraints compatible with the conversation poems on which he would soon embark with Coleridge. Dorothy Wordsworth's presence in William's life during their formative, adolescent years was a periodic and epistolary one; that is, she was a presence that had to be anticipated or summoned up in order to be addressed. Anticipating Dorothy caused William to develop a particularized poetic form; anticipating William, on the other hand, led Dorothy to copious letters that were clear forerunners of the journals written to William as much as for herself.

William's conception of his life with Dorothy in the Lake District makes sense as an anticipation and a double plotting; he expresses it as a doubled self in the 1798 "Tintern Abbey" where Dorothy is not just the sister-maiden addressed but a second or prior self, a more naturalized self. The second self repeats and sustains the primary self through a doubled voice or expression; because the sister feels in a manner equivalent to, and makes present, the poet's prior self of 1793, her voice is subsumed by her expression, which repeats or doubles that of the youthful self. Thus, when only the Poet speaks in the poems of meditation and address of 1798, his voice is nonetheless doubled in himself and doubled in his sister: doubly plotted and doubly gendered. And, as both "Tintern Abbey" and her journals indicate, the sister agreed to her secondary role and secondary self. But Dorothy Wordsworth viewed her voice as collaborative rather than subsumed, as productive rather than repetitive. And regardless of William's doubling of voice and self in the poetry, Dorothy's bodily voice and linguistic aptitude had a special potency for him when he composed. Between the drama of siblinghood and poethood lies a verbal space structured by voice and dialogue, a mutual space where selves meet.

Presiding at these alternate plots of being is the sense of a historically implicated self that exists despite the romantic ability to conceptualize the poetic self anew — the contextual man in despite of the original genius. But whereas Coleridge and Byron conceive of themselves as doubled and therefore ironically ambiguous, Wordsworth's double plot in "Tintern Abbey" (the second visit to the ruins with Dorothy in 1798 mapped over the first visit in 1793)[10] resolves, or attempts to resolve, itself into a single map or chart. It is this attempt at unitary voice and vision that Victorian and modernist readers hang on to, but Wordsworth also complicates the attempt by undercutting it and by doing so *resolutely.* That is to say, pulled toward voicing a Burkean national vision, Wordsworth is also always compelled by the voices that most resound in his imagination, and he dramatizes the oppositional pull of these voices in his poetry. And because the literary is, in the case of the Wordsworths, also a domestic routine, this dramatization extends beyond the composition of words to the composition of self, that is, to the performative. However, whereas Coleridge and Byron dance off the stage molded by their ambivalent public roles, Wordsworth contains that stage in 1798 by embodying and envoicing it and does not leave it again, even in his travels.

To say this is to say something about staging and projected roles. Byron and Coleridge scholarship absorbs performance metaphors from the texts and lives of the two poets, writing "naturally" of Byron's masks and Coleridge's personas.[11] If double plotting marks the period's most significant poetic productions, so does staging and self-direction. But what is still indeterminate is the gendering of the stage and the roles played. Coleridge and Byron occupy masculine worlds that are centered by stages that they can spin across in brilliant performance, en route to some other place and always anticipating a return visit. This in-and-out relation to the site of being is in stark contrast to the seated stage of W. Wordsworth's world, and if spinning across a stage constitutes the masculine vision, then William's self-stationing retains a feminine prospect. Certainly the attraction of the sentimental and melancholic postures for Wordsworth argues a predisposition toward the feminine even though Coleridge considered him the most masculine of poets. But even more spectacular is the epical manly project Coleridge urges on Wordsworth and which Wordsworth can never take on, *The Recluse*. The ground on which this epic is to grow is Grasmere and its surrounds; what could be more doubling to a feminine, pastoral seating than the superimposition of a masculine, sublime vision? Charlotte Smith's novel, *Ethelinde; or, The Recluse of the Lake* (1789), offers an interesting and provocative insight into this aesthetic problem.

As a novel of poetic proportions, *Ethelinde* provides a singled vision framed at beginning and end with descriptions of Grasmere. However, not only is the ground made female here, but so is the (female) Recluse, and by the hand of a woman writer Wordsworth felt artistic affinities for. Imaginatively stimulated by a feminine model and a masculine plan, Wordsworth can only reject one or embrace both. But by the time the failed trip with Dorothy and Coleridge to Germany is over, the embrace of both has become deeply embedded in William's imagination *as* an embrace of Dorothy and the pastoral, of the pastoral sublime (as Lucy), and of a problematic and troubling masculine sublime represented by the elusive spontaneity of the present/absent Coleridge. The embrace of all these, although William can only admit this years later, forecloses on the masculinist epic and prevents its viability. What differentiates Wordsworth's mapping and his world, then, is not simply that Smith informs its terms or that Dorothy's presence allows him to distribute space in interesting ways but that the ground itself is differently gendered for him than for his poet brothers.[12]

Michael Friedman argues that Wordsworth turned from the radical oedipal de-fathering of the French Revolution, which was to replace monarchy with brotherhood, to the internalized father that the traditional Lake society represented for him. Setting aside Charlotte Smith's feminized Lakes, it seems difficult to accept both the hystericizing Revolution and the traditional society of the Lakes as masculine within the terms Wordsworth sets out in his lyrical and epic poetry. However masculine the poet's political vision was, the French and native social realities in front of him epitomize feminine rather than masculine being, mother rather than father.

Wordsworth himself is caught between these two gendered fronts, literally caught between the chastening narratives of suffering offered up by the literary woman — what Marlon Ross has called the "sociomoral handmaiden" — and the masculinist poet's urge to "father culture from the power of isolated natural desire" (*Contours,* 192). Charlotte Smith's novel offers two models for the sociomoral handmaiden, Ethelinde and the melancholic mother of the man she marries. Both are arguably "the Recluse" of the lake, each harboring her own sorrow and her own affinities with the landscape. Smith's affinities, however, are more questionable; her descriptions read like guidebook transcriptions and set scenes which stand out from the narrative's singleminded portrayal of each "recluse" as a moral guide to the men related to her. Indeed, Smith's landscapes contain enough picturesque and pictorial language, as well as inaccurate detail, that they could be based on any of the available watercolor sketchbooks of the Lakes as easily as on her own memories.[13] What does draw the line of comparison between Smith's novel and Wordsworthian Life is her feminization of the Lakes' aesthetic. This is particularly clear in the heroine as a source of consolation for the owner of the abbey, whose own wife detests the Lakes:

> driven from her by haughty reserve, or petulant retort, he was compelled to resort for consolation to the mild and reasonable conversation of Ethelinde. An hour's reading with her, a walk with her, or some little poem repeated by memory as they rambled together on the banks of the lake, restored to his wounded spirit its wonted composure. [*Ethelinde,* 1:36–37].

Ethelinde's maidenhood is stunningly close to Dorothy's, each woman serving the momentarily needy man with a spiritual artistry that builds a bridge between his alienation and the nature around him.

Although *Ethelinde* does not provide a philosophic epical treatment of the meditative life as Wordsworth aimed to do, it does treat the reclusive sensibility. However, the book's genre and gendered landscape tender its critical reception in other ways: That Smith's Recluse project is a novel allows Scott to review the work as properly feminine and, like all her work, an appropriate delineation of character and social status befitting a woman's eye for detail.[14] By way of contrast, Scott interposes Coleridge's troubadour poem, "Love," into his critique of Smith. Scott uses the lines "Few sorrows hath she of her own, / . . . She loves me best, whene'er I sing / The songs that make her grieve," to help him explain why readers enjoy the heavy melancholy of Smith's novels. But the poet-speaker in this poem critiques his lady as too artful, too easily read, too silly for masculine aesthetics to condone. Scott's choice of a calculating speaker devised by a poet deeply aware of the genre and gender implications of his poem transfers the naive superficiality of the speaker's lady onto Smith's novel readers who similarly "love the tales which call forth a sympathy for which their own feelings give little occasion" (*Scott on Novelists*, 189), thereby effeminizing those readers who "wept with pity and delight" ("Love"). Anyone with troubles of their own would rather read an uplifting work, Scott adds, thus neatly finishing off any reader fond of such feminizing melancholy. If, in Scott's view, Smith may be excused for her poetics of sorrow by the misfortunes of her own life, there is nothing in his review to excuse the reader who finds more than simply "many pleasant hours derived from the perusal of Mrs. Smith's works" (190). The impasse between the critical male and sociomoral female poets via the third, male poet-sage, forces a displacement of rebuke onto the reader who would take Smith's ethos too seriously.

A sociomoral handmaiden, Smith feelingly writes of her pain and thus makes us feel, although only sentimentally or artificially so. Like other lady novelists, she affords readerly "amusement" only through the feminine ability to "veil and clothe forms with drapery easily." Such artifice is not the domain of the feeling and sorrowful (and manly) poet, nor is *Ethelinde* the most interesting of Smith's narratives for Scott. However, this review of Smith's oeuvre did not appear until 1827, nearly thirty years after her novel was published, and Coleridge's "Love" was soon followed by the self-dramatizing and deeply melancholic "Dejection" ode, a poem that rewrites "Love" into a questing after the poet's own aesthetic gendering. But when Smith's novel appeared, her feminization of Lake terrain accomplished a gendering of pain and tragedy, a dalliance with the "socio-moral" aspects of nature–self correlations through the sympathetic powers. By displacing Smith's novelism with narrative poetry, Wordsworth (and Scott after him) effaces the troubling implications of female art, even as he opens his own art up to the charge of difference by leaning so heavily into feminized territory, however its forms are veiled and clothed with drapery.

Difference is hardly provident, as Wordsworth's publishing difficulties attest. After Wordsworth's early taste of women writers and then continental influence, the parliamentary Burke provides an obvious alternative, an (ambivalently) masculine and certainly British face to put to William's self-disciplining and distributive mapping. To Wordsworth's stabilizing female ground or base, Burke's patrician judgments provide masculine grids that allow the self freedom of movement because the stage itself has been put in place or demobilized. This is a belief Coleridge and Byron cannot entertain, since their worlding (both public and private) is so masculine that it becomes constituted by slippage, by what will not hold. The romantic irony represented by the worlds of "Dejection: An Ode" or *Don Juan* charges those worlds with a rapidity of change such that the speaker is caught between the flux of the world and the stable but untrustworthy stage. World momentum produces a reluctant and lax hero who nonetheless finds the domestic stage too confining to inhabit for long. Hence, his alienated character derives from a world that cannot hold him, a fact he veils to great effect by claiming that the world has instead rejected him. The Byronic hero, however, is no Wordsworthian deject, no wanderer of his own valley and centering stage. In contrast, Wordsworth's worlding produces a stable home precisely because he chooses it for its femininity: its pastoral aesthetic, its Smithian mythos, its domesticating nests. Already marked as containing picturesque and pastoral scenes, the Lake District is a region whose balding heights display a vast geophysical age and therefore a different kind of timekeeping. Grasmere and its surrounds are ripe for the discipline of mapmaking—in part because everything is already in its place.

Coleridge is still grappling with his own vision of the world during this period, but statesman Burke provides an apt and stable English model because he has already marked the world as sublime or beautiful, courtly or common, mannered or roguish. As a mapmaker, Burke's *Annual Register* might seem more relevant than his *Enquiry* or his 1790 *Reflections on the Revolution in France*. Begun in 1758 the *Register* surveyed the year's events, providing a model for organizational mapping. The 1793 *Register*, for instance, divides the phenomenal year into eleven discrete categories that separate historical and political events from the local and domestic, the scientific from the aesthetic, yet that together recreate a connective narrative of the recent past.[15] On the other hand, the *Reflections* appears overtly antithetical to Wordsworth's thinking in that it speaks against substituting speculative conceptual frames for traditional order and values. Yet, here as throughout his writings, Burke appeals to an achievable universal order through self-examination and self-criticism to integrate man's inner life with the outer world. Against the sentimental ethos of quick, sure judgment, Burke urges critical care and a reliance on custom.

Burke's system for mapping the world offers a substantive model even though he did not seem to practice it fully himself.[16] But its moral atmosphere and dependence on moral will can result in guilt for those who do not efface or wall off painful memories. So 1798 must contain and mediate 1793 not because Rousseau is no longer viable but because Wordsworth's 1793 is rife with terrible memories and terrible guilt — not the least of which is William's disloyal support of France against his own country (Chandler, 11). The turmoil of this year was nothing less than a horrifying revolution in Wordsworth's own "moral nature," an emotion-racked experience he equates with the political revolution taking place in the Parisian streets. The double mapping Wordsworth reads onto these months from the perspective of later years is a vision of streets and street activity mapped over a grid of mental hierarchies in uproar. As he recalls from the standpoint of 1805,

Through months, through years, long after the last beat
Of those atrocities . . .

Such ghastly visions had I of despair,
And tyranny, and implements of death,
And long orations which in dreams I pleaded

Before unjust tribunals, with a voice
Labouring, a brain confounded, and a sense
Of treachery and desertion in the place
The holiest that I knew of — my own soul.
[*Prelude* X][17]

The external and internal coalesce disturbingly in a man-made sublime. When compared to the imperceptible sublime of his alpine crossing, this horror of the streets is too much present and intrusive. Its aftereffects are a horror, a violation of the self, an abjection. This sublimity begins to haunt his vision of the world, activating personal trauma and guilt at unantici- pated moments. Even the threatened nervous breakdown in 1793 was secreted, buried as too dangerous to mention or remember.[18]

After rejoining his countrymen in 1792 — in fact, to garner funds se- cretly for his mistress Annette and their child — William wanders his na- tion in walking tours, attempting to fix it in his mind, to fix himself as well, or to find a place for himself. He finally rejoins Dorothy in 1794 in Halifax, but they do not settle down until the next year, and in the meantime William has nursed Raisley Calvert in the same fashion he will claim in *The Prelude* that Dorothy nurses him during this period. Thus despair over France resolves into a rejection of certain memories, a displacement of them onto the landscape which is hidden from sight and visited only by chance, and a symbolic valuation on the act of nurturance. Sublimation of the French terror, as well as his own guilty fatherhood and desertion, provokes a prescriptive distancing and silence: The sublime is recognized by its extreme silence or by its unknowable voices; it cannot in any case be the occasion for company or easy conversation.

In contrast to the masculine solitude of sublime imaginings, the pas- toral demands a second self or conversant; this is the case even in apparent solitude. In part, the pastoral necessitates company because it is the genre of talk and persuasion. But within the general map in Wordsworth's head, the pastoral is also defined by the feminine coordinates of domestic care and friendly company. The activity of each sphere is accorded not by virtue of Kantian will or mental discipline, however Wordsworth worried over these concerns, but by the easy proximity to, or haunting distance from, a central core of comfort, nurture, and affection. This core is best described as the *chora,* a space Julia Kristeva theorizes as nested between mother and child, recollected by the adult artist as the wellspring of nurture and poetic voice. When too distanced from the chora, the artist finds himself in a place Kristeva calls the *thetic,* a place of blocked voice and alienation from the verbal or conversing community.[19] Thus the prelingual and nurturing chora is productive of the pastoral quadrant, while the disruptive thetic produces the dreamscape of melancholy musing. The chora is discoverable by maternal murmur (the babbling sounds of nature or maidens as represented in William's poetry), whereas the thetic is recognized by untranslatable sounds, unmeaningful words, or awful silence.

Rousseau does not prepare his readers for such complex notions about nature, and Wordsworth's schema is traceable more to native English traditions, as well as to his own artistic sensitivities. Burke is the more obvious proponent of moral life once radical philosophy proved fallible. The neoconservative restoration of an earlier innocent world can, through the gift of mapping, cure the sick heart. Nor is it just the revolution sympathizer who needs healing in the period of Rousseau's ascendancy: Because W. Wordsworth has internalized the political disaster as a melancholy illness or breakdown, his double mapping must also undergo a cure. Effectively, the healing process under Dorothy's steady nursing of the poetic spirit entails an inversion of the mapping process, a redistribution of thetic and choral spaces that reinstates nesting and walls off psychic disturbance. The cure is to turn "out" the internalized street grid of social and mental revolution onto the outer scene, still double-mapped but now as reflection rather than revolution. This performative heals the poetic spirit by allowing it to impose its mind on the outer scene. By implementing control over how the world is to be perceived, the disastrous months of 1793 can be buried in the mind, veiled from that which is chosen for the performative by a literary aesthetic rather than a social one. At the same time, as he explains in his *Prelude* panegyric to Dorothy, she also helped him see the healing qualities of feminine ways of seeing and being when his harsher masculine vision made him ill. It is not just the literary and aesthetic but the feminine-centered mapping that prevails and that allows for other things maternal — sublime terror, single mothers — to be so centered as to be submerged and sectioned off.

The implications of double mapping are enormous, particularly as cura-

tive. In his new vision, the world becomes divisively sectioned by a series of axes: pastoral-epic, rural-urban, domestic-political, privacy-fame.
Quite simply, these binaries allow Wordsworth to structure his universe
by value and by gender, thus controlling what in 1793 had so raged out of
control for him. It is convenient to think of these axes as overlying one
another, as in transparencies that overlie the mother map or matrix; construing the situation in this manner follows Wordsworth's consistent gendering of the binaries. Whether as Nature or as Dorothy, axes defined by
the feminine mark off that part of the world that nurses or heals the poet:
pastoral, domestic, ease. Those axes defined as masculine by William's
own sense of poetic endeavor and social responsibility mark off spaces
of brotherhood, transcendence, and fame. Constituted in this way, the
Wordsworthian world can project simultaneously the poet of gentlemanly
reflection and ease (the Burkean Man of Taste) and the poet who deeply
feels (the sentimental melancholic). And such projection is directly assim-
ilable into literary taste as an ascetic mode, a lens through which every
aspect of a constructed life can be filtered. Literary taste becomes for
William, as for no other member of his present or future household,
so inculcated that later, when Edward Quillinan becomes Dora Wordsworth's suitor, Stephen Gill remarks that despite William's disapproval of
the match "[h]e had come to respect his [Quillinan's] literary judgement,
which for him was always an indication of a person's morals and character" (*William Wordsworth*, 401).

It had become in the 1790s, then, Wordsworth's poetic project to represent this doubled nature as taking in both the feminine and masculine
aspects of his selving, and both the private and public faces to this self. He
must inhabit, as it were, both Dorothy *and* himself. The project entails
living as much as writing within the plotted or matrixed vision, and it
entails constituting a community of like-minded inhabitants to people its
quadrants. The writing that sustains the vision must replicate the structure
of the vision as a philosophical endeavor, one whose complex epical character adequately expresses the careful adjudication of conceptual space
that Wordsworth then transfers onto the visual world. Its projected plan
cannot correlate to this schema. But what we do have is a corrective to
what could not be written of *The Recluse:* the final 1849–50 arrangement
of Wordsworth's works, which groups poems in an architectural order;

and Wordsworthian Life itself. This study depends on these two artifacts to temper the grid in William's head with the fictional drama, the closet drama, that Dorothy agreed to play out with him in their pastoral valley and garden.

Thus Wordsworth's assimilation of the Rousseauistic or French aesthetic to the feminine quadrants allows him to silence Annette Vallon and their child by burying them in the maternal ground of the domestic and picturesque. Thus, too, can he bury the hysteria of revolution gone wrong in the sanctifying hills of Mother Nature. The subsequent embrace of Burkean or English aesthetic is then assimilated to the masculine quadrants. Whether Dorothy, William, and Coleridge are familiar and comfortable inhabitants of these grid spaces depends on their relation to the French or English (or for Coleridge, German) philosophical attitudes toward nature and the local or worldly sensibilities underlying those attitudes. Nature herself becomes a keystone to the structural matrices of this Wordsworthian world; Nature is most available or tangible in the feminine quadrants, and Dorothy is most deeply implicated here.

Part of W. Wordsworth's innovative amelioration of the solitary poet's mythos, and part of his textual entrance into the fiction of self, was to use romantic siblinghood to redress the nature of the subjective trial. Dorothy thus underlies his response to solitary pain in a way that the romance beloved cannot, as she assumes for him a role of the sister-self. By addressing his sibling, who shared his (romanticized) youth and who has absorbed his speech as an attentive listener and respondent, William can negotiate the subject–object divide that threatens the other romantics with the specter of a silencing alienation. The sibling does not so much allow the poet to achieve the semblance of a unified self as she provides a correspondent who can help him mediate the terrors of a hostile Mother Nature simply by allowing him to cross the self–other divide — for she is both other (that which is addressed) and self (a second, earlier self).

The addresses to Dorothy are part of a larger group of poems similar to the conversation genre developed by Coleridge, a group I call the address-to-women. But whereas Coleridge's poems are meditative monologues, these addresses to women can be read as an attempt at true romantic "conversation." The lyric poem itself enacts an utterance, a direct address. Internalizing the addressed maiden's speech gives the poet strength and wards off silence or madness as Coleridge's silent babe in "Frost at Midnight" cannot. At the same time, the apostrophe to her maps the female reader into a maiden template of sentimental values in order to recompose her as a reader of Wordsworthian taste. The sentimental (which demands sacrifice, unlike sensibility) as much as the pastoral demands a reformation of the reader before the aesthetic formula can seem natural. When Wordsworth writes in the 1800 Preface that part of what distinguishes his lyrical ballads "from the popular Poetry of the day . . . is this, that the feeling therein developed gives importance to the action and situation, and not the action and situation to the feeling," he is exalting the reader's naturalized template of response over the familiar set pieces of gothic horror and other self-indulgent genres. But at the same time he seats the terms such that the sentimental is taken to be "natural," in order that the male reader experiences the differential of Wordsworthian poetry from "the popular Poetry of the day" as necessarily true because sincere, precisely because its sincerity is based on female sacrifice, loss, or absence from the temporal plane.

Still, what has the maiden sacrificed, and how willingly, so that the poet may speak? Dorothy Wordsworth finds herself suspended between form and formative and reformative agencies; in addition, she is the addressee in the poem as well as out of it. She also seems to have queried the cost of this relationship; her own addresses to women, written in her later years, do not invoke silenced or nonverbal beings, nor do they gather strength from the young woman addressed by absorbing her voice as William's speaker does. If D. Wordsworth does not use the address to the same end as her brother, it is perhaps because her relation to her addressee is predicated on her own prior status as maiden; as poet she must occupy both subject and object positions whereas W. Wordsworth can only absorb the object by assuming it/her into his prior self. William's is clearly a temporal and therefore a linguistically metaphorical solution as much as it is a colonizing and therefore metonymic solution. He seeks the sister or maiden's aid for a homeostasis that will enable him to transcend physical sense; D. Wordsworth's poetic energies are directed toward enabling another maiden to achieve something so that they both may remain in the pastoral present, contingently grounded by each other's mutual aid.

However, the schematics of the address-to-women in William's rendition of this peculiarly Wordsworthian form instill a subdued threat in its insistent relation between the maiden and Nature as mother. Recurrently, the address-to-women poems move to bring the woman addressed to an enclosed place in nature, a grove or bower; such a move integrates the structural link between Nature and maiden into the form of the address itself: "Dear Child of Nature . . . / —There is a nest in a green dale, / A harbour and a hold" ("To a Young Lady"). In this natural garden, which closes off the open spaces of eighteenth-century locodescriptive and picturesque vistas, the maiden can commune with Nature in the poet's presence, allowing him safe access to that threshold which so intrigues him. Those addresses that view nature itself as an alternative to the confines of the domestic interior call the maiden to an open rather than a closed space: poems like "To My Sister," where the maiden must "yield / To the bare trees, and mountains bare, / And grass in the green field." At the same time they perceive the open fields as spaces that also define Nature's bodily and psychic presence, the "universal birth" and the "blessing in the air" recalling the maternal function of Nature. Nature operates as both holding space and comforter, birth-giver to life and natural love, Eden and idyll all at once; she confuses inner and outer, closet and stage. Such confusion defers time, isolating the valley and elevating it to special status.

Thus the address-to-women participates in an Arcadia in which temporality is held back, cordoned off from the historicity of the industrial city.[20] Set in opposition to industry, societal affairs, and "the principle of the State," the pastoral provides a ground on which the hero can struggle. Standing in the edenic valley, the shepherd hero or poet is alone among men, self-made and self-proclaimed. His antagonists are the patriarch of the legislative State and maternal Nature. If the patriarch is the civic authority against whom the poet wages, against whom the *Lyrical Ballads* (with its realistic rustics, unlovely privations, and pain) were written, then the mother is the archaic or "phallic" mother of epic imagination who inspirits Nature outside the valley through fear, mortality, hallucination. She is the mother who underlies the romantic imagination but whose rejection into a "radical exteriority" beyond the child's ego's boundaries come to represent "the mobile *chora* of the subject in process / on trial" (Kristeva, *Revolution*, 148).

The archaic mother is encountered through the poet's memories of childhood in *The Prelude,* most particularly in the spots of time such as the poet's childhood encounter in Book XI with a place of death in which the hanged man's name was "engraven" on the grass — that is, both graven and synecdochically the murderer's grave. The graven is a "monumental writing," in W. Wordsworth's sense of the monument, inscribing both men's drive toward death and Nature's embodiment of it: "Oh mystery of man," he comments, "from what a depth / Proceed thy honours! I am lost, but see / In simple childhood something of the base / On which thy greatness stands — ." The move from human depths to greatness is both imaginative and natural, for the child's visionlike experience is followed by what is both natural and imaginative, a naturalized or grounded woman holding a pitcher on her head and bending with difficulty against the strong wind. The wind itself is the mother's breath, the romantic breeze as a tumultuous formative power for the emergent poet. The silent woman, the "melancholy beacon" above, "the visionary dreariness" all recount the negative drives associated with the archaic mother. But the pitcher, resonant of the urn-shape that for Kristeva constitutes something even anterior to the womb which she calls the chora, embodies both creative and destructive energies, and the mature poet recalls that this spot of time transforms from terror to "[t]he spirit of pleasure and youth's golden gleam — / . . . with radiance more divine / From these remembrances, and from the power / They left behind." Indeed, the force of the archaic mother is in part to prevent the poet from succumbing to a civic dismissal of the gentler pastoral Nature:

> In truth, this degradation . . . aggravated by the times,
> Which with their passionate sounds might often make
> The milder minstrelsies of rural scenes
> Inaudible — was transient.[21]

The various intensities of Nature's visionary power are connected to the bounded pastoral self as a way to prevent dismissal. The mother claims her "chosen son" through the chora, a psychic form that haunts W. Wordsworth's idylls occasionally as a pitcher or even urn-shaped vale but more typically as a grove or nestlike bower. The grove is itself a choral space of supportive sympathy, for the displacement of the mother from the ego terrain (the atemporal bounded edenic valley) onto the imaginative (the visionary spots of time that demonstrate to the poet his imagination at work) allows for the presence of pastoral nature. This Mother Nature, who personifies the valley itself and whom W. Wordsworth links to the gentle maiden as an intrinsic aspect of her own "nature," is the mother whose bodily chora or nest/grove provides the marked space in which poet and nature commune via semiotic discourse (breezes, rhythmic echoes, rippling streams). Pastoralized Nature supports the hero's endeavors and nurtures his ambitions. She is his lyric muse and the alternative to the sterner epic inspiration of the archaic mother.

The maiden, both inside and outside the address form, suffers from the ambivalence the poet exhibits concerning her powerful relation to the archaic mother and her disempowering relation to poetic voice. In part, William's geographical imagination and aesthetic charting work to sort out this ambivalence and to offer Dorothy a place from which to speak within his own vision and his own ambulatory status. Where she certainly does find a voice is within her own poetic prose and the construction of their mutual Life, and this voiced presence is strong enough at times to assert itself in William's poetic utterance while at others it serves to establish the authority of her self-fiction in a way that the maiden of the addresses is conspicuously denied.

To understand the weight of Dorothy's word, we must first accept Bakhtin's premise that all utterance is address, a phenomenon W. Wordsworth's address-to-women textually inscribes and D. Wordsworth's carries out. In Bakhtin's sense, only the meaningful word exists; "there is only the word as address" (*Dostoevsky's Poetics,* 237). Thus every poetic utterance is double-oriented, directed both toward the object of utterance (the thing or idea or person talked about) and toward the addressee (receiver of the talk). This notion of the word drastically alters our reading of Dorothy's *Grasmere Journals* to assess her entries as always directed toward her brother-self and brother-other as much as toward her own self as reader. The object or referent *provokes* an attitude verging on apostrophe (because it cannot answer back); apostrophe then *invokes* the object (for the romantics, nature or an aspect of nature) but speaks *to* the listener as ally and witness. The listener can be near, as in a textual auditor; historically near, as in the reader; or distant, as in an unsympathetic or hostile audience.[22] In W. Wordsworth's address-to-women, the maiden (based on the historical Dorothy) is constructed as unquestioningly sympathetic, existing to fulfill both these functions of listener and interlocutor. She is summoned as *the* ally against the weight of solitude and silence.

The crucial point here is that unlike courtly love poetry, where the beloved is the object of the utterance without the ability to respond textually, the maiden is the poet's listener and anticipated respondent and so becomes not his object but his audience and interlocutor. In this arrangement, then, Nature must take woman's traditional place as praised or blamed object around which the utterance is structured. The maiden's sympathetic function as listener of the poetic meditation allies her on the one hand with Nature (as female/muse counterpart), and on the other with the Poet (as discursive partner). Her closeness to both permits the lyric form itself to arise, whereas a doubting or masterful listener would provoke an entirely different genre, as when Coleridge provokes the epic *Prelude,* or when Sara inspires Coleridge's half-doubting play on courtly love, "The Eolian Harp."

Yet, in our literary tradition, this split stands behind the internal or external voice poetically understood as the Muse. Behind that hinge between inner and outer worlds of the self is a space that defies verbalization and actualizing performance, a space we have been speaking of as the chora, a preverbal space where the infant's bond with the mother is formative for creative energies. For Kristeva, style and creativity function in response to the speaker's degree of nearness or distance to the maternal space of the chora, but this is a creative function as well as a mythic one; artists continually depict this choral space as multivoiced or as the place where the muse speaks.[23] And if William Wordsworth shrouds his "spots of time" or moments of choral activity in great mystery, Dorothy Wordsworth's journals — perhaps more than her poetry — are permeated with this energy and its sensitivities. The increased recognition of this presence in Dorothy's poetic voice substantiates not that she is more liable to its sway but that she is sensitive to William's placing her in its space as maiden and muse. In the case of Dorothy as listener, not only is the maiden (1) bound to Nature and (2) overly sensitive herself to multiple voicings, but (3) she has been trained to read by the very brother whose words address her. Indeed, it is in her journals most of all, texts written for a communal eye, that layered voicing occurs: Prosed voices interact and intersect, descriptions sit next to lists of chores and accounts of others' dialogues, and William's thoughts, postures, hopes are interlaced with Dorothy's own.

D. Wordsworth's contrasting despair about her poetry would be, in Margaret Homans's view, one of a badly needed but missing muse. Homans reads the equation as Dorothy's maternal muse balanced by William's social fathering; such literary paternity would signify a voice-silencing, body-absenting force that operates to refuse Dorothy poetic status.[24] Certainly, William's poems that do not directly address her represent Dorothy as a bird- or streamlike presence whose babbling murmur comforts and envoices him, particularly in "Home at Grasmere." Yet the evidence of her journals is that she apostrophizes him in order to call him into presence when she is alone in precisely the same manner that his poems address and invoke her. And if Dorothy expected the whisper of the divine Muse instead, a sound both William and Coleridge claim to hear, then naturally she mourns her impoverished ear; yet her journals belie such poverty. If D. Wordsworth's struggle with the muse remained deeply conflicted, her experience with musing was that of inspiring her brother through words rather than beauty or essence (as the two Hutchinson sisters are protrayed as doing in William's and Coleridge's lyrics). Nor is William a traditional patriarchal muse, authorizing the woman writer to create; although she writes that she desires to "please him," she responds to his request that she record an incident only briefly and prosaically.[25] It is through the Wordsworths' interactive relationship that Dorothy is released from the traditional gendered role of the silent muse-woman. Likewise, William is able to refute his gendered role (except for the Lucy poems) of troubled poet-lover because of his sister's supporting voice. A literate/literal thoughtful muse, Dorothy's deft descriptions, particularly of scenes William did not himself witness, and her stories from or of childhood appear as poetry in his hands.

In William Wordsworth's work, however, the traditional Muse is not replaced by Dorothy's supportive voice but displaced onto Nature. His rendering of the divine Muse as Nature's ghostly whisper is the sound of the uncanny — identifiable as rhythmic sounds emanating from the maternal chora. The winds, Nature's breath, inspire the poet with the mystery of words. In poetic language, such inspiration results from the appropriation of "this archaic, instinctual, and maternal territory" of the chora (or Nature) as the "passage into and through the forbidden" (Kristeva, *Desire*, 136). Of this mystery, W. Wordsworth writes:

There darkness makes abode, and all the host
Of shadowy things do work their changes there
As in a mansion like their proper home.
Even forms and substances are circumfused
By that transparent veil with light divine,
And through the turnings intricate of verse
Present themselves as objects recognised
In flashes, and with a glory scarce their own.
[*Prelude* V.622–29]

The mansion and proper home where shadowy things operate underneath and behind the turnings of words suggests Kristeva's notion of the chora as a "receptacle" or space anterior to conscious language use which structures that usage.

Such an interpretation must also remind us of Dorothy Wordsworth's function in "Tintern Abbey," to recall her brother "in after years / . . . when thy mind / Shall be a mansion for all lovely forms, / Thy memory be as a dwelling-place." But I construe her function as more integral than this famous passage suggests, for she stands in as that threshold space between mother and infant and internalized by the child, which we have been calling the chora. Her frustration with the muse is that she never hears Nature's cavernous whispers because her voice and her body/abode are in the wrong place. In the romantic mythology of poethood, this choral space is both interior and exterior, locatable in the nestlike enclosures of grove and bower in Mother Nature representing the externalized interior psychic space. Because the Western tradition aligns women with Nature biologically and maternally, they therefore inherit safe access to this choral space. But according to this view, women's alliance with this space means it cannot be their quest object because it is not otherly to them; it is the quest of the male artist alone. This sought-for encounter with feminized, mystical otherness is for Kristeva an encounter of communion, the *sacra conversazione*.[26] Part of Dorothy Wordsworth's "becoming" is to invest herself in this halfway space with all the literary and creative self-making she can summon, to try on the part and make it hers to such an extent that her brother cannot make do without her. If he is allowed to participate in the sacred conversation, it is only with her aid.

Like Dorothy's, part of W. Wordsworth's "becoming," and the accompanying process of text making, is the everyday act of being in the valley. However, when W. Wordsworth walks in nature, he domesticates, appropriates, and rewrites all that he surveys. A woman working in the fields fixates the speaker with her strange tongue, and he in turn fixes her there in the landscape where she remains the Solitary Reaper. She has been pastoralized in that she no longer possesses her self, her voice, or her affect and has become a natural entity. The process by which pastoralization, even colonization, occurs is by a masterful deployment of the symbolic. The symbolic, which is verbal and structurally oriented toward metaphor and absence, and the semiotic, which is preverbal and rhythmically oriented toward metonymy and presence, designate poles of communicative possibility. Whereas the semiotic manifests *impulsion* or the drive to express, the symbolic reveals *compulsion* or the conscious manipulation of symbol, power, or desire to express meaning, to repress dissension, and to enact beliefs, wants, thoughts. When one speaker controls the discourse so as to reduce the other speaker's utterance to music, whisper, nonsense, or animal sound, speakers become communicative poles but do not communicate. They represent but they do not mean, and the conversation is shifted entirely to an anterior set of discourse participants, the author and reader. This shift should give the author tighter control over the text; however, W. Wordsworth purposefully impairs the regulation of otherness through a figure's mystical silence or babble in order to problematize voice. Both Keats and De Quincey misconstrue the dangers of this power relation at the level of author-reader, viewing Wordsworth's anxiety over this play with selfness as signifying weakness. But Wordsworth seeks to reconfigure traditional ways of meaning; pastoralization is one such model, but it is incomplete. What he continually rediscovers is that it is only in addressing the sister-maiden (whose voice is never problematized because she is never the other) that he precludes objectifying or silencing the other, and thus precludes the theft of another's subjectivity. It is only then that conversation occurs at the level of the figure.

However, and this is an important intervention in the Wordsworthian Life, the figure is not always this or that, never simply an alternate version of the self (Dorothy as Maiden) or the other (the Solitary Reaper as rustic maid). Rather, the figure in its epic and solitary form is always also the subject-on-trial, the subjectivity that knows itself as visionary and speaker. It is easier to conceive this nonunitary being if we consider the pastoral as a state of mind, a place to inhabit figuratively as well as literally, and, above all, heroically. With the gentrification of the country as a place of retirement from city life for the upper classes, pastoral poetry serves to embody thise sense of privileged seclusion, leisure, and pleasure. This is in itself a paradoxical relation because, as William Empson remarks, pastoral is literature of the country but ignores the country laborer for whom it was never written to be read.[27] Wordsworth acknowledges the pastoral's essence in his desire to rewrite it as the habitation of both rustic and poet, as the literature of and, at least ostensibly, for the rustic. This essence for Empson is the condensation of nation and populace; for Wordsworth it is the social turned into a landed condensation, country with countryside. In both cases, pastoral works metaphorically to produce a savior, a "natural" man of heroic stature capable of shepherding the country. This is a role intrinsically suited to a poet of Wordsworth's guilt, ambitions, and simultaneous desire for seclusion.

If Empson's pastoral is a manly tale of salvation, Charlotte Smith's *Ethelinde* describes a feminine land closely associated with the female sensibility, especially melancholy. The pastoral can further be read as halfway between these two genderings, and Marlon Ross analyzes the Wordsworthian pastoral landscape as terrain predicated on a grounding of the female (see "Naturalizing Gender"). The sublimation of the female body into static detail enables the poet to transcend nature, while objectifying the body disables women for romantic poethood. The scale becomes that of nation-country-ground, and of populace-countryside-landscaped women. This arbitrated middle ground provides the pasture out of which the hero of natural genius will arise, a hero who is quite naturally male.

The pastoral thus provides an amiable plot for mapping and overlays.

Its antecedent status, however, is subordinate to that of tragic and epic plots: the rustic underside to the gentleman's tale. As subplot, pastoral makes legitimate the main plot by its return to native ground and the Noble Savage (or at least Anglo-Saxon laborer) who inhabits it. The return itself is accomplished both as plot formation and in the person of the tale-teller, who moves from city or courtly plot to country plot and back in order to interweave the two sides of our human and national nature. Wordsworth's poet-gentleman clearly partakes of the courtier-shepherd, a figure validated by both monarch and nature. Ideologically, the result is self as ideal citizen, as this structure which is both outer narrative and inner ego formation (civic state and citizen) resolves into double plot.

If, as Empson notes, eighteenth-century thinkers saw the pastoral meta-phorically as ripe ground for political satire and commentary, the early romantics reacted by seeing pastoral as the literal ground of its utopian dreams and the gateway to sublime aspirations, not proleptically urban but antiurban. The romantic version of pastoral is normally the habitation of the beautiful, an aesthetic state opposed to the awful sublime of gla-ciers, oceans, and other remainders of catastrophic prehistory. The sub-lime itself is conceptually complex and variable; we can view it here as simultaneously an aesthetic mode, a theological principle, an imaginative experience, and a philosophical category. Sublimity, subliming, liminality, and sublimation are all facets of the ecstasy and fatality of sublime tran-scendence; according to the pastoral double plot, all exist outside the pale of the pastoral valley, yet the hero is uneasily aware of their seductive threat beyond the pale. Sublimity lies on the other side of beauty just as pastoral by a sudden turn can become epic; the whole becomes a dance of mystical proportions with only the poet as (privileged) spectator. Where the pastoral results from the need to inscribe nation on ground, the sub-lime as we consider it here inhabits an interpretive space which can come into presence at any point. The sublime, then, cannot be equated with epic, and the epic tale could no longer drive the visionary project: Words-worth's lyricized *Prelude* demonstrates to what point the sublime will allow the poet's touch.

Twenty-five years after his initializing encounter with Grasmere's lyric terrain, William began translating *The Aeneid* as an experimental attempt to improve on Dryden's translation, and indeed, he was not planning to go beyond the fourth book.[28] In London with Dorothy that year, 1823, Wordsworth met with several friends, including Coleridge, who told him his translation was a waste of time. The narration of Rome's founding does not replace the romantic poet's quest for the sublime. Wordsworth must find his frontier within his own mind as it portrays itself on the native landscape. William's spots of time are not Roman but romantic encapsulations of heroic liminality, not godhead but natural inspiration. In fact, as Don Bialostosky argues, Wordsworth proposes himself to his reading nation as representing "a cultivated 'intellectual universe,' a recognizable 'advance' which widens 'the sphere of human sensibility' . . . in the domain of poetic art."[29] Yet the landscaping of this heroic relation to the poet's readership is driven by a more personal relation, not of hero to tribe, of native son to natural (or chosen) habitat, but of individual to his blood-family, of orphaned romantic to his siblings and friends who together create the nest that sustains him. It is the nesting community that metonymically becomes the reading nation. Metonymically doubled readership demands an equally complex poetic mastery.

The threshold status of double plot, then, offers Wordsworthian myth a significant gain over a plot–subplot structure: William as dominant plot (cultural leader) and rustics as subplot (natural laborers) are supplanted by a doubled sense of writing, indeed, feeling oneself into being through familial and communal relations. Within the tradition of pastoral heroics this structure emplots what Empson has called "covert deification." The hero knows himself as a sacrificial king/Christ figure, whose death is "something like an atonement for his tribe that put[s] it in harmony with God or nature" (Empson, 29). This is not specifically Wordsworthian, since sacrifice is typically feminized or rustic in William's native tale (it is Virginie who dies in Saint-Pierre's heroic pastoral). But the Wordsworthian poet *is* tribal visionary and guilt atoner, striving for harmony with God and nature through rhyme and theme. Pastoral infrastructure is thus the perfect bed for romantic genius to root itself, genius as the mediation between God and man, nature and culture. *The Prelude* narrates a life of epic events cradled in the pastoral, with a hero who is Nature's son born to save the nation through his vision. This is the tale the Wordsworths' life in Grasmere underwrites. In fact, it is a tale composed while William paced the terraced walk at Lancrigg in Easedale while Dorothy sat on the slope and took transcription. However, such a tale is supported by two coinciding perspectives. Both poet and sibling-sister, youth and maiden, must be represented as present and empathetic, and they can be so because Wordsworthian myth displaces sacrifice and deity from the human onto nature, and into "natural objects" such as rustic laborers and naturalized women.

In D. Wordsworth's writing, this schematized or mapped pastoralization is harder to decipher. When writing of peers, children, or natural entities she is respectful of selfhood and the capacity for self-representation. But when she writes of beggars, the dispossessed, and local laborers, or when she redesigns a natural scene, the issue is not so clear. In other words, pastoralization is part of living within the Wordsworths' ideological landscape. At the same time, she is in danger of being herself pastoralized through the sister–beloved–mother matrix. Homans reads D. Wordsworth's career as indeed so crippled and sees her as accepting her silencing Lucy-like place in Mother Nature. But Dorothy is not pastoralized in those poems that address her as sister, as twin, and as envoiced. How she regards, returns, and resists pastoralization depends on how she employs the other two components of Wordsworthian Life: affect and discourse. And if as historical sister she responds with enthusiasm to these addresses to her fictive self, she indicates later in her own poetry a refusal to disregard another's subjecthood.

How Dorothy Wordsworth regards affect, the pastoral component for which she is most praised, depends strongly on how William regards it. In general, romanticism considers two categorical emotive possibilities: love (affect) and melancholy (lack of affect). Love comprises (1) sublimity and fusion, (2) aesthetic appreciation as affection (the beautiful), and (3) domestic affection as nurturance. Melancholy comprises (1) depression as alienation and disaffection, (2) romantic dejection (an aesthetic sensibility) and (3) abjection (the grotesque or the ugly). In the Wordsworthian schema, the ideas in both first categorical levels are masculine domains which William inhabits as a solitary, whereas both third-categorical concepts are feminine domains which Dorothy inhabits alone even while in relation to William. The secondary formulations for both categories are middle ground between the primary terrain which is William's and the tertiary ground which is Dorothy's; on this middle affectional meetingplace the siblings walk together not only as equals but as lovers and lovers of nature.

What I have just described as the Wordsworthian schema, obviously, is William's rendering of it; it is a model which D. Wordsworth both complied with and deviated from. William's bounded self, resulting from the painful memories of his French experiences, now had difficulty with the practice, if not the theory, of sympathy, while De Quincey's famous comment on the quickness of Dorothy's sympathetic powers attests to the ongoing importance she gives it. In D. Wordsworth's less divisible comprehension of the world, sympathy crosses all categories, for it is what allows her always to step into the shoes of another, as well as to study nature's intricacies. Similarly, Dorothy's understanding of melancholy differs from her brother's. Melancholy is a poetic disposition characterized by specular display of disturbance and includes a tearing away of the self and a questing for the self-knows-not-what, but this is typically a masculine definition. For D. Wordsworth this sensibility translates into melancholy as an excess of affect (the second formulation rather than the first), an overburden of pleasure that brings tears. When the tears brought on by a glorious landscape, however, are aesthetic tears they are not dis-pleasure but a distillation of pleasure, not an essentializing of nature as object but an essentializing of emotion as self. Melancholy is then that which comprises the aesthetic mood and displaces the first-level melancholy of emptiness and despair. But underlying this sorrow is the negation of the self in abjection, not the realm of the deject where William's solitaries wander but the abjecting of the bodily self in a state of the grotesque or the ugly. This is Dorothy's particular state, a negative state not shared by William in its bodily disgust but dictated by his scheme as a feminine sublime. It concerns us because Wordsworthian affections do not account for abjection in the bodily sense as a subjective state; Dorothy's poetic exploration of this paradoxical position gets close, then, to what it is to be one of William's landscaped figures. That is to say, it allows her to touch what her literary character would be without an intervening verbal intercourse.

At the same time, D. Wordsworth does not want to change women's role as Wollstonecraft or Hays strive to do but wants to redesign it to suit her self-production. The performative "becoming" for D. Wordsworth is defining herself pastorally, as a member of this new poetic community in which lines are fluid, brothers and friends are spiritual lovers (William, John, Coleridge, De Quincey), friends are sisters (the Hutchinsons), and domestic activities have no set time or place. But such pastoral definition is beset by literary and folkloric traditions. Both William and De Quincey refer, for instance, to Dorothy's gypsy tan, a reference both to her bohemian life and to the nut-brown maid. The maid, to be treated more fully later, is a pastoral figure of folk balladry. For romantic poets she appears most influentially in Goethe as a daughter of the valley who represents wildness of spirit and natural sexuality.

Yet neither she nor the sexually untamed gypsy fits Dorothy Wordsworth's self-characterization or pastoral performance; these are instead male attempts to force her back into a conventional sexualization that has dangerous connotations. Peter Gay points out that the nineteenth century "abounded in assertions that 'Jewesses' or gypsies or other 'exotics' were 'hot-blooded,'" because such distancing allowed for men's illegitimate sexual longings to be displaced onto the undomesticated as a prevention against incest (*Bourgeois Experience,* 392). To compare Dorothy to gypsies or the nut-brown maid (by midcentury a phrase that indicated the beauty of the Mediterranean olive complexion)[30] is to thrust her uneasily further into the sentimental role of sexual victim. But in general this male unease with Dorothy's self-definition is muted, in part because her self-positioning is not outrageous or disturbing but pastoral and supportive, that is, second-place and positively mythified as such by William's poetry. It is not that D. Wordsworth is not capable of a radical individuality such as Wollstonecraft's, whose biography she read, but that she refuses a Wollstonecraftian independence and sexuality. Her femininity, then, is partly defined by her relation to the male figure on whom she depends. Such a dependence also defines how much social disapproval she can afford, disapproval which could cripple her but not William after his early rebellious treks through Europe or his refusal to enter a conventional profession. D. Wordsworth's letters reveal that, for her, being feminine is predicated on dependence but does not include such conventional femininities as flirtation or ribbons or social balls. Yet she accepts fully the expectations that women exhibit care, charity, nurture — that they treat community as family, others as self. But she also excepts and celebrates the exchange of words between siblings as a performative act that crosses gendering to act as literary accomplice to self-creation and twinship. The exchange of words in its simplest form is the basis of Wordsworthian Life.

⌁   *The Wordsworthian Life*

The vision of a poetic life begins with the consciously wrought daydream world. It is a world whose construction D. Wordsworth called building castles ("I assure you I am a very skilful architect"),[31] and throughout the Wordsworths' work this shared daydream always consists of a cottage (or parsonage) in a dell. This world is thoroughly doubled, pregnant with the textual and oral voices of both Wordsworths, and continually crossing mind–body boundaries. It is also infiltrated by the voices of their circle, their community, their literary predecessors, their memories, all of which participate (with or without their knowledge) in the relation between bodily and mental modalities the Wordsworths incorporate as "naturally" and explicitly pastoral—and also public because incorporated into the poetry William publishes.

With the French republican rhetoric of a utopian family-nation the discourse of domesticity becomes a discourse of nation, and siblinghood spells a new utopian relation.[32] Within that rhetoric siblinghood is not only a specific construct, whose development is carved out by revolutionary ideology as well as by eighteenth-century novels of preromantic sensibility, but a construct that must be carefully tended and updated and carefully opposed to that of the solitary spirit.[33] Whereas republican rhetoric displaced public onto private, novels and poems of sensibility confused the boundaries between sibling and sexual relations, Platonic love and passion. Romantic novels and poetry either followed this trajectory to its obvious end—the spiritualization of the incestuously loved sister, as in P. B. Shelley's work—or revised sibling roles beyond those of refined feeling to new possibilities of what a brother and sister can mean to each other, as did the Lambs. The Wordsworths followed this last option, but each conceives siblinghood differently, and as their understanding of themselves and the world alters, this difference informs the way they produced their lives and thus their texts.

Yet, despite the importance of life together, the curiosity of that Life is

William Wordsworth's compulsion toward both the solitary as well as the social figure. In his poetry he often renders these as two ideologically separate figures, as in *The Excursion*'s Solitary and speaker, or as one figure forced by circumstance and despair into solitude, like Margaret of "The Ruined Cottage." Wordsworth's is only a more sophisticated version of Goethe's and Rousseau's celebrated solitaries who yearn for the social but despise society. The self cannot enter society in silence because linguistic competence defines that entrance; nor can the self conceptualize "self" without language. Silence or incoherence signifies the only true alienation, lingual characteristics W. Wordsworth associates with the feminine, and at times with Dorothy. The solitary beggar is often unclassed, thrown out of the social predicate. In contrast to the one who does not speak, Wordsworth's socially coherent speaker is not outcast but cast up into a welcome solitude. That he is vulnerable to the extremes of silence and mad babble on either side of him is an aspect of romantic poethood that weighs heavily on each of the romantic poets. The heft of such fear leads Shelley and Keats to explore these possibilities, while it leads Wordsworth to exert a pressure on his speakers to seek an ally.

Where Nature proves too unstable and indeterminate to lean on, W. Wordsworth finds the perfect fictional and literal support in his sister; second self and complement, she absorbs his self-alienating silence into herself so that he may address her about Nature. In his poetry he absorbs her presence into himself so that he is accompanied in his solitude. In the Wordsworths' daily life, when she then responds to his address, he further incorporates her voice in his art by fashioning poems around her journal entries. These poems stabilize what he had experienced in sublime or supernatural Nature as alienating or disfamiliar: Our conception of William Wordsworth, Poet, stems from the firm voice which is both their voices. Together, William and Dorothy *are* "Wordsworth," as they exercise the myths that can produce the master poet of the age.

In line with the concept of valley existence, there are two particular lines of critical thought concerning D. Wordsworth's relationship to her brother's poetic enterprise that problematize her place in the Wordsworthian myth. The first of these lines, here represented by Margaret Homans and Susan Levin, finds a literalness of thought and expression in Dorothy's writings that is accountable by gender. Homans writes that Dorothy speaks for the literal (Mother) Nature silenced in William's texts, "literalization reproduc[ing] the literal language of daughterhood, of the mother's continued presence" (*Bearing the Word,* 56). Homans argues for the ability of D. Wordsworth's language to represent reality mimetically through a nonsymbolic discourse that "does not demand the distance or absence of the referent" (53), but Levin formulates the formal literalness of D. Wordsworth's writing somewhat more helpfully: "One way of explaining Dorothy's faithfulness to objects, her continual cataloguing, is as a kind of perpetual reality testing" which involves an "insistence on detail, on naming, and minutely describing what goes on around her" (*Dorothy Wordsworth,* 4–5).

Homans and Levin argue that D. Wordsworth's texts reenact female desire for preservation of the other and for a disengagement from transcendent activities.[34] Indeed, Dorothy Wordsworth does exhibit an ambivalence toward mythmaking and a partial preference for the literalness of experiential reality. Despite her adolescent "romantic dreams" used to "amuse my fancy" (*EY,* DW to JP, 16 February 1788), the urge toward literality clearly marks her commentary on entering Calais with William: "Nothing in romance was ever half so beautiful" (29 July 1802). Such a remark would seem a critique of W. Wordsworth's romanticizing and mythic tendencies, given that in the story of his life, *The Prelude,* he displaces the story of his affair with Annette Vallon (whom he and Dorothy were on their way to visit when passing through Calais) with the allegorically pastoral and deliteralizing "Vaudracour and Julia."[35] Romance, for William, protects the self from truth; for Dorothy it also protects one from literal beauty. For example, after William's marriage to Mary Hutchinson, Dorothy maintained written contact with her "sister" Annette Vallon, while William preferred to overwrite the memory of his love affair, his guilt and sorrow, and even blocked Dorothy's wish to visit Annette, Caroline, and then her children, except on two greatly delayed occasions.

The second line of critical thought conflicts with this first account of D. Wordsworth's feminine affinity for the material literal and instead offers an account of how through reading we will ourselves into myth. Whereas the first line involves the concept of literalness, the second is a concept of literariness. Phyllis Rose and Terry Lovell, working from very different methodologies, both offer insights into the need we have to fictionalize ourselves into being. We are socially constructed as readers, and what we read constructs us and our myths of being. Robert Gittings and Jo Manton, who represent this second line of thought in Dorothy Wordsworth scholarship, uphold that particular texts were crucial in D. Wordsworth's conception of herself. Influenced in adolescence by Richardson's *Clarissa*, Dorothy corresponded with her friend Jane Pollard in the sentimental language of Richardson's heroine and imagined her misery in her grandparents' house as a version of Clarissa's female romance. William also read *Clarissa*, but at a less formative age: She was fourteen, while he read the novel instead of preparing for exams at St. John's. Commenting on what they see as the oddity of D. Wordsworth's later reading obsessions — Thomas Clarkson's two-volume history of the antislavery movement and Fox's *Book of Martyrs* — Gittings and Manton fail to relate the thematic similarity of these texts to the Clarissa story and to Mary Wordsworth's comment, " — Poor dear Dorothy! I have been sorry that she should have been such a Slave" (Darlington, 115). Mary's reference is in a May 1812 letter to William; both parents are away on different trips, and Mary's concern is less with Dorothy's devotion to the Wordsworths' ill children than with the extent of the illnesses and her own absence from the site. However, its terms are remarkably consistent with the victimization the adolescent Dorothy found resonant in *Clarissa*, lives of the martyred saints, and in the histories of enslaved peoples that she read later. These are all analogues for D. Wordsworth's own slavish self-identification in others' houses[36] or, at least, for how she chooses to portray these identifications to others and to herself.

Sinking into victimization for Dorothy may also have been the vision of how others perceived her. Like the victimized Clarissa, she is or is expected to be selfless and so cannot/should not equally share in the fused selfhood of William's complementarity. In terms of collaboration — particularly as a kind of twinship — slavishness is the very inversion of the poetic enterprise. It is interesting to discover, then, that D. Wordsworth read the martyr books *before* her life with William and *after* his marriage to Mary. *During* the years of the Alfoxden and Grasmere journals, however, Dorothy is instead most influenced by the fictional paradigm of collaborative twinship. Twinship inverts slaveship, and this is the mode Dorothy and William both discover in the widely read sentimental idyll *Paul et*

Virginie (1788). Gittings and Manton note that both William and Dorothy were much impressed by Bernardin de Saint-Pierre's romantic idyll and that their life at Alfoxden and then at Grasmere was faithfully modeled on this French pastoral of collaborative existence. Their library later contained the novel in Italian, French, Spanish, and English,[37] and their enthusiasm was not singular. Hazlitt records reading *Paul et Virginie* while staying at a country inn, one of his favorite retirements for romance reading because inns are natural habitations, a part of nature;[38] Claire Clairmont reads it as part of her reading program; and Erasmus Darwin includes it in his suggested reading for girls.[39]

The literary paradigm is immanently recognizable: Paul and Virginie grow up in small cottages in an isolated edenic valley where they learn the joys of fraternal love, tend their nestlike cottage and its garden, name their favorite places in nature, and find in each other intersubjective fulfillment. Although the sentimental plot demands Virginie's chaste and self-inflicted death at the conclusion, the novel's emphasis is on her collaborative productivity with her soul twin, Paul. William was so enamored of the novel's most popular English translator, herself a radical poet, that one of his earliest sonnets is a response to "On Seeing Miss Helen Maria Williams Weep at a Tale of Distress" (1787; signed Axiologus). But this early literary representation, written the year he enters St. John's, is of his "full heart . . . swell'd to dear delicious pain," rather than of an address to the re-presenter of the Saint-Pierre idyll. The story of how his sensibility was affected revises the woman's identity; the sonnet is on rather than to the woman, and on a woman listener, moreover, who herself "wept" rather than on a woman poet who stirs emotion by writing. This is a poem written the same year "An Evening Walk" was begun, yet it is only the latter poem that engages the sister's discourse through direct address. The former poem disallows the woman language, so that she communicates only by an emotive identity which easily recalls the Saint-Pierre tale and its pastoral nature. The force of the literary is that the authoring Williams is pastoralized and silenced as a self-representation of linguistic rhythm, while the sister walks into the role of Virginie and converse in the valley.

In addition to Saint-Pierre, Charlotte Smith's novels of sentiment (including *Ethelinde; or, The Recluse of the Lake*) are relevant to the creation of a fictive life, as are the works of Saint-Pierre's friend, Rousseau. Indeed,

despite W. Wordsworth's eventual refutation of Rousseau, it is not difficult to find the parallels before his embrace of Burke between Rousseau's
early life and his own years in France.[40] William and Dorothy Wordsworth's educational views, particularly in regard to their "child," Basil
Montague, are blatantly Rousseauistic.[41] Rousseau's late work, *The Reveries of the Solitary Walker* (1782), has particular relevance to the Wordsworths' fascination with long walks along "public ways," their ambulatory
mediations, William's poems that record the encounter in the road with
another, and even the particular mode of Dorothy's journal keeping. Any
discussion of this work should at least note Charlotte Smith's *Rural Walks:
in dialogues. Intended for the use of young persons,* in its third edition by 1798.
As complement to both *Paul et Virginie* and *Clarissa,* both Rousseau's and
Smith's solitaries help expose a literariness or text making to William and
Dorothy's collaborative life.[42]

Such implications drive the Wordsworths' determination that their life
be read as a controlled text, an autobiography or Life they could inscribe, a
"Home at Grasmere." There, reading life, this life, could be manipulated to
produce the "correct" meaning. But De Quincey's magazine version, written more than thirty years after the events he describes and available to the
wrong (novel-reading) public, offers another reading, at once demeaning
and de-meaning. He is particularly hard on the Wordsworths' less-than-
mythic existence. Oddly, he is also severe with others' ridicule of the
Wordsworthian pastoral. He censures the joke notice in the 9 October
1802 *Morning Post* of William and Mary's marriage, chiding its "most
ludicrous terms of silly pastoral sentimentality," its "puerile slang," and its
"style of allegorial trifling about the muses, &c." De Quincey includes with
this attack on property he considers his own a critique of the event: "the
most interesting circumstance in this marriage, the one which perplexed us
exceedingly, was the very possibility that it should ever have been brought
to bear. For we could not conceive of Wordsworth as submitting his
faculties to the humilities and devotion of courtship" (184–85).

De Quincey outdoes Coleridge in describing Wordsworth as a man of
"high sexual pride" who would sooner lecture a woman than court her.
Wordsworth's "masculine and severe taste" as well as "the eminence of his
own intellectual superiority" make him unfit for the romance and feminizing devotion to a lady, or for childish pastoral games. Thus he looks

"down even upon the lady of his heart, as upon the rest of the world" (186). This portrait of an unyielding and demanding man (second only in "irritable temperament" to Dorothy) cuttingly contradicts the Wordsworths' pastoral fiction. And at the same time that De Quincey explains for the wrong reasons William's position against courtly love, he makes the very notion of a sibling love impossible: "easily enough it might happen, that any apprehension of an unkind word should with [Dorothy] kindle a dispute . . . rare it did happen — and this was the more remarkable, as I have been assured that both were, in childhood, irritable or even ill-tempered" (188). What's more, De Quincey had it both ways. William is too masculine, lacking the feminine sensitivity necessary to an impassioned lover; he is too irascible, making the pastoral closed to him. And Dorothy is not feminine but never reads or writes enough for fear of "bluestockingism," of being unfeminine. There could not be a more thorough debunking of their carefully wrought life, or a more conflicted and Victorian one. De Quincey has misread because he has himself outgrown the valley. His Victorian skepticism allows us to believe with F. W. Bateson that this is still "much the best biography of Wordsworth," that De Quincey has cut to the core of Wordsworth's grand act. But to believe this dissenting voice, rather than to study what it does to the prior discourse, is to dismiss the Wordsworths' fabricated pastoral, the love poems, and Dorothy's own writing — as we do.

De Quincey's misreading might not rest solely in the Victorian light of his recollections. His discontent expressed in the passages above are with the older poet's refusal of a Werther-like passion such as Coleridge and De Quincey himself demonstrate. What De Quincey misses, then, is his own courtly passion, for De Quincey, too, is a courtly lover who declares, as Wordsworth will not, "Too happy if I might be permitted to lay all things [i.e., intellect, power, empire] at her feet. . . . These things were not of the nature of, had no common nature with, did not resemble, were no approximation to, the sweet angelic power — her virgin dowry" (187). But Wordsworth has indeed thought carefully about the role of courtly love in his pastoral valley; what De Quincey does not notice is that against such ardor William places sibling affection, domestic love, and lyrical formulations of these. The Wordsworthian pastoral rests on a more considered and temperate affect system than De Quincey admires, but at the same time it depends on a sufficient silence and a tempered sympathy that belies its early roots in the literature of sensibility. De Quincey's frustration comes in part from William's reference to these roots with his addresses to women, for both the addresses and the women no longer signify what they would have done for an earlier poet.

W. Wordsworth's interest in addressing female figures is actually within the context of the innumerable eighteenth-century poems addressed to friends, spouses, and lovers. But William tailors the form to provoke particular imaginative interactions; Walpole's addresses to women, for instance — "To Madame du Chatelet," "To the Countess of Upper Ossory," "To Lady Cecilia Johnston" — never actually address the supposed addressee but instead share a perspective with her derived from a shared social circle. But, like Walpole ("Oh, would divine Cecilia deign, / With her brave warrior to augment the train, / From every castle famed in days of yore, / Of which, or poets or romancers tell" ["To Lady Cecilia Johnston," 1777]), Wordsworth also harkens back to the much earlier and nearly immured courtly love lyric. Wordsworth owned a volume of troubadour lyrics, *Histoire littéraire des troubadours*,[43] and his interest in the troubadour lyric is clear from early as well as late poems that explore or denounce courtly love. In a late lyric, "Ere with cold beads of midnight dew" (1827), he exhorts the youth to cease his suit for the fair Geraldine and to "crouch no more on suppliant knee, / But scorn with scorn outbrave." His turn away from the troubadour mistress is a turn toward a more rewarding beloved, Nature. Yet this love relationship also presents the poet with difficulties he needs help in surmounting, particularly when Nature is represented as inaccessible. It is through Wordsworth's treatment of the courtly love lyric — rather than his perusal of Spenser or Chaucer — that he understands its enslaving formula, one which could never adequately be redirected toward Nature without intervention of one more comfortably in proximity to Nature. And thus he comprehends the virtues of sibling love, a concept entertained at least since addressing his adolescent "An Evening Walk" to Dorothy in 1787–89. This lengthy exercise begins to explore the difficulty of substituting maternal Nature for a human beloved, as well as the need for a new formula for doing so. Such formulaic exploration continues in early poems such as "Beauty and Moonlight," and although this particular experiment proved dissatisfying,

Coleridge finds it close enough to his own interest to romanticize the poem later as "Lewti, or the Circassian Love-chaunt" (1798).

It is the addresses to Dorothy worked out as a formula that finally prove an adequate intervention in the quest for affective fusion with Nature. And, as Chapter 2 illustrates, the poems addressing Dorothy could never function adequately without the necessary ground of the Grasmere valley. As for the Paul and Virginie fiction, it is the welcoming and maternal quality of the pastoral vale that makes possible life in the idyllic garden; it is this quality Coleridge so longs for, most plausibly because William and Dorothy are already achieving its intensity. For all three, the draw is that for the romantic poet the garden is where that voice is most likely to come — a statement that says much about Dorothy Wordsworth.

The Charted Valley

*The first commonplace of taste is contained
in the proposition, with which every tasteless
person proposes to avoid blame:* everyone has
his own taste. *That is as much as to say that
the determining ground of this judgement is
merely subjective . . . and that judgement
has no right to the necessary assent of others.*

KANT, Critique of Judgement

One proposition laid out in the first chapter about Wordsworthian aesthetics is that mapmaking is as much a metaphysical as a geographical species of "worlding."[1] Cartography is especially essential to the romantic poet whose quest is to reenvision the world and the place of the self in it. Making the fit between maps and one's externalizable self marks as justifiable what can be turned out for poetic scrutiny, a consumable self-representation that is entirely "sincere." Because sincerity marks the site of romantic "taste," as William Wordsworth reinforces in his Preface to the *Lyrical Ballads,* a second proposition would seem to be that taste must not be subjective but must be naturally induced according to the sensitivity and poetic capacity of the one judging. Thus, although not "merely subjective," the Wordsworthian landscape — "the determining ground of this judgement," which incorporates the terrain of both the judgment and the mapping vision — need not be determined by "the necessary assent of others."

This chapter questions the claims of romantic aesthetic ground and revises the second proposition to read that, given the performative nature of romantic sincerity, judgments of taste are themselves performative decisions that require an assent not only to the chosen object of taste but to the subjective state of *being in relation* to those whose words either reinforce or combat that choice. This is a differentially gendered state, in that voicing taste calls it into being; naming objects of taste places them on the aesthetic map; invocation and nomination are masculine prerogatives; therefore, women who invoke taste will achieve their ends more easily by providing assent to the choice of others.

Taste in this sense is not a categorical imperative. Yet the Wordsworthian aesthetic is very much grounded in eighteenth-century and Georgian perspectival and landscaping theory. In this sense it firmly supports Kant's claim in *The Critique of Judgement* (1790) about the grounds of taste that, "in respect of an object with a definite internal purpose, [a judgement of taste] can only be pure if either the person judging has no concept of this purpose or else abstracts from it in his judgement" (67). That is, the functional beauty — or internal purpose — of natural objects can be conceived of as pure beauty *if* the viewer is not conscious of that intermediary lens determining the object's valence as positive. Taking Kant's point, we can say that the supporting ground of Nature as seen through the lens of Wordsworthian schematics demands the unconscious assent of others through its very worlding, which cannot operate otherwise than by what Keats calls Wordsworth's "egotistical sublime" (which subsumes assent) and simultaneously by the domestic imperative of valley ground (which inculcates assent).

To function poetically, a visionary and lived assent must be continually replicated in a daily practice of Wordsworthian living-in-the-moment in order to replicate itself through a taste so natural as to be blessed by Nature. It is occasioned by the close association among being, textuality, and aesthetic taste. It is marked by a collaborative text-ing and a sense of self-placement that does not question but rather habitually inscribes the grounds of taste into the moment. Yet this stabilizing lifestyle is complicated by its difference from the romantic myth of masculine alienation and questing. The Wordsworths turn this difference to account by making their life poetry as much as they made poetry their life. Walking in the woods at midnight, staying up until three in the morning to talk literature and ideas, waking at noon — these are not radical but rather idyllically pastoral acts. They are made "natural" because they fit the Wordworths' chosen lyricized genre of pastoral, and because they play already-texted scenarios that specify both William's and Dorothy's roles in these activities. William's scenarios, lyrics written to and about Dorothy as much as to and about himself, incorporate both their voices within the pastoral mode. These texts employ sibling relation to engage a mutual discourse on sense, affect, the known, and the unknown. They also articulate the Wordsworths' productive relation, their converse, their complicitous self-gendering, and a structure of domesticity in the ancient minstrel land of the Lakes.

This chapter examines first the address-to-women as a specifically poetic schemata — a map of sorts — that defines the writing of self and other into the valley terrain. With that in place I will then argue that the charted valley lies underneath the addresses and makes them real, true to the Life, and therefore dangerous in their very stabilizing effect for a Life so performative, that any stability William longs for will ultimately destroy the aesthetic conditions of life with Dorothy. Finally, the most mythopoetic aspect of valley terrain, the grove or nest, must be assessed in terms of its importance to William's creativity and to Dorothy's subjective status.

⇆ The Address-to-Women

The most literally collaborative of Wordsworthian writing is that which is most doubly plotted and therefore also most doubly voiced: William's lyrics of and with Dorothy, Dorothy's journal entries of and to William. Both pastorally embed the other, re-creating each other as pastoral hero and heroine but also as an aspect of the writing self, a dis-alienating presence. And it is William's representation of Dorothy as Maiden that not only underpins pastoral life in Grasmere for the Wordsworths but underwrites his poetry, indeed, the heroism of his poetics.

William's development of the address-to-women, the lyric form he uses to implicate Dorothy in his register, involves the circulation of texts among the mythic, fictive, social, and psychological literalizing strata within the multiple moment of writing and being written. In the literal sense, inscription for the Wordsworths is not so much what was for them a purely scribal activity of committing words to paper but the transcription of pastoral or sublime worlds. Transcription is most clearly associated with the poems on writing worlds into being ("Home at Grasmere" and, *The Prelude*), and the Lines poems ("Lines left upon a seat in a Yew-tree," "Lines to my Sister," "Lines written a few miles above Tintern Abbey"), where a prior note or verse on the scene is itself the subject of the new poem. But transcription is literally the task of the amanuensis, Dorothy's self-appointed task of taking dictation and copying over drafts. Thus William actively utters and inscribes while Dorothy is passively registered and passively transcribes his lines. If active male and passive female locate this relation as typical, Dorothy's atypical importance to William's creative identity is not. Her sibling status links her not with fictive brothering (Coleridge) or literal brotherhood (John) but with the siblinghood of sensibility. Alan Liu understands fictive brothering rhetorically as a metonymic relation that displaces the metaphorics of father law (*Wordsworth*, 280–86), but Dorothy's siblinghood is neither in metonymic relation ("like"-family) to brother William nor in metaphoric relation (*nom de père*) nor in symbolic relation (Lucy-love). Rather, she achieves a virtual status that places her within the pastoral myth as the native hero's heroine, the native poet's "eyes and ears." She is not William's muse, for this is the figural Lucy's role, but her literary status as Maiden causes an easy confusion between her and Lucy which Coleridge believed when he declared the Lucy poems to be actually about Dorothy (see "The Rhetorical Sublime and the Lyrical Sublime" in Chapter 4).

   Much of William Wordsworth's anxiety over actually achieving communion with Mother Nature stems from his early political enthusiasms which cut social affairs off from the natural. Keeping company with women became difficult in this early period in which separation from Dorothy coincided with separation from Cumbria itself, as well as with a deep immersion in the masculinity of Cambridge and London. Even so, William's first published poem, "An Evening Walk" (1793), evinces a dependence on the sister-maiden already in place.[2] Subtitled "An Epistle; in Verse. Addressed to a Young Lady, from the Lakes of the North of England," the poem begins with an address to the sister-maiden as a framework for the narrative: "Far from my dearest friend, 'tis mine to rove / Thro' bare grey dell, high wood, and pastoral cove." "Evening Walk" contains many of the elements Wordsworth is soon to codify into the address-to-women form: the woman addressed, the grove, the speaker's interpretive meditation, and Nature as the object of his regard. What Wordsworth has not yet incorporated is the immediacy of the meditative interaction, the collaborative quality of the maiden's copresence, and his desire for both participation in and transcendence of Nature's presence.

The sister receives not an address but a narrative: "Say, will my friend, with soft affections' ear, / The history of a poet's ev'ning hear?" Here the poet's immediate address is not to the sister but to inhabitants of Nature, such as the "Fair swan! by all a mother's joys caress'd, / Haply some wretch has eye'd, and called thee bless'd." As in this first address to Dorothy, William will never historicize her by placing her *in* the narrative proper; her presence must be for the lyric moment only, for it is the writing present memorialized in lyric that demands the maiden's intervention, her sympathetic sharing of value judgments and attitudes, her "choral support."

Perhaps because this poem partakes of the locodescriptive genre, it cannot fully initiate the address-to-women form. But more importantly, Dorothy Wordsworth had not yet come to play her mythopoetic role in William's vision of the world; he has written this poem while still separated from her, and brother and sister are only just coming to know each other. "To My Sister," "Nutting," and "Tintern Abbey," all composed five years later in 1798, exhibit a much fuller working out of the address form, though they all integrate it with other generic types: the carpe diem, the romantic quest, and the irregular ode.[3] Together, these three poems create and actuate the maiden myth as William Wordsworth continued to use it throughout his career; it is the myth to which Dorothy Wordsworth responded well into her sixties.

"Nutting" provides a productive entree into these 1798 lyrics because as a quest-address, it is a transitional poem in Wordsworth's reworking of the courtly love lyric tradition. The knight sets off "fearless of a rival":

> sallying forth . . .
> Tow'rd some far-distant wood, a Figure quaint,
> Tricked out in proud disguise of cast-off weeds . . .

> Forcing my way, I came to one dear nook
> Unvisited, where not a broken bough
> Drooped with its withered leaves, ungracious sign
> Of devastation . . . A virgin scene!

Entering the wood of error, the knight neglects to rescue the mistress. Even worse, instead of rescue he commits a crime against the beloved objectified as "the spirit of the place," a rape against Nature herself.

To read "Nutting" as a continuum between the human mother and Nature as mother forces this poem to enact oedipal rage against a parental ethos. This is a model which, Homans argues, Dorothy Wordsworth finds discontinuous and disconcerting since "[t]he objects of her love are divided" forcibly between brother-love and nature-love (*Women Writers,* 50). If Dorothy cannot share her brother's maternal vision of nature, in this poem he does not attempt to portray her attitude as nonconflicted. Where Nature's generosity, despite the rape, points out the presence of maternal benevolence toward the poet-son, her gentleness manifests itself in the retrospectively invoked maiden whose bodily presence protects the poet even in the act of remembering/writing ("unless I now / Confound my present feelings with the past") from the consequences of his transgressive and violent act. Yet the maiden is not entirely one with the poet if he feels compelled to issue his caveat regarding her behavior. The son's own oedipal fear of punishment complicates the success of his venture ("I turned / Exulting, rich beyond the wealth of kings") so that when he "dragged to earth both branch and bough with crash / And merciless ravage,

> the green and mossy bower,
> Deformed and sullied, patiently gave up
> Their quiet being. . . .
> I felt a sense of pain when I beheld
> The silent trees, and saw the intruding sky —

Yet when he translates this fear into warning for the sister-maiden, the twin self who helps him to recapture elusive joy, there is also an understanding that she stands apart and thus needs the addressed caveat. As sibling, the maiden is in some sense responsible for the act committed against the parent; however, as female, the status of her purity or pollution is more open to question than is the male child's. Thus she is in draft the original transgressor, the grove's Eve who in subsequent revision is tamed from her childish sexual energy to a sisterly innocence and purity. And once rapine and guilt are appropriated to the male self, nicely inverting Christian theology and thus desexualizing the sister-maiden, the blame for the transgression shifts from the speaker's "natural" act in "the mutilated bower" to the maiden's potential for violation and pollution:[4]

> Then, dearest Maiden, move along these shades
> In gentleness of heart; with gentle hand
> Touch — for there is a spirit in the woods.

The lesson learned is one not uncommon in the "Poems Founded on the Affections": that of having initially valued the wrong things. Guilt results from the ransack of the benevolent mother's body while "stocks and stones," that is, inanimate things, receive his prior attention. Although the Lucy poems will later radicalize this notion, reverberating in the "waste" of sympathy on the "things" of the diurnal earth, in "Nutting" the "heart luxuriates with indifferent things, / Wasting its kindliness on stocks and stones, / And on the vacant air."

The maiden's task, then, is to learn the speaker's lesson and to treat the correct recipient of romantic love, the spirit of Nature (the new courtly beloved), with the gentleness of her own heart rather than the aggression of the poet's desire. It is this lesson Dorothy Wordsworth repeats to another little boy who she, too, fears hasn't learned when to love correctly (and so wastes his sympathy on "things") in her own poem, "Loving & Liking." Although this poem is written in 1832, it purposefully recalls "Nutting" and proves that, though "I would not preach," she has learned the lesson well.

That the maiden shares in the blame in "Nutting" means that the "one dear nook" can then remain accessible to the poet as he tranquilly re-collects it, his pain and guilt expiated. The Wordsworthian speaker's need to gain control of the maternal is that essential step in the oedipal process, a step Dorothy Wordsworth unfailingly avoids in her own work. Success there determines the success of his transcendent project to become with

Coleridge a "Prophet of Nature," speaking to others "[a] lasting inspiration, sanctified / By reason and by truth; what we have loved / Others will love, and we may teach them how" (*Prelude* XIII). The pluralized archaic mother, she who must be achieved, is present, as Richard Onorato demonstrates, in Wordsworth's texts as "Nature's disembodied voice, 'the ghostly language of the ancient earth'" (Onorato, 106–15). To absorb this voice ("Thence did I drink the visionary power") is to attempt to control "the mystery of words" which the mother "embodies" (*Prelude* V). It is this very drive to pull together the disparate voices of the natural scene that signifies the epic rather than the pastoral. Using Freudian schemata, Onorato posits visionary drinking as the necessary precedent to spiritual revelation: Mother Nature precedes God the Father. Kristeva, also drawing on Freud, similarly explains that the other tale the male poet narrates is the brotherhood of sons armed against the Father's law. Such an agon imposes "*one* logic, *one* ethics, *one* signified" against the Father's mastery (*Revolution,* 152). Both forces irrupt into and against the patriarchal text in order to formulate a new mastery, a new poetics, and a new readership. It is this monologic mastery that Wordsworth, in the company of his brother poets, seeks to incorporate into his very *being* as poet and seer in his sublime modes (*The Prelude, The Excursion,* the dreamed-of *Recluse*) in the belief that the sublime *is* a mastery of voice that necessarily sublimates the pastoralized body of Nature. But against this control rests the contradictory goal of achieving aesthetic sublimity, producing a double bind of laxity and control. Yet within this uneasy double goal, W. Wordsworth comprehends that (re)pressing nature into the politicized service of God the Father evokes the same disturbing possibilities as does the troubadour's silencing of the lady for political ends: Univocal control is not finally realizable because sublimation of the other eventuates a return of the repressed voice. Like the pastoral, the sublime moment of epic is thoroughly dialogized, thoroughly out of the hero's control, hallucinogenic.

Thus the address-to-women will, as in the case of "Nutting," endorse Nature's vocality and anticipate the maiden's expected utterance at the same time that it queries the male poet's role against that of his brethren. The sibling-maiden is the poet-speaker's one ally in the threatened divide between the State (where the sons symbolically gain mastery over the father — troped as epic quest) and the Family (where the mother's enabling of verbalization and language turns to silence if the State is dominant). Between brother and sister all monologic and dialogic configurations are possible because together they represent both the integrative and the fragmented self. The address, then, is the mode in which the pastoral finds the core of its double plot and the exploratory space for resolution.

The State–Family structure of the pastoral double plot characterizes romantic concerns, both civic and artistic. But while its force is best found in W. Wordsworth's version of the pastoral, and in particular in his lyrical ballads and celebrations of the pastoral, Dorothy Wordsworth's poetry reveals that she does not agree with the sons' quest to master the Father's mastery at the expense of the mother. It is worth noting Dorothy's dissent at this juncture, because "Nutting" is dialogized with dissent, initially mocking the heroic quest by playing on medieval archetypes (the boy as questing knight in "quaint weeds," the bower as lady in distress, the nuts as treasure to be gained). Kristeva remarks that the quest romance "is a test of phallic endurance" (*Revolution,* 93), a test Wordsworth's speaker both celebrates having passed and feels guilty about having undertaken. Similarly, "To My Sister" recuperates to romantic myth another aged form with similarly troubling and dissenting features, the carpe diem. In some sense the form itself cannot retain its value in a revolutionary age where desire seeks a utopian, pastoral stability and not a forceful confrontation with mutability. When the address is to the sister rather than the beloved, desire needs a double voice; the result is a discarding of both State and Family and a reversion to siblinghood as the grounding text for affection. William Wordsworth interestingly locates "To My Sister" in one of the last classifications of his 1849–50 collected work, the "Poems of Sentiment and Reflection," where it works as a symmetrical counterpart to the "Poems Founded on the Affections" and to its related "Poems Referring to the Period of Childhood." Together these categories represent where William locates Dorothy herself both in myth and in the placement of her poems.

W. Wordsworth's earlier title for this address to the sister, "Lines Written at a Small Distance from my House and sent by my little boy to the person to whom they are addressed," shows the poem to have been intended for a different genre altogether—the Lines poems which rewrite the locodescriptive form.[5] Stephen Gill notes that the importance of this lyric goes beyond the scope of mere genre revision: "This poem, no less than the more complex 'Tintern Abbey' published in the same volume of *Lyrical Ballads,* expresses some of the fundamental convictions on which the whole of W[ordsworth]'s poetry is based" (*Oxford Authors,* 688). In "To My Sister," the idea of a spirit that dwells in Nature also dwells in the human mind; but this time it exists only in its positive, nurturing aspect, and the speaker names it "Love." The speaker sends a young boy to call the sister to come with poet and child to the grove. Although the child is not the speaker's "little boy" at all, he was historically in the care of both William and Dorothy, and their coming together in the poem forms a family triad.[6] The maiden as mother to the child ("My Sister! . . . / Come forth and feel the sun. / Edward will come with you") thus becomes both sibling and mother. Complicating matters, the little boy, rather than the maiden, tropes the speaker's earlier self, "what once I was" ("Tintern Abbey"). Together man and child will experience not only the maiden's maternal love but, through her presence, Nature's maternal love as well:

> Love, now a universal birth,
> From heart to heart is stealing,
> From earth to man, from man to earth
> —It is the hour of feeling.

The communion of mind and earth through the spirit of Nature's love will teach the trio how to feel, and "One moment now" of feeling "may give us more / Than years of toiling reason." That feeling represents the maternal gift; it is what *The Prelude*'s narrator first learned from his human mother and then learned from Nature herself, and it gives him the visionary power: In order to see, the poet must first feel. The sister-maiden is not easily manipulated here, and the reader begins to doubt the poet's absolute power in his priestly role when he has to beseech not once but twice for "My Sister" to put off further chores and to forgo reading ("And bring no book") so that she may accompany him in his reading of the textual body of Nature:

My Sister! ('tis a wish of mine)
Now that our morning meal is done,
Make haste, your morning task resign . . .

Then come, my sister! Come, I pray.

This poem is the most explicit address to Dorothy herself; interestingly, it exhibits the most resistance on the maiden's part. She must be cajoled, she must be transformed from domestic worker to forest nymph by putting on her "woodland dress," for just as "Nutting"'s speaker becomes a knight by wearing "quaint weeds," the sister must wear naturalized clothing to be placed in a mythic setting. Sublimating the sister's resistance is the overpowering characterization of Nature's beneficent nurture: "And from the blessed power that rolls / About, below, above, / We'll frame the measure of our souls, / They shall be tuned to love." The "living Calendar" that "No joyless forms shall regulate" presents Nature as animate, perpetual rather than cyclic, and presents us with the joyful pastoral, an antigeorgic in which labor and the domicile are traded in favor of "grass in the green field." Yet sisterly resistance, however quieted, can be read as the addressee's response to the carpe diem's hail. "To My Sister" responds powerfully to "Corinna's Going a-Maying," one of the most celebrated carpe diems in English literature. Herrick's poem begins "Get up! get up for shame! . . . Get up, sweet Slug-a-bed, and see."[7] The sister, too, must be seduced into leaving the domestic interior to attend to leaves other than her books contain, a turn toward indolent ease. While Corinna's uprising is a blooming forth, an unfurling of foliage to be put on, the sister is called to "yield" and "Come forth," verbs emphasizing her resistance to love itself. This is not Corinna's maidenly resistance but a bookish, laboring resistance that if not abated will "murder to dissect" ("The Tables Turned"). Within the carpe diem's context of love there is no place for the mystery of words or its "dark abode" of sublime landscape, and the pastoral opposes the "Visionary power / Attend[ing] upon the motions of the winds / Embodied in the mystery of words" (*Prelude* II). The vision inherent in pastoral joy is that of "the blessed power [from which w]e'll frame the measure of our souls" ("To My Sister"). Wordsworth rewrites the notion of the sleepy girl, assigning industry to the maid and idleness to himself: "('tis a wish of mine)." Though her industry has no place in nature, neither does the industry Corinna's speaker has in mind: "And some have wept, and wooed, and plighted troth, / And chose their priest, ere we can cast off sloth" ("Corinna"). The love the maiden-sister must come help celebrate in idleness is rather "the blessed power that rolls / About, below, above" ("To My Sister").

In "Tintern Abbey" "the measure of our souls" takes a darker resonance and itself casts off flirtation. Five years have passed since the poet was last here, and the pain of experience has caused the "groves and copses," "pastoral farms," and "These waters, rolling from their mountain-springs / With a soft inland murmur," to "impress / Thoughts of more deep seclusion" than this already "wild secluded scene." Marjorie Levinson has pointed out the title's proleptic reference to Bastille Day ("Composed . . . July 13, 1798") and the implied analogy between the prison's inhabitants set free and the abbey's ruined walls harboring vagrants during the 1790s (*Fragment Poem*). The date makes this secluded yet "wild" landscape radically historical: Is wilderness defined as the sublime "steep and lofty cliffs" or as the seemingly "sportive wood run wild" which he traces on a landscape composed of well-regulated "pastoral farms"? And if this is a pastoral and not sublime landscape, what is the relation of this wild pastoral to the "wild eyes" of his sister or the "wild ecstasies" of her being in nature to which he addresses himself at the poem's end?

Quite seriously, and through the wild yet domestic sister's presence, both landscapes can present themselves to the eye at once. The poet and Man of Taste, in addition, uses meditation to reconcile both scapes to himself. "Thoughts of more deep seclusion" visit the speaker as he reclines under a "dark sycamore" and views the landscape. This poem, which begins as a beautifully modulated conversation poem and ends as an address-to-women, is made the antithesis to "My Sister" by the entire sense of darkness, wildness, seclusion, emotional fatigue, even as the sister stands there beside him. Although belonging to the same Lines genre, the bright lyricism of the pastoral song is in deep contrast to the sublime odic despair of "Tintern Abbey." Despite various groves in the landscape, the real grove here is in the speaker's mind, a "more deep seclusion." It is to this mental "grove" that the poem recurs when the speaker finally turns to address the sister, exhorting her to create the very same "grove" or "dwelling-place" in her own mind. This internal grove will serve to hold nature's sounds, "all sweet sounds and harmonies" for future need.

Similarly, in "To My Sister," the speaker proclaims:

> And from the blessed power that rolls
> About, below, above,
> We'll frame the measure of our souls,
> They shall be tuned to love.

In the pastoral, souls are instruments that are tuned to feel a measure which is at once nature's rhythm and the soul's weight or achievement. But in "Tintern Abbey" the soul's measure has been taken and found wanting, and "the blessed power that rolls / About" takes on a troubling sublimity:

> And I have felt
> A presence that disturbs me with the joy
> Of elevated thoughts; a sense sublime
> Of something far more deeply interfused . . .
>
> A motion and a spirit, that impels
> All thinking things, all objects of all thought,
> And rolls through all things.
> $\qquad$ [93–96, 100–2]

The sister's presence in the midst of this despairing mood over "the heavy and the weary weight / Of all this unintelligible world" (39–40) leads the speaker to intone: "The dreary intercourse of daily life, / Shall ne'er prevail against us" (131–32). She complements his thought and mood — her excitement with his despair, her present observation with his past memory — assuring him at this disturbing juncture in his poetic and political career that her presence there will insure that his devotion to Nature is not forgotten, and that Nature will not forget that he came there as such a worshiper (151–53). Through this communion, the maiden's future thoughts of present times will function to heal him:

> oh! then,
> If solitude, or fear, or pain, or grief,
> Should be thy portion, with what healing thought
> Of tender joy wilt thou remember me,
> And these my exhortations!
>
> [142–46]

The poignancy of "these my exhortations" reveals that now the brother must face being reduced to rocks and stones and trees with the unfeeling nonmemory of death, while the sister must embalm him in her mind even as she houses the grove within her. Yet even this task must be performed at his desire and not from her own impetus, since it is he who is "Prophet of Nature." In effect, his prayer deposits in Dorothy *as chora* or grove the semiotic energy that will enable *her* if not him to poetic language in future years. And it is when he is no longer writing the pastoralized verses of his middle years that Dorothy takes up poetry herself. "Thoughts on my sickbed," (discussed in detail later), the poem that specifically recalls William's "exhortations," replies both rhetorically (yes, I did remember) and materially with its very production as proof of the enablement to poetic voice.

"Tintern Abbey" is seminal in W. Wordsworth's poetry and poetics; the presence of the address-to-women in its peroration indicates the essential nature of this form for Wordsworth's thought. That the address-to-women does not become its own fully conceived form until several years into Wordsworth's poetic career says two things: that its development was part and parcel of the tumult of finding new combinations of genre forms, and that as an informing concept it held great importance for William Wordsworth's artistic thought.[8]

"To a Young Lady who had been reproached for taking long walks in the Country," composed three years later in 1801, is an almost pure example of the address-to-women form. It begins: "Dear Child of Nature, let them rail! / —There is a nest in a green dale, / A harbour and a hold." In just those three first lines nearly the full address-to-women form is configured: the address to the maiden, the adult speaker who views her as the child / daughter of Mother Nature, the invitation to the maiden to escape from society and to come alone with the poet into nature, and the grove or nest. And equally important, the nest within the dale which is "A harbour and a hold" is the answer to the question the narrator of *The Prelude* will ask himself: "in what Vale / Shall be my harbour? Underneath what grove / Shall I take up my home . . . ?" (1805, I). It is a question that appears in the 1805 *Prelude* but not the 1799 version, and its repetition of the bridging 1801 lyric "To a Young Lady" finds its echo in a letter of doubt for the future which Dorothy writes in 1804 to her friend Catherine Clarkson:

> Mr. Clarkson spoke of the Cheapness of the land in Kent and perhaps we might all settle there. . . . But oh my dear Friend it will be a hard thing when we leave these dear Mountains. . . . As long as Sara and Tom Hutchinson are at Park House there will be one *Hold* for us. [*EY*, 420; emphasis is DW's]

The Hold's importance is revealed in "To a Young Lady" as a physical space to hold and cling to as the babes cling to the Young Lady, a domestic nest differentiated from the grove by its extreme association of the maidenly with the maternal:

> A harbour and a hold;
> Where thou, a Wife and Friend, shalt see
> Thy own heart-stirring days, and be
> A light to young and old.

If the maternal Young Lady, a very type for the Dorothy figure with which William peopled his world, is the ultimate expression of the nest's harboring character, then the nest as a home and holding space is even more clearly drawn here as a (house)hold of domesticity ruled by the motherly maiden.

The harbor and hold serve first to anchor the poet in the choral nest of inspiration out of which poetic discourse irrupts, but they also function as an atemporal space to which he resorts as a return to the mother. The naturally formed grove and domestic nest also anchors the maiden, but with all the implications of the atemporal pastoral mode she is rather the ship anchored than the pilot in safe haven:

> There, healthy as a shepherd boy,
> And treading among flowers of joy

Which at no season fade,
Thou, while thy babes around these cling,
Shalt show us how divine a thing
A woman may be made.

The Young Lady receives four capitalized epithets in the poem: Wife, Child, Friend, and Woman. Together they compose her whole being and her whole meaning for the speaker. She is at once the sister-companion who allows for a fuller experience in nature and the exemplary, divine woman who resonates back to the characterization of Mary, that phantom of delight. The maiden's dual identity necessitates an extreme harnessing of the maiden's sexuality and temporality in these roles: At the same time she is the mother's communicant and the speaker's virginal younger sister. As Child, shepherd boy, Young Lady, and divine woman, the maiden in this address must be as pure and timeless as Lucy.

Purity resists desire, and in the address-to-woman, purity differentiates the virginal maiden from Nature as the site of romantic desire. The male artist's intent toward the object of desire, in Kristevan theory, is to possess and master the mother in both her nurturing and her powerful aspects. Kristeva writes that the artist's conceptual possession of the mother figure "Provides motherhood, that mute border, with a language; although in doing so, he deprives it of any right to real existence . . . the point is to reach the threshold of repression . . . where maternal jouissance, alone impassable, is arrayed" (*Desire,* 249). Yet William's play with this threshold is a dangerous one, and as much as he recognizes its importance for strong poetic voice, he also recognizes its threat to his repressed and guilty pain.

The mother, whose attention always turns away from the artist as male adult, can be innovatively mediated by turning instead to the listening, voiced maiden. Her jouissance replaces maternal mystery with an already experienced and very romantic joy: "Dear Child of Nature, let them rail!"—that is, come out and play. The poet-hero at once battles the patriarchal State and maternal silence; if the maiden never fully separates from her identification with the mother, she rigorously avoids maternal jouissance so as not to be sited at the point of repression. Likened to a shepherd boy, she is instead planted in pastoral ground; "lovely as a Lapland night," she is that white night. She is that eternal space of serene purity that follows the dance among unfading flowers of timeless joy. The speaker praises her "light" not as that of the muse but for the same sightedness for which the sister's "wild eyes" are praised in "Tintern Abbey." To see correctly in the address-to-women is not a silent activity but rather a part of the oral/aural relation.

V. N. Vološinov asks how the poet senses auditory presence, and answers, "To put it figuratively, the listener normally stands *side by side* with the author as his ally."[9] William literalizes the trope, writing of Dorothy, "The thought of her was like . . . an unseen companionship . . . we . . . walk abreast . . . / With undivided steps" ("Home at Grasmere"). The essential trait of the maiden is that she does not stand at the poet's side; as second self she not only accompanies but attends the poet's words in the dialogic sense of "the listener whom the author himself takes into account . . . and who, consequently, intrinsically determines the work's structure" ("Discourse in Life, *Freudianism,* 110). Standing at the poet's side, the maiden shares his purview and so remains a nonvisible presence sharing in the view.

The final verse of "To a Young Lady" reads,

Thy thoughts and feelings shall not die,
Nor leave thee, when grey hairs are nigh,
A melancholy slave;
But an old age serene and bright,
And lovely as a Lapland night,
Shall lead thee to thy grave.

The maiden as recipient of the word becomes the object of intruction rather than of desire, and the three "thou shalts" of the poem inform the relation of stanza to stanza: Thou shalt see, thou shalt show, and thou shall be led. Outside the pastoral vale, her increasing passivity from active though directed seeing to being the thing seen leads finally to her own agedness and death. But the voice that instructs the maiden is a voice at the mercy of her willing companionship; the voice cannot dialogically engage those who rail. She therefore retains some vestige of power ("divine," "serene") despite her journey toward a temporal death in the civic State, and it is this retention of power that makes the maiden a companion

and not a (silent/dead) beloved. However, the sister-maiden who remains within the bounds of pastoral is more powerfully present than this
maiden whom the poet must entice away from societal constraints.

In "To —— on her first ascent to the summit Helvellyn" (1816), the
speaker metaphorically brings the maiden to a mountain summit which is
on the edge between pastoral beauty and epic sublimity:

> Inmate of a mountain-dwelling,
> Thou has clomb aloft, and gazed
> From the watch-towers of Helvellyn;
> Awed, delighted, and amazed!

A true act of the imagination, this poem is entirely envisioned as the
speaker recapitulates what he imagines took place on Helvellyn. The
speaker "watches" as the personified Helvellyn casts a spell on the maiden,
and the Ether as Nature's breath embraces her as the mother's embrace of
the daughter—an embrace the speaker does not share. The speaker regards the maiden's transformation and invokes her new power, crying:

> Maiden! now take flight; —inherit
> Alps or Andes—they are thine!
> With the morning's roseate Spirit
> Sweep their length of snowy line;
> Or survey their bright dominions . . .
> For the power of the hills is on thee.

The power of the hills here represents the coming together of Nature's
power and her human communicant. The maiden receives the Ether's
essence, and like the Ether she can now be airborne. This interestingly
reverses the idea of poetic inspiration to the involuntary act of breathing,
and the function of the poetic muse to inspire divine thoughts into the
poet. Here it is the maiden who receives the muse's breath, and the Ether
lifts her up in ecstasy, in place of the would-be transcendent poet. To her
now belong the beauty and wonder of Nature's elements: land ("inherit /
Alps or Andes—they are thine!"), water ("Thine are all the choral foun-

tains"), and air ("For blue Ether's arms, flung round thee"). Still, it is the speaker who invokes them and commands her, "Maiden! now take flight." By giving voice to Nature the speaker establishes his priestly role in the proceedings: The maiden participates in Nature's acts, but the poet has the knowledge to comprehend the scene.

This lyric relates the maiden's mythic role to the Faustian myth, particularly as it is played out in Byron's *Manfred*. Comparing the two works, both written in the same year, clarifies the poetic quest embodied in the two works. Manfred is himself the Promethean questor for knowledge and power, the very type for the romantic poet. His drama plays itself out in a bipolar field that alternates between an inner domestic space and the outside sublime space of the Jungfrau, virgin or maiden alp.

W. Wordsworth reserves a Manfred-like Promethean desire for his speaker-poet, who uses it to manipulate others rather than to attain supernatural powers himself. In Goethe's *Faust,* the questor seeks to endow himself with the ability to make himself invisible, to travel like the wind to distant places, to transcend the elements; in Wordsworth's poem, it is the maiden the speaker wishes to endow with these Mephistophelian abilities:

> Maiden! now take flight . . . or halt,
> To Niphates' top invited,
> Whither spiteful Satan steered.

The quest becomes the search not for the knowledge that enables the Poet to transcend the elements but for the power to manipulate another's transcendence. The Wordsworthian speaker is presented, as always, as the passive witness to the event on which he gazes or imagines, and what he witnesses is the maiden's active gazing: "Inmate of a mountain dwelling, / Thou hast clomb aloft, and gazed." The interactive visualizing of speaker and maiden recalls the manner in which the Wordsworths took their walks, Dorothy actively regarding while William meditatively gazed, so that she comes away with a record of the scene while he brings home a vision.[10] Even in their reciprocal acts of seeing/envisioning, the speaker and the maiden accomplish together what was once a unified and emblematic process of poethood. As in Coleridge's "Lime Tree Bower" and

"Vale of Chamouni" odes, the speaker is not actually present but only imaginatively taking part in the gazing; that is, envisioning both the landscape and its inhabitant's inner thoughts and experience. Coleridge details the negative space of his speaker's absence in the landscape whereas this lyric offers the reader few clues as to the speaker's actual place in the poem. Like Lucy, he is at once nowhere and everywhere. His own supplanting of a Lucy-spirit of the place who mutely both embodies and inhabits Nature reveals the poet here to have crossed the chasm of "A Slumber did my spirit seal" that separated him in his humanity from what it is Lucy becomes in her fusion with the earth. But unlike Lucy's semiotic status, this speaker does have access to symbolic language, and he performs not as local spirit but as wizard, similar to Manfred's Witch of the Alps.

The question is, to what purpose has Wordsworth reversed the gender conventions of witch/spirit as female and questor/poet as male? Manfred's first speech from the Jungfrau complains that "The spirits I have raised abandoned me . . . My mother earth! / And though fresh breaking day, and you, ye mountains, / Why are ye beautiful? I cannot love ye" (I.ii). Wordsworth's speaker also acts to raise the spirits, but because he raises them for the daughter-maiden, an anthropomorphized Jungfrau, they do not abandon him, nor does his quest interfere with his ability to love Nature. The textualized search in "To ——— on her first ascent" is not Manfred's but that of transforming the Promethean project into the terms of the maiden myth. W. Wordsworth's textual quest rewrites, as a formal feat, the sublime romantic project into a lyric genre.

The prior act that permits this transformative inscription of the questor's gaze, this re-vision that links maiden's gaze with onlooking poet's, is anticipated in the much earlier "Tintern Abbey." There the speaker meditates at length on the "coarser pleasures" and "glad animal movements" of his passionate, indeed "dizzying" and "aching," younger days and compares the effect of what we would call the semiotic — "The sounding cataract" that "[h]aunted me like a passion," the "colours and . . . forms" that "were then to me / An appetite," "a feeling and a love" — to his sister's "wild eyes" in which he "catch[es] . . . these gleams / Of past existence," as in her voice he "catch[es] / The *language of my former heart*" (emphasis added). Dorothy herself embodies the semiotic as her eyes speak the discourse of affect and display the energy of the drives in their "shooting lights." Though the speaker tells her that what he seeks is the chance to "read / My former pleasures" in those shooting lights, what is more fundamentally important is that they stand together gazing. This act of doubled viewing / envisioning is what transports Dorothy from the role of object / other (the alterity Kristeva points to as the place the dis-placed, rejected mother occupies after the child's oedipal trauma) to the shared role of poet making. William does not accede to her the capacity to make *poetry,* but she may help make the *poet* with her kindred gaze, her sympathetic memory, her activity as *witness.* Witnessing, in Vološinov's dialogic model, supports and enables the speaker, whose word would otherwise falter into uncertainty and silence. Indeed, D. Wordsworth's sister voice impels the poet's own, as "in thy *voice* I catch / The language of my former heart" (emphasis added). Dorothy Wordsworth herself shared this notion of the doubled poet, the sibling-couple who gaze together — not with one as witness to the other but both as witness to nature's endlessly differentiated features. In the following journal entry, Dorothy describes gazing with her other "brother," Coleridge, achieving the same doubling effect as if he were William:

> April 23rd, 1802: We left William sitting on the stones feasting with silence — and C. and I sate down upon a rocky seat. . . . After we had lingered long looking into the vales — Ambleside vale with the copses the village under the hill and the green fields — Rydale with a lake all alive and glittering yet but little stirred by Breezes, and our own dear Grasmere first making a little round lake of nature's own with never a house never a green field but the copses and the bare hills enclosing it and the river flowing out of it.

The sense here of sitting together above the pastoral valley and lovingly gazing down on the pastoralized scene is partly attributable to the communal nature of pastoral beauty versus the solitary activity of gazing up at sublime scenes, but it is also the dialogizing voice that speaks its own experience yet sees that experience as itself communal. The difference between the twinship of William Wordsworth's addresses to sister-maidens and that of Dorothy Wordsworth's doubling voice involves primacy. Whereas

William's speaker takes the sister's voice into his own as a multiplying effect that opens up his own consciousness, Dorothy Wordsworth's narrative voice in the pastoral journals dialogizes others and otherness so as to acknowledge being within her community of siblings, her garden valley, and the natural landscape.

⌇ *Living in the Landscape*

In order to think about Dove Cottage as both heart and household, the iconic and physical structure can be helpfully thought of in terms of embedded domestic space: the nest and the closet. In the lives of privileged eighteenth-century women, the closet was a small retreat where letters could be written and journals kept, more private than the bedchamber itself. In the Middle Ages the closet was a private space outside the house, for example, the closet in the queen's garden, but it was more usually a small chamber in the private quarters, often called a bower. Traditionally the closet had also been a domestically located place for prayer and meditation, associated with both genders, and also a place for scholarly labor and for authorship. Both from traditions of domestic space and from modern social manners, then, the closet became a retreat from disturbance, a nest within the home, and by implication an interior space not of resistance to the outer order but of submission to divine law.

Ironically, the deeply personal and internal submission to divine law is intimately related to the social relations that force us "out" into history. Historicization of the individual is both a private and a public act. If in the twentieth-century closet one is what one should be, and so a public figuration, then coming out of the closet is a way of controlling the information known about us, thus making it a private act. Byron, Coleridge, and Anna Seward understood the closet in this modern and very dramatic sense.[11] But in the nexus between eighteenth- and nineteenth-century culture, the establishment of the closet as transformative, as capable of blurring public–private distinctions, as closet drama, also occurs. The closet in this sense is figured as the love bower or even as the small "blue" rooms favored by salon hostesses. It is taken to be a dramatic space of poetic language where body colludes with performative desires, a nest where fictions can be dallied with and tried on as commonplace acts. Closet dramas as lived fictions become public property when they are recorded in journals, commonplace books, and lyric poetry.

The Wordsworthian closet, however, extends to become the entire cottage, the cottage transforming into bower and conversation room. The house itself becomes the imaginative space where the child as romantic original can be replayed daily. And because the closet is a space that can be transported from the literal house walls and projected on an external setting, its boundaries are variable. In his "Naming of Places" poem to Dorothy, William dedicates a natural spot to her and remarks, "— Soon did the spot become my other home, / My dwelling, and my out-of-doors abode." The imaginary closet structure can either be placed tangentially or superimposed as habitual domesticity. It is a place that stands halfway between the truly private and a self-proposing romantic conversation. Stepping out should be the individual resistance to group expectations, but whether for Byron, Shelley, or Wordsworth, closeting is the moment of resistance, and stepping out becomes speaking for the nation. The romantic poet is "a man speaking to men" (1800 Preface), but he is also Childe Harold striding through Europe. Being public becomes an overtly symbolic act in which poetic language is contained within ritual discourse befitting the public role. Romantic poets are expected to be "out" and to speak in a mode that seems most private when it speaks for us all. What is not seen in this role is the poet coming home to revise his utterances within the familial space where closeting may or may not take place while he works.

Connecting both places is cottage business. If Dorothy's rhythmic record of chores keeps the accounts for the cottage,[12] her maternal discourse, especially when conjoined with a *Paul et Virginie* lovers' discourse, represents not the daily history of rustic life but the mythic history which was part of the Wordsworths' business to construct: closet talk. William's business specifically was to dally with this and other talk to produce valley histories, Wordsworthian tales.

When Dorothy records a fishing trip in which she and William part, her narration turns a business trip into one of idyllic idleness and nurture:

W. and I went into Langdale to fish. . . . When W. went down to the water
to fish I lay under the wind my head pillowed upon a mossy rock. . . . We
ate our dinner together and parted again. Wm was afraid he had lost his line
and sought me. [23 June 1800]

Dorothy does not actually fish, although several entries in the journals
record her fishing alone. She sits at the lake's edge and notes the landscape
("The view exquisitely beautiful"); then she lies higher up "under the
wind" but is not inspired. William's fishing, accomplished alone, ends in
defeat; his fear, his seeking out of the other part of himself that is temporarily lost to him, is echoed in miniature by the loss (or feared loss) of the
line. William then continues the business of fishing by moving on to Rydal
while Dorothy walks home alone. Her entry turns from William's small
fear to an encounter she has with an old man as she returns home. He asks
where she is headed and informs her she is taking the wrong way, saying,
"It's well I saw you or you'd ha' been lost." William's fear of no account, his
loss of line and therefore of productive labor during their partial separation, becomes for Dorothy a possible frightening loss/lostness when they
are really apart. Her account for that day, which begins with the loss of a
father ("Mr Simpson called in the morning. Tommy's Father dead"),
repeats a cycle of real and possible losses, comfort and the impossibility of
comfort. What is also chronicled is the interrelation of history (a village
death, the fishing trip, encountering the old man) with aesthetic production (three lengthy sentences describing views, plus the extended anecdote of encountering the old man, which also renders his dialogue and
dialect). Facing the possibility of becoming lost, Dorothy recounts the
old man's speech as if she were living through one of William's lyrical
ballads in which the dialogic encounter *is* the plotted action.[13] She observes not the old man's appearance or clothing but rather the character of
his utterance: "Why says he it's well I saw you ye were gane to Little
Langdale by Wrynose, and several other places, which he ran over with a
mixture of triumph, good-nature, and wit." Her treatment of this anecdote is markedly different from the solemnity of the rest of the entry; a day
marked by acute headache begins with a father's death, is punctuated by a
maternal act, and takes a turn for the better when a father figure preserves
her in such a way that she can laugh at and with him. Recovering the

father, at least temporarily, in a community of parentless siblings—a pastoral valley of romantic children now adult—draws another circle, one that relates to closet-bound origination.

In the Preface to his *Second Discourse,* Rousseau observes that it is necessary to know or "to have precise notions" (or perhaps boundaries) about man's origins regardless of the possible fictionality of that prefallen state, its possible impossibility. But while the prerevolutionary Rousseau is obsessively concerned with undoing what is already done in order to reinvent beginnings, William Wordsworth is most concerned in his pastoral lyrics with being and presence—not what was so much as the stillness of the present moment.

Above all, romantic presence problematizes being in history. A historical representation that held particular interest for the Wordsworths was the "Life" genre. The growth of the biography's popularity is connected to the rise of the novel but more intimately to the rise of bourgeois self-representation. In the *Alfoxden Journal,* D. Wordsworth notes that Godwin's newly published biography of Mary Wollstonecraft has arrived and, in the *Grasmere Journals,* that she is reading Boswell's *Life of Samuel Johnson,* the lives of the Scottish poets Robert Fergusson, Michael Bruce, John Logan, Smollett's life, and Ben Jonson's life. The reading of these literary lives, often but not always accompanied by reading the literature produced by the subjects of these lives, calls attention to the life Dorothy is recording. Johnson's *Lives of the English Poets* propelled the critical biography, but the Life itself dramatically enacted within the pastoral valley must reject the analytic eye in favor of a gentler vision.[14] The "autobiography" that Dorothy Wordsworth constructs through selective recording and careful description/depiction is a tale of origins like William's *Prelude,* particularly in its correspondence with Saint-Pierre's *Paul et Virginie* and with Richardson's *Clarissa.*[15]

D. Wordsworth's early letters to Jane Pollard, her best friend in Halifax where she was first sent after her mother's death, document the misery of now having to live with her grandparents and uncle Christopher. Her account takes the air of the fairy-tale princess locked up by ogres: In her first letter to Jane, she writes that, even though she is reunited with her brothers, "We have been told thousands of times that we were liars" by disapproving grandparents and contemptuous servants. In addition, "I can bear the ill nature of all my relations, for the affection of my brothers consoles me in all my Griefs, but how soon alas! shall I be deprived of this consolation! and how soon shall I become melancholy, even more melancholy than before," and she begs to be known in Halifax as "poor Dolly" (*EY*, July 1787). *Clarissa Harlowe* was part of her favorite reading as an adolescent;[16] it is a novel that plays out the childish fantasy of imprisonment, cruel relatives, betrayal by servants, and isolation from a desired social milieu. Dorothy can read herself in Clarissa, whose sole outlet for her despair is the lengthy letters written to a close girlfriend. She also reveals her penchant for fictitious living in doing so, for melancholic poses, and for redistributing truth toward more pleasing scenarios.

Not unlike the fairy-tale princess, D. Wordsworth is rescued by her uncle William Cookson, who first sets about giving her time for her lessons, for letter writing, and for tutoring her—all of which her grandmother thought unfit occupations for a young woman. No longer having literally to steal time to read, Dorothy comes to see Uncle William as the antecedent for her beloved brother: a closet provider. Clergyman, tutor, and the supporter of a literary life, her uncle as fairy prince will next provide the cottage in the country where Dorothy can escape her familial or antifamily imprisonment: "if I do not flatter myself . . . he will soon be married, I must certainly in a little time go to see him and then I shall visit Halifax. I assure you I am a very skilful architect I have so many different plans for building one Castle, so many contrivances! Do you ever Build Castles?" (*EY*, DW to JP, 6–16 December 1787).

With his marriage to Dorothy Cowper, William Cookson sets up the model for life in Racedown, Alfoxden, Goslar, and finally Grasmere: a William and Dorothy setting up house in a rustic country village with "charming" gardens. D. Wordsworth has become a member of this William–Dorothy family, accompanying (as she will later do for her brother and sister-in-law) her uncle and new aunt to their wedding, honeymoon, and new home. Literary life is continued there, for "after breakfast is over we are to read, write, and I am to improve myself in French . . . and after tea my Uncle will sit with us and either read to us or not as he and we find ourselves inclined" (*EY*, DW to JP, 7–8 December 1788). D. Wordsworth's self-identification in this new family, like her later self-location in her brother's new family, alternates between "we" as all three members, and "we" as the sister-selves. The two Dorothys of the Cookson family structure the relation Dorothy will have with her friend and future relative, "my sister" Mary.

When Uncle William briefly moves the whole family to Windsor, D. Wordsworth reports to Jane that she has met two young women who are, like most "country ladies," "of course fond of the country lady's amusement, walking." Together the three of them "had several very charming little excursions into the country," a happy opportunity where young women cannot walk about alone (*EY,* DW to JP, 16 October 1792). Walking with country ladies, whom Dorothy "of course" understands, not only shows her preference for country over city ladies but also places Dorothy as a heroine in a sentimental "lady's" novel. How does she turn into a deeply serious, romantically sentimental, and deeply creative inhabitant of a Wordsworthian landscape where few "ladies" stroll about?

The threads of this conversion are already present in her description of Windsor: the fairy-tale presentation, imagining the self within a scape, the amount of space devoted to the scene and environment. By the time that Wordsworthian Life has taken hold, so has the assertion of Saint-Pierre over Richardson. Bernardin de Saint-Pierre calls attention to his pastoral, and very sentimental, models in his foreword (1788): Colonized worlds like the Ile de France

> only lack poets like Theocritus and Virgil to present us with pictures at least as interesting as those of our country. I am aware that travellers, men of taste, have given us enchanting descriptions of several of the South-sea isles; but the ways of their inhabitants and more especially those of the European settlers often spoil the scenery. My wish has been to blend with the beauty of tropical nature, the moral beauty of a small society. [vii]

This explanation also works to correct Robinson Crusoe's self-centered colonization of "his" island, in which the self-sufficient Crusoe is blind to its beauties because he has no time for "men of taste." At the same time it replaces classical pastoral experience with that of "a small society," thus offering the picturesque tourist a pastoral vision from the edenic inhabitants' perspective. In adopting the role of Virginie over that of Clarissa or a fairy-tale princess, Dorothy Wordsworth begins the process of Wordsworthian aestheticization, an act of self-reformation which results in part from having been hailed by a Man of Taste in "An Evening Walk."

Aesthetic reformation demands a new way of viewing the self, of writing the self into being. Kurt Heinzelman writes that "one of the Wordsworths' critical tasks . . . [was] to write their household into being, even as they were engaged in the material process of shaping [it]" (56). We have seen this process already at work in Dorothy's early letters. Specifically, writing-into-being, a process of self-creation as much as it is a process of shaping the domicile, reflects a potent social fantasy at once utopian, sentimental, escapist, picturesque. We could call this social figuration the georgic pastoral, which it certainly was, and explain the Grasmere experiment in terms of this classical ideal—which for the Wordsworths interweaves idleness and labor in a "truer" pastoral existence than the pure idleness increasingly sought by Londoners escaping the city. By calling it the Wordsworthian georgic or Wordsworthian pastoral, however, we can avoid some of these configurations.

We must, in any case, add the other influences that the Wordsworths mapped onto the classical and literary ones. Most specifically, the Wordsworthian georgic responds to a strong cultural fantasy,[17] often equally sentimental, which resulted from the conflation of public into private life during the tumultuous years of the French Revolution. The dangerous signification of "private" as against revolutionary or communal interests resulted in a reactionary drive toward the private throughout Europe. Lynn Hunt remarks that "[a]n ever-expanding publicity of life, especially between 1789 and 1794, provided an impetus for the romantic withdrawal into the self and withdrawal of the family into a more clearly defined domestic space" (13). It is interesting to think about William and Dorothy's year in Goslar in terms of this drive toward a privatization of the self, for that was a year alone in a cottage, in the harshest weather in decades, that proved utter misery. Subject to nature's storms rather than its blessing, the Wordsworths lived a private life that resulted not from choice but from alienation and misunderstanding. Ostracized from polite company in the small German town where Dorothy as sister was culturally translated into Dorothy as mistress, privacy took on a new meaning: privation. The four Lucy poems written in this year create a dreamlike rendition of the pastoral in its most elegiac and melancholic moment. Their abstract quality, which is not replicated in the later sixth Lucy poem ("Among all lovely things"), reveals the hallucinatory quality of a privacy so extreme that the domestic myth turns on itself.

Yet the Wordsworths did not interpret their year in Germany as revealing an innate flaw in their plan; they returned with renewed desire to live in a pastoral setting and perhaps even build the home they would inhabit together. Their early daydreams of living in a cottage alone becomes in Grasmere a life in which their increasing circle of friends inhabit their cottage nest as members of the Grasmere "family," replicating utopian communal structures. The drive toward privacy which failed with the Goslar experiment is turned to success in Grasmere by double-plotting the private as pastoralized staging. Moving outside the cottage is moving not into the public but into a nature with bountiful nests. Moving into the public in order to speak for the nation, on the other hand, is only to speak as a deeply private man and poet and to express deeply personal (but also political) sentiments. Dorothy is deeply implicated in the first move but deleted from the second. The doubleness of roles and spaces thus marks the home as a site of community, even as it marks off space as gendered. However, gendered boundaries are physically and visually fluid; in the doubly gendered natural scape, William continues to seek solitude and privacy as he walks through the landscape. Even when accompanied by Dorothy and Coleridge, he often chooses to isolate himself slightly from them in order to contemplate in private. "We left William sitting on the stones feasting with silence — and C[oleridge] and I sate down upon a rocky seat. . . . He was below us and we could see him" (*Grasmere Journals*, 23 April 1802).

What did William — or both Wordsworths, or Dorothy alone — dwell on as they walked or sat or lay on the slopes of the landscape in which they had located their dwelling? Much of their notion of gazing is itself a social fantasy (see n. 10 to this chapter), drawing most obviously from the formulaic aesthetic of the picturesque. The Wordsworthian sensibility is not just a literarily derived aesthetic but a visual or painterly one as well, in which tableaus and stillpoints provide a correlation between the two genres. It is no accident that in the first year of the Wordsworths' residence in Grasmere they obtained and read Richard Payne Knight's *The Land-scape: A Didactic Poem in Three Books* (1794) or that D. Wordsworth's entry noting Knight's poem details at length the afternoon's foray to the lake, beginning: "We lay a long time looking at the lake" (26 July 1800).

However, the question of picturesque aesthetics in Wordsworthian myth is a complex one. Picturesque attitudes organize nature into surface features at the same time that they organize one's view(ing), teaching one to read nature in a particular way. Both the Wordsworths are compelled by such attitudes in the early Grasmere period not least because, as John Murdoch points out, Virgil's "et in Arcadia ego" came to equate upland landscape with pastoral and the lost state of childhood, while the flatlands nearer London took on georgic, postlapsarian identification.[18] With the eighteenth-century aestheticization of poetic terrain the Lake District came to embody the very notion of the picturesque. But the picturesque tourist is problematic, wanting to find the untouched natural landscape and at the same time wanting to "improve" it. For instance, the first entries of D. Wordsworth's *Grasmere Journal* detail the improvements she is making on their cottage; later, William will improve the "orchard" and garden. If in his poetry W. Wordsworth opposes any kind of "beautification" of the landscape, and if his lyric tale "Rural Architecture" laughs at the notion of embellishing scapes with fanciful, nonnative structures such as John Plaw recommends in his *Rural Architecture* (1794), this was contradicted by numerous acts of beautification carried out by the Wordsworths. Dorothy even reworks nature by transplanting wildflowers from one place to another, and hard labor went into the construction of their garden "bower."

Thomas Gray, master of the natural sublime whom the young Wordsworth admired and emulated, wrote a journal of his visit to the Lake District in 1769. W. Wordsworth's 1776 edition of Gray contained his poems, letters, and this journal, and in it William would have read of Gray being particularly charmed by the village of Grasmere.[19] For both Gray and W. Wordsworth, the hamlet is the pastoral ideal: "no flaring gentleman's house or garden wall breaks in upon this little unsuspected paradise; but all is peace, rusticity, and happy poverty," writes Gray, and the Wordsworths improve on this only to provide a romantic redefinition of "happy poverty" as proud independence. Yet William found that when Grasmere is not in its undifferentiated aspect as viewed by the tourist it loses Gray's "rusticity" to attain the Wordsworthian pastoral quality of domesticated sublimity within it. If, as Southey suggests, pastoral is a state of mind, then for W. Wordsworth the sublime is also discoverable in vistas other than the sublime scape.[20] This is not to say that the same landscape can always provoke both pastoral and epic but that a pastoral setting with sheep, stone wall, and grass can suddenly induce a spot of time and pre-monition of death: "And afterwards . . . / The single sheep, and the one blasted tree, / And the bleak music of that old stone wall . . . / All these were spectacles and sounds to which / I often would repair" (*Prelude* XI). Wordsworth's pastoralization, then, moves beyond eighteenth-century aesthetic conventions of pastoral as calm picturesque rusticity, where country manors are situated, so that picturesque views (scenes corre-sponding to prescribed proportions and arrangements of natural features, suitable for framing) are available at each large window. For Wordsworth, the picturesque is artificially imposed on nature and therefore cannot be associated with epic poetry. Instead of the discernment of guides, nature best expresses the division between the beautiful and the sublime to the discerning mind. Attempts to describe the supernatural aspects of land-scape can even draw contempt from the youthful poet: "See a description of an appearance of this kind in Clark's 'Survey of the Lakes,' accompanied with vouchers of its veracity that may amuse the reader" (original note to 1793 "Evening Walk").

Although Wordsworth is usually considered a sublime, Miltonic poet on the strength of Coleridge's assertions and his own posthumous *Prelude,* several critics read W. Wordsworth as primarily a pastoral rather than a sublime or questor poet. David Ferry, Raymond Williams, and Michael Squiers see Wordsworth as a poet who combines traditional pastoral con-ventions, eighteenth-century rewriting of that literary tradition (the counter- or antipastoral), and the variations of modern or realistic pas-toral. Many of the poems written for the second volume of *Lyrical Ballads* are entitled pastorals whether or not they underwrite or counter the tradi-tional pastoral form: "The Pet-Lamb. A Pastoral," "The Idle Shepherd-boys. A Pastoral," "Michael. A Pastoral Poem," "The Oak and the Broom. A Pastoral." Pastoral is characterized not merely by habitat but by inhabit-ants as well. Even before he settled in Grasmere, Wordsworth's particular concern was the rustics about whom and for whom the 1798 *Lyrical Bal-lads* was written as a replacement for the chapbooks of halfpenny ballads that circulated.[21] The comparatively large number of "statesmen" or rustic freeholders in the valley was one aspect of Wordsworth's chosen homeland that most accorded with his republican beliefs, a disproportionate 26 out of a population of 270.[22]

Dorothy Wordsworth, however, appreciated the farmer less because of political position than from a north-country inclination for rural communities. All of the daydreams and castle building she records prior to living with her brother are pastorally situated, and she does not look to London as her Scottish contemporary Joanna Baillie does. When Dorothy learns she is to accompany her uncle William Cookson and his new wife to the living he has been given in Forncett, she writes to her best friend Jane of her delight in the prospect of living in the "country": "You know how partial I always was to country life, but I almost despaired of it. . . . Forncet[t] is a little village entirely inhabited by farmers, who seem very decent kind of people" (*EY*, DW to JP, 7–8 December 1788). Later she is enough a part of this new community that she will teach school to the village children, reporting proudly of their progress. However, her building of communal ties through a nurture of local children is at odds with William's conception of the rustic child.

With romanticism's focus on the child's birthright as a natural and spiritual alignment, and of childhood as an arcadian existence for which one feels nostalgic yearnings, the child came to be figured as a shepherd.[23] The shepherd child as poet is protected from the pain of death and loss because in his passage through the pastoral realm toward civic maturity he is nurtured by nature and sheltered by its timelessness and Virgilian celestial light as in the "Immortality" ode. Still, what does W. Wordsworth seek from the shepherd lad beyond an image for the protected self communing with nature? Or, conversely, how does Wordsworth recount his childhood in relation to the adult shepherd, the figuration for Empson's native hero of the people?

In Book VIII of *The Prelude,* the pastoral book that explores the union and natural energies in the landscapes of his childhood, W. Wordsworth announces that the first people he learned to love were shepherds, their undegenerate character proving a kind of native "noble savage." Shoring up his bond to these men was Nature's influence on his developing social and political values. " 'Twas thy power" which compelled

Love human to the creature in himself
As he appeared, a stranger in my path,
Before my eyes a brother of this world —
. . . A shepherd in the bottom of a vale,
. . . Man free, man working for himself, with choice
Of time, and place, and object.

The description here is of a utopian existence in a world separate from the vulgar life of the city, where the shepherd figure bridges the imaginary realm of the visual ("A shepherd in the bottom of a vale"), with the symbolic: a creature "spiritual almost / As those of books, but more exalted far, / Far more of an imaginative form."[24] He exists in opposition to the classical arcadian inhabitant, "a Corin of the groves, who lives / For his own fancies, or to dance by the hour / In coronal, with Phyllis in the midst" (*Prelude* VIII). The ancient lover's idle hours and songs, despite the picture of leisure and retirement conjured, does not lure the young poet for he lacks heroism. Rather, the shepherd poet prefigures the ideal ego of the adult poet, a heroic version as at home in a Miltonic landscape as sublime questors. For Wordsworth, the poet patriarch who writes as majestically of retirement and paradise as he does of heavenly battles, (re)fathers pastoral as well as Christian epic. Both modes locate the shepherd ideally;[25] however, to pastoralize this shepherd requires a nostalgia that combines Nature's love, native heroism, and an idealized version of the poetic ego. The arcadian shepherd child answers the requisite conditions, yet because he precedes the adult poet he cannot be out of time in the same sense as the rustic shepherd "in the bottom of a vale." The child must grow into the adult poet, and thus grow into mortal time. Wordsworthian myth accounts for the difference between shepherd self and shepherd other through language. And it is the clash between poetic lyricism and the real languages used by shepherds that repels the Wordsworthian imagination, directing it toward a reconfigured reality.[26]

W. Wordsworth does not want to emulate the "natural" shepherd himself but wants to behold him populating the pastoral valley and filling it with rustic wisdom and affect. Poetically and mythically his emphasis is clearly heavier on Nature and the ideally populated vale than on the vale's historical inhabitants. He describes coming back to Hawkshead during summer break at Cambridge, and when he walks out of the cottage into nature,

> Gently did my soul
> Put off her veil, and, self-transmuted, stood
> Naked as in the presence of her God.
> [*Prelude* IV]

Pastoral transport is a self-transmutation and a nakedness in Nature's presence. This gentle unveiling is a rendering of truly sublime transport, "as in the presence," but it also speaks to the protected moment of self-birthing; this is not shepherding but breathing anew, redefining the pastoral moment as mystically (rather than naturally) sublime and fully accessible to the child-man. When the adult poet does ascend into divine presence, as in the Helvellyn episode of *The Prelude*'s Book XIII, the poet's transport will be unprotected by pastoral nature; instead, it is a violently wrenching transformation that does not "put off" the outer shell to reveal the soul but pulls the self out into the sublime's vast vacuum. Pastoral, in contrast, contains promise as well as protection, and Dorothy Wordsworth's later reading notes indicate that she shared William's rather than Rousseau's notion of pastoralization as a cultivated practice. Her reading of a travelogue of Africa indicates that she agreed with its author that the "Boshiesmen" are enemies to peaceful, pastoral life without any of the skills of British peasants,[27] an assessment in accord with the Saint-Pierre analysis of native interference in pastoral life, quoted above.

⟜ *The Bower as Nest*

Both William and Dorothy Wordsworth's sense of pastoral involves the nest as an image of protection in Nature's motherly bosom. But whereas Dorothy stops at the notion of the nest or even bower as architected or domestic space, nests abound in William's poetry from the "Poems Referring to the Period of Childhood" to the sublimity of *The Excursion*. The primary significance of the nest is its secure enclosure which negates the anxiety of separation, isolation, and death implicit in intrusions of reality into the Wordsworthian life. The nest also retells the story of the Wordsworths' childhood before the death of both parents. The historical loss of the mother, followed by that of the father, came back with the full force of mortality in 1805 with John's death: William writes to his older brother, "God keep the rest of us together! the set is now broken" (*EY,* WW to RW, 11 February). William and Dorothy's recurrent use of "hold" and "harbor" to describe the safety of the Grasmere vale visualizes the pastoral in terms of John's mariner lexicon, an indication of how the nestling bonds refuse to break. In the imaginable nest, the set will stay intact, preserved from external harm by the nest's maternal boundaries.

The Wordsworths' own harbor and hold, their "dear, dear cottage," was the home around which their pastorally poetic life centered. Even its original name, Dove and Olive Inn, fits W. Wordsworth's poetic lexicon with the nesting mother dove imaging the very essence of a nostalgic sense of security, maternity, and peace. The cottage's former name links the harboring hold with the antediluvian ark and its shepherding mission, but it is also linked with the other house names in the vicinity: The Dove and Olive Inn, Bird's Nest (Brougham Hall, built by James Bird), and Dove Nest (owned by the Wordsworths' landlord, John Benson). The Wordsworths' cottage was located in Town End with two smaller cottages, all three of which nestled on the old road to Rydal, separated from the rest of the village.[28]

In Book I of *The Prelude,* the book that sets the architectural framework of both the epical text and the Wordsworthian venture, the speaker seeks a vale, harbor, and grove in which to "take up my home"; temporarily resting "in the sheltered grove where I was couched. I made a choice / Of one sweet vale whither my steps should turn," but meanwhile "Thus long I lay / Cheared by the genial pillow of the earth . . . [in] the grove of oaks / Where was my bed." While in this mediative, seeking mood, he realizes that

> The mind itself,
> The mediative mind, best pleased perhaps
> While she as duteous as the mother dove
> Sits brooding, lives not always to that end,

> But hath less quiet instincts — goadings on
> That drive her as in trouble through the groves.
>
> [*Prelude* I]

W. Wordsworth's characterization of nature's groves as homes and nests figures Nature as mind on the pastoral, lyric level. Though critics most often recognize W. Wordsworth's assertion of the fit of mind to Nature in the transcendent thirteenth book of *The Prelude,* here he makes the same formulation in lyric terms, particularly in the addresses to women.

The bower, on the other hand, becomes a variant of both the familial nest and the choral grove. Because the bower retains neither the maternal quality of the former nor the mystical aspect of the latter, yet replicates the structure of either space, it becomes a favorite haunt of both the Wordsworthian child and poet. It also provides the perfect image of domestic Wordsworthian space, containing Spenserian or romantically medievalized allusions as well as alluding to a very real chamber in the traditional cottage. The bower, then, calls to mind the tended or georgic garden of Eden, as well as Spenser's bower; W. Wordsworth recalls it as a space of natural music:

> Once more should I have made those bowers resound,
> and intermingled strains of thankfulness
> With their own thoughtless melodies
>
> [*Prelude* V]

"Thoughtless" contrasts here with both the concept of Nature's presence in the landscape as a shaping "mind" and the poet's own artistically wrought "strains of thankfulness." The bower is a domesticated space of comfort, a resting spot which has lost, through its taming, the grove's terrific link to divine inspiration. The bower is not a choral but a nonlingual space, a holding place or (house)hold of "perfect stillness" where the poet is "soothed by a sense of touch / From the warm ground, that balanced me . . . I lingered here / Contented" (*Prelude* I).[29] In contrast, the grove is a space of poetic anxiety where the Wordsworthian speaker comes to gain inspiration, not always finding it ("But no wind / Sweeps now along . . . Not even a zephyr stirs" ["The Haunted Tree: To ——— "]).

W. Wordsworth sometimes figures the entire valley as an extended bower with a blessed domesticity that compels him:

Ah! if I wished to follow where the sight
Of all that is before my eyes, the voice
Which is as a presiding Spirit here
Would lead me, I should say unto myself:
They who are dwellers in this holy place
. . . are blessed.
["Home at Grasmere"]

The valley-bower comforts through its maternal embrace — "Embrace me, then, ye Hills, and close me in" — much like the maternal and permissive trees of "Nutting." "Home at Grasmere" itself works to domesticate the valley, to rewrite the history of the vale from one of successful labor to an embowered utopia that welcomes the poet as its special son. That is, he transforms pastoral from the ground, out of which a savior hero rises, to a bower that protects and embeds the poet son. The bower itself is a highly specialized space, however; more central to Wordsworthian myth is the family nest, a space in which familial and sibling connection is intimately experienced.

"The Sparrow's Nest," composed in 1801, perhaps best illustrates the importance of the nest, both in its nostalgic association with pastoral childhood and in its connection to the sacred grove. The year 1801 was one of intense poetic production in William and Dorothy's cooperative existence, a relation that would change radically with William's marriage one year later.[30] Perhaps because of these pressures, "Sparrow's Nest" refers back to an earlier shared experience between the poet and his sister "Emmeline." As in the addresses to women, the incident is shared, but the male poet is the active viewer whose gaze (stage)-directs that of the experiencing maiden:

Behold, within the leafy shade,
Those bright blue eggs together laid!
On me the chance-discovered sight
Gleamed like a vision of delight.

> I started — seeming to espy
> The home and sheltered bed,
> The Sparrow's dwelling, which, hard by
> My Father's house, in wet or dry
> My sister Emmeline and I
>   Together visited.

Just as the greater romantic lyrics "Tintern Abbey" and "Nutting" entertain the poet's vision and meditation in seeming solitude until he addresses the maiden at the end, we are not aware of the maiden's existence until the last two lines of this half of the poem. The space between this and the second stanza recalls the structure of Lucy's horrible and comforting death in "A Slumber did my spirit seal" but here produces only Emmeline's fear — a fear intimately connected with her brother-directed gaze:

> She looked at it and seemed to fear it;
> Dreading, tho' wishing, to be near it:
> Such heart was in her, being then
> A little Prattler among men . . .
> She gave me eyes, she gave me ears.

The structuring components established all come into play in the addresses to women: child-sister to older brother, poet-seer directing the maiden's gaze, the poet's vision having previously been educated by her natural ability to observe, the maiden's emotional capacity. They are also all, as here, intimately connected with the notion of the nest. Emmeline, the "little Prattler," like the Dorothy of "Tintern Abbey," "Nutting," and "Home at Grasmere," is significantly younger than William. The diminution of Dorothy's age and status reveals a fundamental assumption in the complementary relationship between poet and maiden: Her "natural" and naive teaching informs his poetic, mature self-education so that his teaching synthesizes human and natural wisdom. Together Poet and Maiden have taught each other, yet their dialectic always ends with the brother older and wiser. In fact, William as Poet places the sister-maiden firmly in the pastoral world of the nest and grove while he occasionally and to his detriment falls into reality; as second self, she is allied with his own former self and relegated to the workings of the fancy, to the poems of childhood and fancy (where Dorothy's poems reside in the collected works), and to the aesthetics of the beautiful.

If the pastoral shepherd presents one type of romantic being in the world, the child as poet or "favored being" (*Prelude* I.364) presents another, and the maiden with her poetic perceptive powers presents yet a third. These positions of identity all participate in William's pastoral myth of romantic existence. What none of them reveals is the labor that produces them, or the work of weaving these stationing modes into the integrity of Grasmere envisioned. This integral structure is secured by those who do not wander, the republican natives who in their tradition-oriented lives produce what the French Revolution should have and didn't: not the paternalistic utopia Rousseau envisages for Emile and Sophie to rule but yeoman life free of the Norman yoke, a self-sufficient husbandry centered on the household.

Grasmere, in this mythic system, is the focal point of the Wordsworthian universe, figuring in small the concept of native land equaling nature. Here the valley contains the cottage as the utopian domicile of the family; Grasmere, valley, and cottage form a series of concentric choral structures within the larger enclosure of the Lake District. On another level, the valley contains not the nest but the sacred grove in which Mother Nature, the Maiden, and the Poet can commune. This concentric structure (poet and muse, grove, valley) spirals upward to the heavens as nonenclosing so that the Poet can transcend this natural choral structure and reach toward God.

Critics often take W. Wordsworth's tripartite mapping of the imaginative growth of poetic selfhood as the romantic model per se. For instance, Anne K. Mellor uses this scheme as a given against which she pits German-influenced romantic irony: "Not all romantic works present a confident movement from innocence to experience to a higher innocence, that circuitous journey which leads the protagonist spiraling upward to a more self-aware and therefore more meaningful communion with the divine" (*Romantic Irony*, 6). Wordsworth employs this scheme for his epic plot of origination and quest; it is a tale critics are more likely to tell than his pastoral myth of natural birth and continued growth. In both plots, however, the poet begins in innocence (childhood), grows into experience (adulthood), and transcends at specific moments to a higher innocence (such as stumps the speaker in "We are Seven"). While the poet himself passes either literally or imaginatively through all three stages, both plots contain various otherly "be-ings" arrested along the way as signposts for the experiential self. They are sign-selves who manifest the idea of each particular stage: the leechgatherer as he who endures, Lucy as the sublimated Beautiful whom only the poet discerns and desires.

W. Wordsworth's tendency toward philosophical rather than "organic" structures reveals itself repeatedly in his poetry (a practice at odds with his daily routines). Even in the last years of his life, he and his family were attempting to reorganize his oeuvre by an alphabetic system.[31] Prior to this, he had repeatedly organized the genre categories of his growing body of work, as evidenced in the 1815 and 1849–50 editions. In his 1815 Preface, Wordsworth explains that he has ordered his poems so as to correspond to the life cycle:

> From each of these considerations, the following Poems have been divided into classes; which, that the work may more obviously correspond with the course of human life, for the sake of exhibiting in it the three requisites of a legitimate whole, a beginning, a middle, and an end, have been arranged, as far as it was possible, according to an order to time, commencing with Childhood and terminating with Old Age, Death, and Immortality. [Owen and Smyser, 3:28]

The classifications as Wordsworth arranges them in the collected works correspond to the different rooms of a spiritual building or home, as well as to the architectonics of the poet's life, the origins of his creativity, and the growth of his intellect to artistic maturity.

It is the poet, and not everyman, whose passage through both epic and pastoral plot is mapped through these three stages; others are there only to teach the poet. The maiden who walks beside the wanderer remains bodily in the pastoral, though her absent presence or the memory of her accompanies him on his epic journeys. So, while romantic ironists such as Byron, Schlegel, and even Coleridge saw the universe as essentially chaotic and incapable of providing true form or meaning, W. Wordsworth created structures like his tripartite one to impose a mythic order on his world;

such structures are analogous to house-building schemes and gardening designs, which were his other passions. The romantic ironist also devises patterns, but they purposefully deconstruct in order to give way to new patterns in the unending process of becoming.[32] W. Wordsworth refuses to relinquish patterns, for they give form to his world, forms that become embalmed in an eternal stasis which itself embodies change. In his address to Dorothy at the end of "Tintern Abbey," William "exhorts" her to preserve her own memories of youth spent in nature within an architectonic structure of the self: "thy mind / Shall be a mansion . . . / Thy memory be as a dwelling-place."

The sublime demands abstractions, unidentifiable places, unrecognizable others, and an experience of dislocation. The georgic or domestic "reality" of Grasmere, with its confluence of pastoral and sublime energies, alternately calls for particularity, language, community. But underlying the Wordsworthian myth as William views it is a more heterogeneous colonizing. To understand pastoral as the birthplace of a native hero instead of the epic questor is to unbalance received conventions of the pastoral lover and epic warrior. Wordsworth redresses his displacement of lover and warrior with poet-hero by commingling his two plots, doubling them. If this is not an original remedy, it is of the romantic idiom by its blurring of genres and traversing of prescribed boundaries. For instance, the first stage of the epic scheme, childhood or innocence, belongs to the world of pastoral. Its dominant faculty is the Fancy, and its dominant characteristic is the Beautiful. Yet isolating pastoral on the heroic level as the child poet who tells verses to the fields (*Prelude* I) denatures the pastoral from the working reality of Grasmere. Thus, in his epical autobiography, Wordsworth refers to Nature's (inferior) "secondary grace" and turns Mother Nature into the Infant Prodigy's "old Grandame Earth . . . grieved to find / The playthings which her love designed for him / Unthought of" (*Prelude* V). That is to say, the penalty for Wordsworthian romanticization of classically defined genres is the denaturing of Nature herself; no longer a powerful mother, she is epically relegated to the stature of an old woman of the village whose "grace" is secondary both to the Imagination and to a larger, patriarchal "Truth." On the other hand, De Quincey's description of Grasmere as one of the Lake District's several "shy pastoral recesses"[33] grasps Wordsworth's utopian vision of community with feminized nature, pleasure and nurturance, even as it is visited by the awful powers of the archaic mother when death enters the valley.[34]

Dorothy Wordsworth's place in William's valley is mediated by her own version of the dramatic stage both as literal vale and as a rendering of Paul and Virginie's valley home in Saint-Pierre's sentimental novel. At the same time, she adjudicates her place in the manufacture of Wordsworthian aesthetics and art. Her relation to Imagination is arguable on two counts: Her artistic production does not bear the trace of sublime acts, and William himself denied her figurative access to undomesticated, unpastoralized terrain. Even D. Wordsworth's participation in romantic discourse is not entirely in her favor here, since the imagination as a sublime enactment assumes a radically monologic character at the liminal moment. If Dorothy's language production does not sublimate itself, it is still not necessary to agree with both William and her critics that she resides in the realm of pastoral Fancy rather than sublime Imagination. D. Wordsworth's place in romantic Imagination will come under scrutiny in the following chapter, but here we must be more concerned with simply her place itself — her relation to Fancy, to the pastoral, and to William's placement of her in his fancy.

Making these discernments calls up specific notions of creativity, gender, and the mind. First, in William Wordsworth's world the fancy is the creative faculty generally understood in terms of the pastoral valley, the generic natural entity (i.e., unspecified, unnamed), and atemporality. It is a feminine-influenced associationism that works metonymically, subordinately, quietly, familiarly. It is associated with the beautiful and the canny or domestic and is the stuff of daydreams and childhood games.

The valley's antipode is the mountain, the Beautiful's is the Sublime, and Fancy's is the Imagination. The romantic imagination works metaphorically by allegoric stills rather than by contiguous or narrative movement. It is uncanny, wild, and sparsely populated by beings whose specified names are part of their haunting selfhood. These are the settings, then, for poetic placement of self. However, only one set allows for twinned being and sibling selves. For this reason alone William would displace Dorothy to the Fancy, since the mountainous sublime is a place he inhabits himself only in the writing moment, the moment of actual pres-

ence. The Fancy is a creative process that embodies community as association; testifying to its difference is William's representation of his moments
of liminal and temporal imagination as always out-of-body.

William Wordsworth's figurations of the domestic nest and the nest
found in nature both manifest a drive toward architecting the world.
Dorothy Wordsworth, too, repeatedly imagines plans for possible homes
and sites nests everywhere. Together they labored to build a moss hut as a
nest within their pastoral cottage garden. Both Wordsworths conceptualize nestedness as domed spaces that nurture and enclose the individual
in safety. Although we can see Dorothy Wordsworth as complicitous in
William's version of the Wordsworthian myth, particularly as she wills
herself into the maiden construct in an inversion of the romantic concept
of will,[35] her writings evince her own sense of how the myth might go.

For D. Wordsworth, valley, bower, nest, and grove are also each differentiated, but she gives them meanings other than her brother's. W.
Wordsworth interprets the bower as a sheltered spot in which to ruminate
in privacy, or from which to "gaze and gaze," both representing acts of
possessing the scape: "Our thoughts at least are ours. . . . / — Soon did
the spot become my other home" ("It was an April Morning"). In her
journal entries, Dorothy reverses William's identification of the bower as a
nurturing, feminine space where one can loll passively, referring to it as a
place she tends and cares for. William rests in the bower for comfort and
nurture; Dorothy nurtures the bower herself. Her attitude of care replicates the maternal nurturance William attributes to Nature and expects to
find in the maiden; it also reverses male appropriation of the physical or
material. Dorothy's transplanting of small wildflowers to bowers found in
nature and her returning to tend them recall Eve's duties in Eden; at stake
is the notion of transplantation, providing orphaned creatures (like the
tragic Green children) with new homes. The gardener transplants for the
sake of harmony and beauty, both of which imply health and vital spirit.
Similarly, the Green children are given new homes by the community
women so that they might thrive.[36]

The bower is also important to D. Wordsworth as a station or vantage
point from which to regard the landscape as a *work* of natural beauty, the
product of natural labor. The bower is a space both interesting in itself and
particularly situated to allow a focusing of attention on the exterior land-

scape, a space from which to frame one's viewing to allow it a pictorial boundary and composition. Composition, in the picturesque sense, requires not only the artful arrangement of natural objects and terrain but also a positioning of the self in order to see in a particular way. Composing the self requires an integration of self with environment; "stationing," an activity required for proper appreciation of a picturesque scape, means standing still as much as it means standing in a particular place. That is, it means transplating oneself as a natural object, at least temporarily. Indeed, Dorothy and William would spend hours sitting in chance spots in order to gaze at the landscape, although they sought out scapes that went beyond the fashionable picturesque to what was more natively resonant, less artificially manufactured from landscape to approximate painterly artifice.

D. Wordsworth's attitude toward the native land as something that is appreciable does not replicate William's sense that the land is *shaped,* that it takes form in order to respond *to him.* In the opening lines of "Home at Grasmere," the chosen homeland is an enlosed sphere whose hills are arms ("Embrace me, then, ye Hills, and close me in"), a "Spot" that is "A Centre . . . / A Whole without dependence or defect, / . . . Unity entire." Even as the poet places the valley, a center "Within the bounds of this huge Concave," so too does the valley position him both spatially and affectively: "It loves us now, this Vale so beautiful / Begins to love us!" even as it wraps him in its maternal arms ("I feel your guardianship; I take it to my heart").[37]

W. Wordsworth's projection of human affect on the land is not replicated in Dorothy's version of living in Grasmere. "The lake looked to me I knew not why dull and melancholy, and the weltering on the shores seemed a heavy sound," is the fifth sentence, a prose poem in itself, of the opening entry of the *Grasmere Journals,* and as such it provides the counterpart to the opening lines of William's "Home at Grasmere." Yet here the valley does not embrace her, does not center her, does not love her, and does not guard her. Her "heart was so full" that only "a flood of tears" makes "my heart easier," for she has been left alone. The lake is not acknowledged as co-respondent in her emotional crisis even as she can only read her sadness in its appearance; despite the poetry of the sentence, she denies its move into poetic sentiment that would reformulate the thing seen. To reject that projective gesture, she writes "I know not why" and turns immediately to detailing nature attentively as it is in itself:

> The woods rich in flowers. A beautiful yellow, palish yellow flower, that looked thick round and double, and smelt very sweet — I supposed it was a ranunculus — Crowfoot, the grassy-leaved Rabbit-toothed white flower, strawberries, geranium — scent-less violet, anemones two kinds, orchises, primroses. The heckberry very beautiful, the crab coming out as a low shrub.

This entry places the colonizing force of romantic poetry, in contrast with the attentive witnessing that is Dorothy's hallmark. Whereas "Home at Grasmere" forcibly makes the valley "our dear Vale" that "Received us . . . with a passionate welcoming," the *Grasmere Journals* begin with a recognition of that valley as it exists *not* for them: "Above rose the Coniston Fells in their own shape and colour. Not Man's hills but all for themselves the sky and the clouds and a few wild creatures" (23 April 1802). Dorothy's careful descriptions of the flowers are followed two entries later by the exclamation, "Oh! that we had a book of botany." Nearly a year later Withering's *Arrangement of British Plants according to the latest Improvements of the Linnean System* was purchased, but even before then D. Wordsworth is referring to flowers by both their proper and local or native names.

If D. Wordsworth's writing does not reveal the colonizing impetus of her brother's poetry[38] or the habituated vision of a native resident, it does reveal a quality I will call cultivation. Dorothy's moss- and flower-gathering activities display an attitude toward nature that is appropriative in the sense of reaping wild harvest, Eve gathering her flowers: "I carried a basket for mosses, and gathered some wild plants"; "Brought down Batchelor's Buttons (Rock Ranunculus) and other plants"; "We got Broom in returning, strawberries etc."; "went down rambling by the lake side — got Lockety Goldings, strawberries etc., and planted." Cultivating her garden rather than making the valley her own makes the garden part of the valley, for the garden is interchangeably mixed with domestic (the peas, radishes, and plants purchased from Matthew Newton) and natural life (mosses, wildflowers). According to Dorothy Wordsworth's notebooks, particularly DCMS 120, homemade remedies and salves were not concocted of wild herbs or other "natural" ingredients but made by recipe from ingredients purchased from the apothecary. Dorothy's botanical interest, then, is purely aesthetic and not housewifery. Not surprisingly, then, when Coleridge "discovered a rock-seat in the orchard. Cleared away the brambles," the domestic is discovered to be natural after all. Indeed, their walks are often punctuated by sitting "down upon a rocky seat" even as they also "sate in the orchard until tea time." This interleaving of nature and domesticity operates in the opposite direction as well, as she and William sit on "seats" on the hillside, or as they walk "the vale opens out more into one vale with somewhat of a cradle Bed" (16 April 1802).

In her record of rambles in the countryside, D. Wordsworth does weave versions of her childhood dream homes in with the realistic landscapes she documents, as she continually sites cottages: "If I had three hundred pounds and could afford to have a bad interest for my money I would buy that estate, and we would build a cottage there to end our days in" (27 May 1800). This, too, is part of her cultivating activity, for dream homes ignore real life and real needs. They focus on the same play-acting that the Wordsworths engage in their idling moments in the landscape. Part of this play-acting, in which bowers are located or planned, is the overlying of landscape viewing (attention to the "reality" of nature) with daydream gazing (transforming the real scape into the dreamscape): "Above at the top of the Rock there is another spot — it is scarce a Bower, a little parlour on[ly]. . . . It had a sweet moss carpet. We resolved to go and plant flowers . . . tomorrow." And, "C. and I sate down upon a rocky seat — a Couch it might be under the Bower of William's Eglantine, Andrew's Broom" (23 April 1802). D. Wordsworth's pastoral bowers, which are not quite Spenser's bower of bliss though she is reading Spenser on and off, need work and care just as does her man-made pastoral home. But the similarity of the care creates an erasure of boundaries rather than an erecting of new walls. The external bower for Dorothy becomes another place to "be" in, similar to the boat she rows on the lake or the homes of others she visits. It is not possessed by her even though she tends it, nor does she require that the native inhabitants of the land recognize it as hers as does

William in his poem to her: "the Shepherds who have seen me there, / . . . When they have cause to speak of this wild place, / May call it by the name of EMMA'S DELL."[39]

The nest as William defines it is a specifically maternal space whose chief impulse is fostering the self as child. When Dorothy describes the nest in her letters and journals, however, she refers to a domestic space, most often in connection with their cottage and the family circle inhabiting it. The nest, too, becomes emblematic of her maternal care as she labors to perfect domesticity. Here the nest turns care for the bower, tending nature as a garden, and attending to nature's minute beauties into domestic cares, chores, and anxieties. Whereas the nest provides William with the utmost security and focuses its energies on him, Dorothy treats the nest as her domain from which she then opens her attention onto the outer world.

It is the grove that poses the greatest difficulty for D. Wordsworth. W. Wordsworth identifies the grove as mysterious, ghostly, supernatural. D. Wordsworth, reading herself into William's lyrics, would recognize the effects of complete complementation of brother-poet and sister-maiden: The poet derives inspiration from the maiden, whose nourishing act results in her own loss of vitality. Male transcendence is an ecstasis, a rising out of the body, but the feminine transcendence that the poet supervises in William's grove drives the female self inward so that it *becomes* the bodily shell, the divine thing.

Dorothy's journals, therefore, avoid William's groves and focus her descriptive powers on open landscapes, vistas she describes without herself becoming an object in the scene. Walking through a natural scene, William participates in it by absorbing its essence, but D. Wordsworth distances herself from that essence by maintaining a vigilance that externalizes her subjectively from it.

Dorothy also views nest making in a manner quite different from William's vision. William's poem "The Sparrow's Nest" locates the bird's nest in a tree, and the nest itself promises rebirth and life with its blue eggs. "I started," the speaker announces, "seeming to espy / The home and sheltered bed, / The Sparrow's dwelling." Dorothy Wordsworth's recorded encounter with a bird's nest contrasts two kinds of birds (whereas no bird enters William's poem). The first is a bird who would have hatched from a tree nest like William's, though without its safety. The second kind of bird — a nesting swallow — is associated with the first only by juxtaposition, and no comparison or identification of one with the other is made. However, a contrast between William's version of the nest and Dorothy's is implicit.

The first bird is a hatchling of a precarious nest in nature, untended by parent birds:

> I spoke of the little birds keeping us company, and William told me that that very morning a bird had perched upon his leg. . . . he thoughtlessly stirred himself to look further at it, and it flew on to the apple tree above him. It was a little young creature, that had just left its nest, equally unacquainted with man, and unaccustomed to struggle against storms and winds. While it was upon the apple tree the wind blew about the stiff boughs, and the bird seemed bemazed, and not strong enough to strive with it. The swallows come to the sitting-room window as if wishing to build, but I am afraid they will not have courage for it, but I believe they will build in my room window. [16 June 1802]

Dorothy records William's tale of the bird and follows it by her own seemingly subjectless observation which allows the swallows to tell their own tale. Her juxtaposition of William's subjective story and her own absence from the story that particularly concerns her is immediately complicated by what comes before: "I wrote to Mary after dinner . . . speaking to [her] about having a cat." Dorothy focuses on the de-nested bird which William frightens, and in a departure from her usual detailed descriptions, she constructs a story about the bird's unpreparedness for the harshness of life.

D. Wordsworth was worried about her emotional, domestic, and financial status after William's impending marriage to Mary, and she encodes her anxiety in these lines.[40] Particularly telling, after the association of Mary with the (bird-eating) cat, is the effect of William's gaze on the vulnerable young bird. William most often likens Dorothy to birds in his poetry; clearly, D. Wordsworth is concerned with the detrimental power of the gaze on the fragile, unnested analogue for herself. The possibility of exclusion from William's life meant loss or diminishment of that intimate

collective poetic effort, as well as possible loss of mythic status and importance in William's schema.

The swallows, by contrast, are a family who will nest in the safety of the
domestic shelter, and in the safety of Dorothy Wordsworth's empathetic
observation. When catastrophe does come, Dorothy's empathy with the
swallows' plight gives comfort as their nest making follows the pattern of
her own continual domestic caretaking:

> It had fallen down. Poor little creatures, they could not themselves be more
> distressed than I was. I went upstairs to look at the ruins. They lay in a large
> heap upon the window ledge; these swallows had been ten days employed
> in building this nest, and it seemed to be almost finished. . . . I watched
> them one morning, when William was at Eusemere, for more than an hour.
> Every now and then there was a feeling motion in their wings, a sort of
> tremulousness, and they sang a low song to one another. [25 June 1802]

What the journal entries tell us about the nest, structurally part of the
family nest-cottage, is that lived experience is not utopian but unstable.
Although William details a seemingly similar instability in "The Ruined
Cottage," there the decay of the cottage-nest represents the irresponsibility
of the mother, her failure in care. That Margaret's cottage goes to ruin and
her baby dies is more a lesson for the Poet as receiver of the Pedlar's word
that an understanding of the dangers of daily "winds and storms."

What D. Wordsworth's two bird accounts relate is that nests as homes
are vulnerable to life's destructive power. For William there is only ultimate maternal presence or ultimate maternal failure, and the nest represents which force dominates; for Dorothy, there is only cottage upkeep.
Significantly, she writes on 8 July 1802, "The swallows stole in and out of
their nest, and sate there, *whiles* quite still, *whiles* they sung low for two
minutes or more at a time just like a muffled robin. William was looking at
The Pedlar when I got up" (emphasis is D. Wordsworth's). The rest of
Dorothy's entry reflects William's version of the ruined cottage, but what
she stresses alongside the coming loss of the (premarital) house she keeps
is the maternal care of her own home, as it is reflected both in the account
of her own chores and in the now successful swallow nest.

This tale is emblematic of the larger whole. Without Dorothy Wordsworth's part of the story, the nest would not be rebuilt but would remain Margaret's ruined cottage; the story would transmute from pastoral sympathy to the melancholy of desertion and ghostly haunting. Chapter 3 investigates the nature of storytelling when the teller knows herself to speak from an impossible, or at least compromised because pastoralized, position and yet feels empowered to speak nonetheless.

THREE

Authoring Selves,
Traversing Ground

Alas! with countless charming names, I have
seen come to life the trees, fountains and rocks
of this place which has since suffered such
convulsion and which, like a field of Greece,
has nothing left to offer but ruins and
moving names.

Paul et Virginie, *39*

Dorothy Wordsworth Senr
D Wordsworth Old Poetess
Miss Wordsworth
D W Sr
M. DWordsworth

[various signatures DW used for her poems]

To remain the secure space of Dorothy Wordsworth's Grasmere terrain, the pastoral valley must avoid the desolate destiny of the scape described by Saint-Pierre in his *Paul et Virginie,* a sentimentally charged scene occasionally pocketed in the Wordsworthian landscape into which the poetic self can wander unaware. Dorothy Wordsworth's achievement can be said to be the production of a congenial halfway space, a safety zone composed of what William Wordsworth repeatedly refers to as a harbor and a hold. This space is the cottage landing, in which one is at once partially private or "closeted" and partially public or "out." Whereas Dorothy's contemporaries maintain for themselves a private closet in the home—either a study, for men, or boudoir, for women—she labors to maintain a circulation of cottage space in which no room is functionally stable, not even the designated sleeping chambers. This style of space presentation conforms to cottage living in the rural sense but is

109

designedly different from any of the middle-class homes Dorothy has grown up in. It thus takes on a bohemian cast that responds to the call of the French Revolution to replace bourgeois private space with the republican space of citizenship. Dove Cottage was not politicized to this extent, but the sentimentalized response to this call for openness, combined with the sentimentality of a *Paul et Virginie*-type pastoral lifestyle, leads to the creation of a felicitous and nestled space in the valley that can answer all the aesthetic demands put upon it.

The home or nest thus provides kind of partial closet where the players are made ready for yet another outing into the valley. This version of the pastoral was already put in place by the very "romantic" life led by the Ladies of Llangollen, whose literary life was intimately related to the changing contours of their Welsh cottage.[1] But the collaborative relationship between these two "beloved"s of Llangollen was contained in working together on everything sentimentally and rationally, while the Wordsworths as "beloved"s understood that their relationship could always involve other partners in the collaboration. Nonetheless, D. Wordsworth's role in the collaborative life as sister and twin is caretaker of that "harbor and hold" productive of Wordsworthian poetry. To denote the curated object as sentimental rather than one of sensibility, however, presupposes a fatal flaw in the arrangement. The flaw, which William so evenly draws out in Margaret's "Ruined Cottage," stems from the conflictive roles of mother-caretaker and heroine-beloved. As sister, Dorothy sits halfway between these roles in an attempt to ameliorate them and at the same time carve out an anomalous yet quintessentially romantic place for herself.

To speak even more aesthetically, we can say that D. Wordsworth curates the setting even while playing Virginie to William's Paul; she as much as William is an authoring self engaged in writing self into being. This is what we understand from her journal entries; William understands something somewhat different. It is not that Dorothy is external to W. Wordsworth's vision of self-in-the-world but that she is selved or twinned: interpolated. As this chapter will argue, such a positioning involves a sharing that goes beyond love to origin, and to Dorothy Wordsworth's own role in romantic origination. It is this dynamic that she picks up and enacts in relation to the sibling-brother whom she has defined not as interpolated self but as self absorbed, that is, as the interpretive self who defines their world.

✑ The Nature of Collaboration

Selving cannot be a purely willed identification, since the Wordsworths do not wear hollow masks, and in fact cannot understand Coleridge when he does eagerly exchange masks. The performative as a taking-on-of-self invokes subject formation, and invokes as well the question of how one is then impelled and compelled by identity. This is the question of how Dorothy comes to both forge and accept her place and her identity in romantic ideology, or at least in William's mythology. Both schemes associate her as object or subject with nature as facilitator for all things related to the pastoral, the maternal, the domestic. To be so compelled, Louis Althusser argues, individuals are socially transformed into subjectivities who subject themselves to ideological subjugation. That is, the subject is interpellated: "There are no subjects except by and for their subjection."[2]

Interpellation operates, Althusser tells us, through the act of hailing, or *direct address*. When the individual recognizes him or herself as the object of address, interpellation has occurred: "the one hailed always recognizes that it is really him being hailed" (174), and so we can understand D. Wordsworth's extreme internalization of William's lyric poetry, which literally hails her. The address involves recognition by the subjectivity as well as one's subjecthood: William's addresses interpellate Dorothy precisely because they do recognize her as an ego-self or twin. W. Wordsworth's mythic ideology, however, can function only because, as members of their society, he and Dorothy are already ideologically subjected through language.[3] As poet-priest, William is the prime *Subject* in which Dorothy recognizes herself as reflected "subject." Althusser explains that God is "the Subject *par excellence*," as is Christ; recall that Wordsworth characterizes himself and Coleridge as Christ figures in the concluding book of *The Prelude* and that Dorothy worships him ("Read L.B. — Blessings on that Brother of mine!"). The interpellation of subjects and of subjection to the Subject causes "absolute guarantee, the subjects 'work,' they 'work by

themselves' . . . the individual is interpellated as a (free) subject in order
that he shall submit freely . . . , i.e. in order that he shall (freely) accept
his subjection" (181–82). Dorothy's complicity in the maiden myth, and
what Mary refers to as her "slavishness," partly results from the compelling
hail by which William continually addresses her in his poetry.

It is also the result of her much earlier interpellation in the Western
ideology of gender identity and the resulting divisions of labor, power,
and privilege. For Althusser, subjectivity is a matter of free will in that
there are "good" subjects who "work by themselves" and "bad" subjects
who provoke the existing order as subversives. Women who through
"freewill" choose to embrace interpellation and, indeed, literalize it by
being "such a Slave" may be conflicted in their complicity by subversive
impulses; eventually such conflict must take its toll. On the other hand,
another preformulation molded D. Wordsworth to the brother's needs.
During her adolescence spent with every mother figure except her own
mother, Dorothy worked from the prism of sentimental fiction to compose herself as a Clarissa-martyr during her worst moments and as a member of a female utopian community in her happiest periods. Both self-
representations were directed through letter writing toward her best and
most sentimentally oriented friend, Jane Pollard; imagining a utopian
future with one or more female friends was a familiar set piece of sentimentalism, most popular among isolated communities of women on both
sides of the Atlantic. This early collaborative self-imagining readies Dorothy for a similar collaboration in selving with her brother which, again,
takes place through the act of writing. But she does return to the early
form when she begins to write her own poetry and needs a model that
turns the lens on William's charted scenario, needs to escape its placement
of her in his topography.

Thus Dorothy Wordsworth's literary activity at once supports W.
Wordsworth's mapmaking and adjusts or subverts it. She is a "salutary
imago" both in William's poetry and in her later years as a poet herself
who, in inscribing the feminine, presents us with an equally complex
figure: a woman addressed who herself addresses others. This is conversation in a new sense from the way Coleridge intends the word. Conversation provides the performative space between valley settings and ways of
being that allows for adjusting and replotting. As conversation, the ex-

change of words need not occur within the print economy that produces William as the poet Wordsworth; the woman who herself addresses exchanges her words in a domestic circulation where poems act as word gifts rather than the labor of art. Romantic conversation, on the other hand, is an aesthetic production. It becomes an important form of pastoral outage, inverting cosmopolitan wit and salon discourse into pastoral sincerity and natural erudition and upstaging the simpler word of women's exchange.

Because D. Wordsworth partook not only in women's words but also in the romantic conversation as W. Wordsworth and Coleridge lived and textualized it, and because she is essential to W. Wordsworth's concern with a gendered universe, she sits at the heart of romantic conflict and revolution. Dorothy is no mere "origin," nor is her writing mere material for the male romantics she knew; she is crucial to the structure of their discourse. De Quincey remarks on the quality of her valuable conversation,[4] yet her voice is so valuable it must be repressed. W. Wordsworth, Coleridge, Samuel Rogers, and De Quincey all provide descriptions of D. Wordsworth's keen eye for detail and her sensitivity and taste, yet none records what she actually said that was of intellectual interest, nor did she herself. Even in William's addresses to her, she is represented foremost as listening, and voiced but in a naturalized key. If the power of her voice threatens, the very form of the address acknowledges that power, addressing her voice yet continually deferring her speech.

For D. Wordsworth, the collaborative relationship cannot be merely one of peer status and conversation, for she writes nothing collaboratively with Coleridge, Mary or Sara Hutchinson, or anyone other than William. Necessary to the collaborative production of poetry is the bond of twinship, D. Wordsworth's version of romantic fusion. Thus she can work together with William because she knows his mind and heart and, more importantly, cares so intensely about them: "William worked at 'The Leech Gatherer' almost incessantly from morning till tea-time. . . . I was oppressed and sick at heart, for he wearied himself to death" (9 May 1802). Yet her respect for the subjectivities of others does not allow her to imagine the fusion of self and other of male romanticism: She and William constitute a close partnership, a literary as well as emotional relation.

Perhaps because of her internalization of collaborative discourse, it is difficult to position Dorothy Wordsworth as a romantic thinker and poet.

The overwhelming power of our notions of male-defined romanticism trains our reading, and William Wordsworth's myth of the sister-maiden is no less constraining. It is problematic whether Dorothy Wordsworth may be classified as a poet at all. In *Women Writers and Poetic Identity* Margaret Homans writes of her that she is "a writer who did not become a poet" and reads Dorothy Wordsworth's poetry as texts for a "resistance to poethood." Even her journals are read by Homans as "such unselfconscious texts as these." Susan Levin comments: "Uneven in quality, Dorothy's poetry sometimes has the effect of making us more appreciative of her talents as a prose writer. But it would have been surprising if any writer living in the Wordsworth household did not attempt to compose poems." Levin, however, does account for Dorothy Wordsworth in relation to romanticism, noting that, "Working in awareness of the great Western myths of masculine power, of authority and fulfillment — helping, in fact, to create one such myth — she presents an alternative to them. It is not what we are accustomed to reading" (*Dorothy Wordsworth*, 3). The romantic quest is unavailable to a woman socialized to adopt the social fiction of the domestic, communal sphere of influence.[5] In the Preface to *Lyrical Ballads* (1800) William Wordsworth explains his attempt in one poem to "displa[y] the strength of fraternal, or to speak more philosophically, of moral attachment when early associated with great and beautiful objects of nature."[6] The poet "Dorothy Wordsworth" is not comprehensible in the terms of those arguments predicated on the importance of male identification and its associations with "moral attachment," beauty, and the natural sublime except in terms of negation. We can, however, read her adaption of social encodings of "properly" female behaviors into positive communal and collaborative experiences that we recognize more readily as romantically bohemian.

Depending on how we define romanticism, D. Wordsworth both is and is not a romantic writer and poet; that is, her romanticism is one of her own making as she rereads Wordsworthian collaboration into a form of community making. William views community as both supportive and constraining to the seeker of the sublime, but the sublime loses its value for Dorothy insofar as temporal community is preferable to an atemporal, nonrepresentative sublime. Dorothy Wordsworth is thus both central and marginal to the male project: Her status as maiden in William's mythic scheme makes her muse and complement to his creative endeavors, but this certainly in itself marginalizes her. As feminist critics have repeatedly demonstrated, the position of the muse relative to the poet is an exclusionary one.[7] At the same time, when the creating self occupies both self and other positions, it fragments. Complementation or twinship provides one way to circumvent a shattered psyche, but it necessitates a fiction to structure itself on more complex than the simple master–slave story that allows people to understand themselves as objects.

Dorothy Wordsworth's poetic self-actualization is puzzling because it does not conform to our expectations of the romantic poet, and it has been tempting for critics to speak of her simply in terms of William's creative complement: muse, nurse, critic, amanuensis. In her *Grasmere Journals,* the work written during the most fully romantically bohemian years of her life, description not only precedes mediation in importance but displaces it as if to deny poetic thought and vision. Her continual effort is to avoid projecting emotions on the landscape and to avoid making self-conscious meditations based on her descriptions. In itself, this avoidance of the main aspects of romantic methodology displaces her from the center. For Dorothy, the object exists almost as a being, in and of itself, yet mutable and beautiful in its changing phases. She takes care not to intrude herself onto the landscape but to be an active observer of it, witness to its integrity and wonder. The subordination of self to object is an aspect of taking care, a maternal involution of self so that the other has room to blossom. Indeed, the archetypal caretaker role of gardener in God's Eden, replicated in Wordsworthian Grasmere, is a role that requires the elevation of object over observing self; even transplantation is a harboring of flowers and mosses where they will best prosper. Caretaking is peculiarly a feminine role, at once a selfishness (that is, a dominance of subject over object) in the act of gathering plants, mothering children, caring for brothers, and a decenteredness (a dominance of object over subject) which causes self-sacrifice, exertion, remembrance. Straddling two worlds, crossing boundaries, occupying self and other simultaneously, this particular mode can also take the form of being outside such roles to act as witness. This ambivalence feeds Dorothy Wordsworth's prose *and* poetry and allows her to feel at home in modes of mythmaking. This practice is essentially antithetical to William's poetical territorializing practice, which Homans calls "the internalizing imagination."

Nature's dual roles as mythic and real replicate D. Wordsworth's own doubled experience as she occupies both self and otherly positions and mythic and temporal schemes. This doubleness creates the problem of making sense of her place in the world, for this is an alterior doubling to William's double plotting. Contrary to William's mythic belief in her inherent female capacity for communing with nature, which reductively places her in a single ontological role aligned with nature, Dorothy's journals and poetry express only a distancing from nature where she is unable to locate the female self comfortably. Dorothy's concern in her journals for the health and moods of others stems from the same impulse as her careful witnessing of nature's changes and moods. An entry that notes "A misty rainy morning — the lake calm" is identical in tone and language with "Wm had slept better. He fell to work, and made himself unwell." As witness, she does not fall into the sentimental trap of overvaluing momentary exigencies but merely records that they exist. Yet the act of recording itself becomes an act of mothering in its notice of another's small moments, those things beneath the notice of great men. The roles of mother and sister are carefully conflated in sentimental literature, but they are also passive roles there. Dorothy does not accept either role as passive or active but uses them to flesh out a collaborative lifestyle with which to replace the conventional life she does not choose to lead.

The creation of unconventionality here reveals the real threat of the sentimental, since it stems from the mother's death. After the loss of Anne Wordsworth, Dorothy Wordsworth's youthful displacement from her own male-dominated family to the more feminine world of her "Aunt" Threlkeld only intensified her need to belong to a tightly knit community.[8] The caretaking of a devised "family" — the circle of friends continually visiting at Dove Cottage — is a reaction to D. Wordsworth's adolescent Shakespearean self-dramatization: "How we are squandered abroad!" It is one of her favorite quotes for troping the physical splaying out of the orphaned Wordsworths, and in Shylock's utterance she adopts a mercantile paradigm for the family's worth being "squandered": The boys must become earners in the capitalist economy, a squandering of talent she and William thoroughly forgo at Racedown. If the mercantile, as opposed to the bohemian, signifies waste and inappropriate valuing — illicit terms for weaving the family into an affective meaning unit — being sent abroad means landing in an undomesticated wasteland of alienating nonconnection. (See Gittings and Manton, 14–15)

Dorothy's energies in the first months at Dove Cottage focus on the creation of a utopian human community as she divides the home as nest from the grove or bower in nature, and where nature presents a nested or embowered space Dorothy feels welcome, cared for, at home. It is in partial response to the protection of the domesticated bower that she and William create their own "bower" in the tiny orchard: "We planted 3/4ths of the Bower. . . . I read The Lover's Complaint to Wm in bed and left him composed . . . A sweet morning. We have Put the finishing stroke to our Bower and here we are sitting in the orchard" (5–6 May 1802). The interweaving of compositional effort — of composing the bower, composing her brother (with a love plaint), and composing the journal entries — are in contrast to William's desire to seek out and inhabit, as a naturalized proclamation of poethood, the nest or sacred grove in nature.

And when Coleridge, William, and Dorothy find two nested bowers on their walk, her journal records imaginative energies expended not on the perfect first bower but on the second spot, which "is scarce a bower, a little parlour on[ly], not *enclosed* by walls, but shaped out for a resting-place by the rocks, and the ground rising about it. It had a sweet moss carpet. We resolved to go and plant flowers in both these places to-morrow" (23 April 1802; emphasis is Dorothy's). Because the first bower exemplifies the enclosing mythic grove where the address-to-women hails the maiden, it excites a tension in Dorothy and a sense of not belonging. D. Wordsworth is uneasy with the elevating myth of maidenhood, a myth which when applied to lived experience disallows her selfhood and aligns her with the sure object of the poet's gaze, Nature. The second, half-completed bower excites no such trepidation because the nest needs human care — gardening and housework — to render it habitable, a bower not of subliming myth but of fictive myth, a bower such as Milton and Spenser wrote of. Her response to nature is most visible in the way she grasps the bower, compared to William's usurping imagination. Her attempt is to comprehend the object's subjectivity and respect its power, not to rewrite Nature but to be witness to it, alive to the details of its presence.[9]

In one sense Dorothy's *Grasmere Journals,* generally accepted as her finest effort in this genre, exemplify William's discussion in his 1800 Preface concerning the nature of poetry versus prose:

> And it would be a most easy task to prove . . . that not only the language of a large portion of every good poem, even of the most elevated character, must necessarily, except with reference to the metre, in no respect differ from that of good prose, but likewise that some of the most interesting parts of the best poems will be found to be strictly the language of prose, when prose is well written. [Owen and Smyser, 1:132]

We might add that, conversely, the language of well-written prose must necessarily, except with reference to the meter, in no respect differ from that of good poetry and that the most interesting parts of the best prose will be found to be strictly the language of poetry. The prose quality of William's poetry and the poetic quality of Dorothy's prose mingle, arising perhaps from the same impulse and a mutual influencing. In the *Grasmere Journals,* mixed among entries such as "Mr and Miss Simpson came in after tea and supped with us" (11 October 1801), "Rain all day" (29 October 1801), or "Baking and starching" (15 December 1800) are passages such as the following: "[I] walked to the Cottage beyond Mr Gell's. One beautiful ash tree sheltered, with yellow leaves, one low one quite green. Some low ashes green. A noise of boys in the rocks hunting some animal" (16 November 1800), or "A rainy morning. A whirlwind came that tossed about the leaves, and tore off the still green leaves of the ashes" (8 November 1800). The following passage demonstrates how discourses are intermixed:

> A very rainy night. I was baking bread in the morning and made a giblet pie. We walked out before dinner to our favourite field. The mists sailed along

the mountains, and rested upon them, enclosing the whole vale. In the evening the Lloyds came. We drank tea with them at Borwick's and played a rubber at whist — stayed supper. Wm looked very well — A fine moonlight night when we came home. [28 October 1800]

But if a poetic language that hums close to the liminal moment of access to the real (Nature) can be located in the journals, so too can poetic language be found that is distinctly artificed. At least one edition has been made that transcribes the poetic passages of the journals into found poems. Pamela Woof has demonstrated the journals' tendency to fall into iambic pentameter, not surprising given D. Wordsworth's extensive trek through Shakespeare during the early Dove Cottage years.[10] William himself must have found Dorothy's prose highly poetic, though it is her observant eye he appreciates most. The felicity of her language allowed him to take over and make use of bits of her journal, so that one finds resonances and even word-for-word borrowings in his poetry. It is a commonplace to speak of William's use of her daffodil passage, but subtler resonances exist: "A very fine evening calm and still" (27 August 1800), for instance, resounds in his "It is a beauteous Evening calm and free."

Dorothy Wordsworth's journals, then, are not only viable sites for the location of her poetic productivity but the only work of any quantity besides her letters from the years when she and William created their romantic version of artistic life together. Her poetry is written so much later that it only offers a retrospective account of these years. D. Wordsworth's standards for her own work, and her understanding of her brother William's, show a critical intellect at work.[11] Coleridge and W. Wordsworth both valued her conversation, and if William was absent she and Coleridge would converse long into the night. William thought so much of her talent that, before the Pinney brothers offered the use of Racedown Lodge, William had proposed his scheme for Dorothy to join him in London where they would try their hands at Grub Street, writing and translating. Yet Dorothy was harshly critical of her own attempts to write both poetry and prose, and the absence of meditation or philosophical thought beyond the moralizing "prosing streaks"[12] shows an unwillingness to incorporate in writing what she engaged in in daily speech. Although, if the journals are notably absent in Wordsworthian metaphysics, they do not record the philosophical dialogues of her male counterparts either: It seems that while W. Wordsworth and Coleridge were consumed with the generic possibilities of the conversational mode, and with turning content into form in their conversation poems, Dorothy left the recording of conversation to them.

The journals are no Boswellian rumination and self-positing. Introspection is strictly, even rigidly, disallowed, and the journals are instead daily recordings of life, a family document intended above all for William's eyes rather than for posterity. Yet far from being selfless, uncentered texts, they are also the documentation of Dorothy's doings and observations; still, the thoughts themselves are rarely recorded, substituted instead by a notation of the act of thinking. The *Grasmere Journals* note unceasingly the daily bodily ills of each of their large circle, the coins spent on mail, charity, and food, the daily weather, and William's tribulations and successes in writing. They also record conversations in native dialect, but not the scintillating conversations of the brotherhood that seduced them into staying up until early morning. Nor does any mention appear of completed works by D. Wordsworth except the fair copies of her brother's poems. We hear only of the failures: "I was tired when I reached home, and could not sit down to reading, and tried to write verses, but alas!" (18 March 1802) is typical of her response to the demands poetry as William defined it made on her. His concern was that each poem have a "*worthy* purpose," that it be written not so much "with a distinct purpose formally conceived" but with a purpose that results from fully formed "habits of meditation." These habits are precisely what Dorothy avoids in her journal. In addition, "[p]oems to which any value can be attached were never produced on any variety of subject but by a man who, being possessed of more than usual organic sensibility, had also thought long and deeply" (Preface to *Lyrical Ballads,* 1802). Although D. Wordsworth possessed the requisite sensibility, the required intellectual apparatus (habits of meditation plus long and deep thought) as well as the specified masculinity (for the Poet is "a man speaking to men") must have been especially daunting.

To Lady Beaumont in 1806 Dorothy wrote of her continuing failures: "I did try one story, but failed so sadly that I was completely discouraged. Believe me, since I received your letter I have made several attempts . . . and have been obliged to give it up in despair (*MY,* 25, 20 April 1806).

Dorothy's insistence on artistic failure, despite the beginnings of poetic output (her first extant poems are composed in 1805 and 1806), reflects an incipient tension, as Homans notes, "between her desire to be a poet and her resistance to this desire" (*Women Writers,* 42). The derogation of "verses . . . or little stories for children" as "all I could be ambitious of doing" (*MY,* 24–25, 20 April 1806) reflects the suppressed desire and repressed will to write "serious" poetry which must consciously or unconsciously inscribe that "worthy purpose" W. Wordsworth insists upon.

The most notable contrast between the writings of the two Wordsworths, beyond William's obsessive awareness of self and Dorothy's denial and decentering of self, is their different emphases on the nature of the phenomenal world. W. Wordsworth's motivation, especially in the poetry of the early years, is to illustrate that the components of daily life have supernatural origin, thus creating a link between the domestic and the sublime. D. Wordsworth's interest is in the domesticity of nature (the realm of the beautiful) and in the naturalness of domestic life. Thus the perfect home is a cottage in the vale, as her first self-conscious bid for poethood attests ("A Winter's Ramble in Grasmere Vale," 1805). The journals, consequently, don't "str[i]ve to decorate the truth" ("Irregular Verses," 4) or to imagine sublime heights. Their currency is in the natural objects so regularly visited and commented on that they are familiarized, yet kept strange, intact, inviolate.

The journals provide relief in both the devastating failure to write at all, a rigorous self-criticism, and the moral weight of attempting poetic sublimity. They are both daily account books for the business of family affairs and an artist's sketchbook to be plumbed later, judgment deferred until that time. During the periods in which William is gone, long descriptive passages follow each other as Dorothy attempts to fill her hours and communicate their essence to the absent brother. The journal thus provides her version of William's union of maiden and Nature in the present tense of the grove: Here, in her loneliness, she sets down words about a past event, which have immediate union with another only on an imaginary plane. Her words wait, embodying the traditional role of women as they attend the intervention of some active agent in their lives; they are written to give another "pleasure by it," yet the journal keeping — in and of itself and apart from the highly poetic flashes — seems to have been more a chore than a delight, more a record of events than an exercising of creative powers. And so the passages that catch the ear have a guardedness that seems to deny the writer's authority to say anything more than that the sunlight appeared to strike the lake in such a manner. Quick sketches, these delineations of a particular scene, are meant to be the raw material for another's "worthy purpose." William later used the following for a ten-line passage in *The Excursion:*

> We lay a long time looking at the lake; the shores all embrowned with the scorching sun. The ferns were turning yellow, that is, here and there one was quite turned. We walked round by Benson's wood home. The lake was now most still, and reflected the beautiful yellow and blue and purple and grey colours of the sky. We heard a strange sound in the Bainriggs wood, as we were floating on the water; it *seemed* in the wood, but it must have been above it, for presently we saw a raven very high above us. It called out, and the dome of the sky seemed to echo the sound. It called again and again as it flew onwards, and the mountains gave back the sound, seeming as if from their center, a musical bell-like answering to the bird's hoarse voice. We heard both the call of the bird, and the echo, after we could see him no longer. [27 July 1800]

Characteristic of this entry is its awareness of otherness, both in the "we" as viewer, rather than a single, isolated viewpoint taking place next to another's, and in the otherness of nature. Interestingly, the act of calling is recognizably self-originated, as an alignment more in tune with her poetry than her journals. Indeed, the calling is itself a poetic act, but an act which responds to and calls forth far more important sounds or voices. The "strange sound" heard while the twinned viewers "were floating on the water" signals the presence of Nature. Her otherly presence causes a sense of isolating disequilibrium similar to the disorientation William's speaker-hero experiences in the ice-skating episode of *The Prelude:* "—yet still the solitary cliffs / Wheeled by me, even as if the earth had rolled / With visible motion her diurnal round" (I.484–86). The disequilibrium, which is at the same time the immersion in Nature and the distancing from the natural world, makes the world itself strange, so that a "strange sound . . . *seemed* in the wood, but it must have been above it" (emphasis as given).

The viewers are protected from the strangeness in their nestlike landscape of water encircled by woods and enclosed with "the dome of the sky," which so encapsulates the "we" that sound bounces back to them, as in a cottage room or as in the arched vault of "Home at Grasmere."

Typical of the journal entries is the use of an accumulative descriptive catalog, which one finds here in the "beautiful yellow and blue and purple and grey colours of the sky," without any attempt to do color analysis (e.g., dove grey, or blue fading to purple). Contiguous cataloging, as opposed to synthesis and reformulation into the symbolic abstract, signals the presence of poetic rhythms and thus of a mind more in tune with the impossible real of Nature. The entry is written in the past tense, yet the temporal moment of the experience is induced in a strange mixture of present with past, so that the reader's eye is led, in a reexperiencing of the moment, with the eye of the twinned viewer around the lake. Through the cataloging of the separate elements that make up the scene — the colors of the sky, the surrounding trees, the bird over the woods — the reader is given all the necessary material for a romantic meditation poem. Yet D. Wordsworth herself refrains from the symbolizing act of making the meditation, or from recording it. The catalog represents the literal eye, whose importance in the project of acting witness to nature Dorothy insists on. It is her tool for acclimating herself to the beautiful, that realm which William claims in *The Prelude* Dorothy taught him to appreciate and truly to see.

Margaret Homans's important and useful reading of Dorothy Wordsworth's tendency to literalize the descriptive moment, and to ascribe imaginative constructions to Nature, nonetheless incorporates an acceptance of the mimetic word as adequate to experience. Thus she concludes that Dorothy is unable to write imaginatively, crippled as she is by societal strictures and by her brother's overpoweringly forceful poetic vision. What Homans does not acknowledge is the discrepancy between the written word (that is, what Dorothy presented to her specific audience) and what she herself later says she would have preferred to write: "I *reverenced* the Poet's skill, / And *might have* nursed a mounting Will / To imitate the tender Lays / Of them who sang in Nature's praise" ("Irregular Verses," emphasis is DW's). To say that D. Wordsworth was incapable of the imaginative act is to take her words as literally as Homans argues Dorothy herself took experience. It is necessary, instead, to argue for Dorothy's lifelong choosing to record only the inarguable, that is, experience as unsubjectively transcribed as possible. Thus, as Homans notes, "Dorothy leaves herself out of every center she proposes" (*Women Writers,* 70). The cost of such an extensive decentering process, for Dorothy, is to renounce, at least to her most immediate audience, the male romantic project. In addition, Homans's response to the literalization that occurs in the journals, a move Woof also notes—"Where Wordsworth connects, Dorothy allows unrelated existence" ("Dorothy Wordsworth," 100)—is to see Dorothy Wordsworth's struggle against the temptation to personify and emotionalize the landscape as the exclusion of

> any language that would permit symbolic readings of nature. This Edenic state brings reunion with William and reunion with (maternal) nature into alignment, because the idea of a world prior to division excludes all subject–object division, sexual division as well as separation between the mind and nature. [*Women Writers,* 56]

Although Homans's observation intends only to establish the preoedipal character of D. Wordsworth's utopian desires, she not only quite helpfully describes the desire for fusion inherent in the bond(age) of twinship but also broaches the framework for Kristeva's semiotic realm of thought and language.

Curiously, Homans's main thesis is to argue that, according to the Freudian schema of family relations, Dorothy should have looked for a paternal presence in nature which would replace the father she had lost, just as William seeks in nature the maternal element. Yet to discuss D. Wordsworth's descriptive language in terms of "[non]symbolic readings of nature" is to contrast William's oedipal, symbolic relationship to the mother figure with Dorothy's refusal to engage in such a splitting of subject and object. Thus William is defined by symbolic language despite his insistence on the importance of the disruptive economy of spots of time; Dorothy, at the same time, is defined as a natural poet, the speaker of "poetic language." And it is true that, by not acknowledging her own artistic subjectivity in her renderings of nature, D. Wordsworth is adhering to a poetic vision of an "edenic state" which is the fusion of mind to nature. Yet the answer to the creation of this Wordsworthian differential is the appeal to Enlightenment reason in both Wordsworths' work. The symbol, as it exists in romantic thought, is the attempt artistically to heal the gap between subject and object; as such, it is an appropriation of the other through Nature as the female principle. D. Wordsworth resists such a falsifying fusion, insisting on the subjective status of all others, at the same time that she also resists clear delineations of what is self and what is other. The uneasiness with symbols and with symbolic language leads her to Nature, while William's needful mythic appropriation of Nature positions her alarmingly as a daughter of Nature.

Although Dorothy Wordsworth rarely refers to her own self-conception as a producer of written works, at least three places in the *Grasmere Journals* gesture toward inner vision. Unwilling to discuss such matters as fully as does William in Book I of *The Prelude,* Dorothy mentions only fleetingly her attitude toward her own poetic aptitude. Walking home in the moonlight alone, she exalts in the "glorious brightness of the moon itself!" and, after a lengthy passage, declares: "I had many very exquisite feelings, and when I saw this lowly Building in the waters, among the dark and lofty hills, with that bright, soft light upon it, it made me more than half a poet" (18 March 1802). Like her brother, D. Wordsworth envisions poethood as something that is given: "it made me" rather than "I felt." This passive acceptance of inspiration does not denominate the muse, but her description of the inspiring scene ascends from picturesque sensibility to sublime sensations (the building seemingly in the water, eerily spotlit and backdropped). As a gift of the otherliness of nature, these sensations are not explored or enumerated, merely described generally, and the passage is prefaced by a long paragraph that incorporates enough raw material to provoke one's own "exquisite feelings." It is not Dorothy's feelings that need to be communicated, the end product of her vision, but instead the material with which to have the experience itself.

Earlier, Dorothy walked alone to Ambleside and then back "round the lakes — a very fine warm evening. I lay upon the steep of Loughrigg, my heart dissolved in what I saw, when I was not startled but re-called from my reverie by a noise as of a child paddling with out shoes" (1 June 1800). Again, the reverie itself, which caused the heart to dissolve, is not recorded, and the creative, poetic mediation is kept private while the events that surrounded it are carefully given. Another entry, "It made my heart almost feel like a vision to me" (20 June 1802), further distances the experience so that it is even more passive, even more tentative.

Finally, Dorothy's recounting of her trip back to Grasmere from William and Mary's marriage mentions that, on passing through Wensley,

> my heart was melted away with dear recollections—the bridge, the little waterspout, the steep hill, the church. They are among the most vivid of my own inner visions, for they were the first objects that I saw after we were left to ourselves, and had turned our whole hearts to Grasmere as a home in which we were to rest. [8 (?) October 1802]

Clearly, for D. Wordsworth, vision and poetic sensibility reside or are stored in the heart, whereas W. Wordsworth places them in the mind. She is also invested in creating a myth of poetic origins based loosely on William's spots of time and his own story of self-creation. "[M]y own inner visions" repeats the Wordsworthian formula for poetic essence while it also answers William's "exhortations" in his odic "Tintern Abbey" that the sister preserve memories of youth to which she can return in later years for succor. This passage, more than the rest, delineates why the vision is important to her, but typically she opts to explain by means of emotional bonds to those she loves rather than to explain the precise significance of the inner visions themselves—a significance her readers would have well been able to imagine for themselves, that is, the farewell to the years of living alone with William.

The manner in which these most important passages in a poet's notebook are glossed over and woven into the more characteristic cataloging of scenic elements ("the bridge, the little waterspout, the steep hill, the church") represents the essential character of the journals, and of the *Grasmere Journals* as raw material for others rather than for D. Wordsworth's own future use. The data compiled for William do not find their way into her own verses (except for rare instances, and then only phrases rather than whole scenes); nor do the necessary preliminaries for her Green narrative, lyrics, or fables appear in the journal.

Written for William, the journal becomes—despite Dorothy's notes of her own activities and moods—his property, one more voice to be absorbed by the territorial will or egotistical sublime. Such an arrangement was congenial to them both, for her insights and recording of data aided in his composing process, while he provided her with an interested and responsive audience, an answering voice. However, since the crafting of Dorothy's language into William's own work often took place several years after her original entries, so that she could never know exactly what it was he might use, the journal must not be mined for her own creations. To do so could mean proprietary conflicts if they wanted to use the same line or image.

The need to separate writing that does not belong to the self from writing that does belong causes a particular kind of conflict. The journal entry in which Dorothy feels "more than half a poet" expresses her poetic desire, but it also records what it is to be that fraction, that half: "I was tired when I reached home, and could not sit down to reading, and tried to write verses, but alas! I gave up expecting William, and went soon to bed." The feeling of poethood was only half-given, and the verses did not come. Expecting verses and expecting William intermingle in the passages expressive of poetic vision: They all take place in his absence, as if William and poetry are synonymous. Her desire for the one intensifies her desire for the other, and the will to compose, which is normally in recession (and perhaps is considered at times a cancer of gnawing frustration), irrupts. The conflict is always whether or not to compete with William on his own ground. The recording of failure in the paradoxically public space of her journal signals not only the effects of competition on her poetic sensibility but also what it is she will let William know. Since William often experienced difficulty and dejection when at work on his poems, her recording of her own failure is not in stark contrast to his success, and her "Poor William" entries are numerous. But the absence of any mention of her own poetry making shows that, at least in the vision they had together created of artistic production, her function in the creative process was as complement rather than as prime agent. D. Wordsworth's entries that record failure are similar in nature to the entries that surround the accounts of William's marriage to Mary: These are all entries that stress her inability to exist independently of William and, as a result, are all demands to be taken care of. The recordings of failure, interestingly, all appear during periods of William's absence from home, so that they function as needful calls that unsuccessfully invoke his coming. Her inability to compose poetry at these moments signals an inability to be independent of her twinned sibling: The danger is that if she could perform his creative labor then she might be perceived as having no need of him.

The balance maintained among the tasks divided between the Wordsworths was delicate, and during the Dove Cottage/*Grasmere Journals* years it was a balance carefully maintained. Dorothy seems early on to have accepted her "mission," to use Ernest de Selincourt's term, as helpmate to William's "vocation" (*Dorothy Wordsworth,* 21). But just as her sense of being "half a poet" shows her awareness of her own fractured state as an artist, her sense of the collaborative project means that she has accepted the Eve role of helpmate. To cite de Selincourt's religious terminology to describe the nature of the Wordsworths' collaborative project is not to overread their literal relationship. William's preparation at university for ordination provided both Dorothy and himself with the opportunity to plan out a future together where she would take care of William's parsonage. William's sense of himself as a poet-priest and as a wearer of priestly robes continued to color their relationship: "to the open fields I told / A prophecy: poetic numbers came / Spontaneously to clothe in priestly robe / A renovated spirit singled out, / Such hope was mine, for holy services" (*Prelude* I.50–54). Although their relatives viewed William's poetic endeavors previous to Dove Cottage as a joint effort of both brother and sister, she does not share equal status in the unnamed collaboration.[13] Dorothy is the most recurrent figure in William's poetry, appearing as beloved, as maiden, and as pupil, but she is not a coauthor of his verses, nor does she share his authority or status as poet. Restricted by gender, she could not be a member of the Lake District's poetic brotherhood; she was instead the founding member of its sisterhood. But what did it mean to be "our Sister Gift-of-God," in Coleridge's phrase, and not only literal sister to William and John Wordsworth but also figurative sister to Coleridge and to the Hutchinson sisters? The term "sister" appears repeatedly in Dorothy's journal, but her notion of sisterhood contrasts with William's meaning of the existence of a well-developed nest with much nurturance (such as the family of sisters his speaker longs after in "Home at Grasmere"). For Dorothy sisterhood implies a utopian female community, such as she knew at her aunt Threlkeld's, but also a collaborative identity in relation to others.

If being a complement to her brother's genius meant halving Dorothy's own sense of poethood, a fracture must then take place between the capacity to write and poetic self-identity. Yet Dorothy's adolescent letters to her friend Jane are authoritative in tone and reveal a self-confidence in her erudition and taste not found in the later writings.[14] Her well-known adult letter to Sara Hutchinson in defense of William's "Leech-gatherer" is a marked contrast. Subsumed under William's critical auspices, Dorothy's independent stance has evaporated, so that the critical method she shares with Sara consists of the supportive attempt to under-stand, that is, to get beneath the reader's own view and change it, rather than the earlier insistence on correcting the *composition* according to preexisting readerly standards: "When you happen to be displeased with what you suppose to be the tendency or moral of any poem which William writes, ask yourself whether you have hit upon the real tendency and true moral . . . and when you feel any poem of his to be tedious, ask yourself in what spirit was it written" (*EY,* 307, 14 June 1802). The radical change in attitude from adolescent confidence to mature dependence signals the effects of collaboration on the helpmate.

The turn from critical confidence to readerly nurturance replicates the question of self and selflessness endlessly repeated in the substructure of D. Wordsworth's writings. A subjectivity defined by gender, her education included service and deference to others. Her early assertion of self becomes in the journals an abasement of self which calls for the support and love of friends. A passage which de Selincourt refers to rather cruelly as "naive simplicity" (*Dorothy Wordsworth,* 141) portrays a devoted sister at her most vulnerable and is an implicit demand that she be taken care of despite William's impending marriage: "My tooth broke today. They will soon be gone. Let that pass, I shall be beloved — I want no more" (31 May 1802). The dejection of this entry is striking in its contrast to her adolescent epistles about curls and clothes. For W. Wordsworth, dejection is aligned with romantic imaginative depths, affective loss, hallucinatory landscapes. For D. Wordsworth, it is aligned with the (aging) female body, an alienation from the natural scape, failure to translate emotion into aesthetic form, and a superabundance of affect. For William the deject is one step from sublimation; for Dorothy the deject is in danger of being integrated into the scene, capable only of translating experience through the semiotic body and so without affective language: "after a flood of tears my heart was easier"; "I had been very melancholy . . . and I could not keep the tears within me"; "I was melancholy and could not talk, but at last I eased my heart by weeping—nervous blubbering says William. It is not so."

D. Wordsworth's melancholy, like her brother's, is in part a literary sensibility. Whereas William derives his dejection as well as his joy from the pastoral, odic, and epic terrain of classical heights and depths, Dorothy has to resort to more contemporary literature: Besides *Clarissa* and *Paul et Virginie,* she read Anna Seward's melancholic sonnets, Beattie's *Minstrel* (Edwin reminds her of William), *Wanly Penson; or, The Melancholy Man,* Oliver Goldsmith's works, and even William's "Descriptive Sketches." When she does not cry, melancholic dejection can be a pleasurable response to the scape: "The air and the lake were still—one cottage light in the vale. . . . I sate till I could hardly drag myself away I grew so sad. 'When pleasant thoughts,' etc." She is quoting from the absent William "In that sweet mood when pleasant thoughts / Bring sad thoughts to the mind" ("Lines written in Early Spring"), yet she literalizes what he intends contemplatively. By embodying his lines, she draws him into presence with her in a process of fusion that melancholy bodily represents for her. When he draws her into presence with his address-to-women she is silenced; when she draws him into presence she gives him (poetic) voice.

Keenly attuned not only to nature's emotive scape but to the affects of others which she re-presented through manifesting her own emotions, Dorothy Wordsworth presents herself as a woman of sensibility. In effect, she parlays her prior self into Wordsworthian maidenhood. And she seems to have provided William with selective information about her childhood with which he could further construct the myth of her self. She recalls one morning when

> we were talking about the pleasure we both always feel at the sight of a butterfly. I told him that I used to chase them a little, but that I was afraid of brushing the dust off their wings, and did not catch them. He told me how

they used to kill all the white ones when he went to school because they
were Frenchmen. [14 March 1802]

The juxtaposition of such feminine gentleness with such masculine aggression is the mythic material Dorothy offers her brother as complementary partner to his mythmaking activities. The mature reality of such gentleness, attested to by several of their community as one of Dorothy's adult
personality traits, is contradicted by the textual history of "Nutting."[15] The
earliest version of "Nutting" has as its hero Lucy, then the boy and Lucy
are both present, and in the final version only the boy remains. Even the
admonition in the final text to the maiden (whose appearance has been
reduced to an unexpected, unnamed presence in the last lines) to "move
along these shades / In gentleness of heart; with gentle hand touch" the
silent trees, which the speaker had himself despoiled, indicates that her
(un)natural tendency might, unlike the maiden figures of the other address poems, veer toward lawlessness. Likewise, the lawless Dora several
years later is understood to be a replica of the early Dorothy whose energy
and lack of decorum her Cookson grandmother deplored.[16]

Romantic or bohemian lawlessness, that which William writes out of
the myth of bounded maidenhood, plays an important part in the female
arena of communal interrelation. But it is also characteristic of the causa-
tive agent of abjection to "not respect borders, positions, rules" since it is
the "in-between, the ambiguous, the composite" (Kristeva, *Powers of Horror*, 4). Lawlessness appears in Dorothy's work as a way to transgress
boundaries between genres, voices, and traditions. The following note is
pasted into one of D. Wordsworth's commonplace books (DCMS 120)
after the fair copy in her hand of "A Holiday at Gwerndovennant":

> *Finis* — and again I say tune up your musical pipes & put on your accommo-
> dating ears — be in good humour & forgive — bad metre, bad rhymes — no
> rhymes — identical rhymes & *all that is lawless* — As to dullness I leave that to
> take care of itself. (Levin, *Dorothy Wordsworth* 195; second emphasis mine)

It is this sense of lawlessness that is both central to Dorothy Wordsworth's
poetic sensibility and also a source of guilt and apology. It appears in her
poetic language as it is fed by the interweaving of the textual with the

social and relational. On the other hand, she expresses guilt at having transgressed the laws of a male romantic poetics with her own version of what might be permissible in poetry making.

While Dorothy's lawlessness is sutured to her domestic cares, so that the maintenance of relational webs validates the weaving of words, what is significant in William's poetry is that his myth of domesticity, "Home at Grasmere," also contains his self-isolating vow of poetic intent: "Urania, I shall need / Thy guidance, or a greater Muse. . . . Come, thou prophetic Spirit, Soul of Man . . . unto me vouchsafe / Thy guidance . . . that my verse may live." This apostrophe specifically disavows his poetic dependence on the maiden, thus cutting even the tie with the complementing sister-self. Like the resolution to *The Prelude,* which he is yet to compose, this apostrophe claims a higher muse and allegiance than Milton, Nature, or the maiden. W. Wordsworth's transcendence of Nature in order to reach toward "the one thought / By which we live, infinity and God" (*Prelude* XIII.183–84), contradicts the desire he expresses in the addresses to women. The words in this *Prelude* passage that would be more familiar to Dorothy preface these lines: "in some green bower / Rest, and be not alone, but have thou there / The one who is thy choice of all the world." *The Prelude*'s speaker asserts, transcends, and so in one sense denies the bower: "There linger, lulled, and lost, and rapt away — / Be happy to thy fill; thou call'st this love, / And so it is, but there is higher love / Than this" (XIII.156–62).

The transcendence and denial of a female space specifically associated with the maiden can only deny his need for the sister's complementary presence. After his transcendence of Nature's bower in which one is "lulled, and lost" to higher aims, the poet walks alone in isolation, for "Thy love is human merely" while the higher love that calls him "proceeds / More from the brooding soul, and is divine" (XIII.164–65). His vocation, which is based in the security of his arcadian family nest yet tempered by his transcendent project, makes it necessary for him to denounce the pastoral convention; it is vital that the reader understand the heroic quality of his undertaking. The address to Emma prepares the reader for the final Miltonic section of "Home at Grasmere," which William later uses for the Prospectus to *The Excursion.* The heroic "I," minus Emma as complement, learns to displace his socialized masculinity onto a different plane: Thus the poet is still the hero-warrior with "foes / To wrestle with and victory to complete, / Bounds to be leapt and darkness to explore" in the conquest of the human mind. The poet's access to this different plane of activity renders pastoral and family incongruous with the epic solitude of the poet. This solitude is not the loneliness earlier feared but the state of continuity with Nature which allows him to leap beyond it.

The difference between Dorothy's and William's attitude toward the voice of Nature lies in the question of gender. In "Home at Grasmere" the voice of Nature encourages William in his poet-priest vocation. For Dorothy, Nature's voice is intrusive and brings an undesired message. In one of her most impressive late poems, "Irregular Verses" (1827), she makes important claims for her own poetic subjectivity, but it has taken her twenty-seven years since "Home at Grasmere" so completely mythologized her to do so. Although "Grasmere — A Fragment" is the intentional complement to "Home at Grasmere," it is "Irregular Verses" that responds to William's claims for epic intent in his poem. In addition to the nest imagery, all five of his other themes are counterpointed in "Verses": the address to a woman, twinship versus poetic selfhood, three stories as models for the self, pastoral versus the real, and the influence of voices as a draw toward transcendence. Counterpoint helps the woman poet position herself in relation to the brother poet, and to reinvent her younger self out of the memory of the fantasy selves she and Jane collaboratively produced, just as "Home" reinvents the pastoral siblings.

Where the two poems differ most intriguingly is in their comprehension of the naturalized mother. In William's version of the domestic valley, the disequilibrium between family life and his solitary quest produces the family's "Strange question" which "answers not itself": Questing means leaving the maternal behind. Dorothy's poem constructs a world of mothers and daughters in which mothers are both positive supports (Jane, the now-grown friend of adolescence) and negative underminers ("the mild maternal smile, / That oft-times would repress, beguile / The over-confidence of youth"). The mother's complicity in the repression of the daughter's poetic desire is contrasted with Jane's "unshaken truth" and "Mother's heart," her cathexis to Julia's correctly "chearful" and tranquil heart. In the speaker's identification with Julia as maiden, Jane becomes the speaker's mother as well, and her "Mother's heart" will respond to the speaker's sad song "with tender pain." The speaker also mothers Julia, the maiden addressed, as she instructs her in the importance of thought and memory, two essential elements in the making of poetry, and thus her mothering revises maidenhood.

For William the maiden occupies a tertiary position between self-poet and other-Nature that allows her no place from which to speak or be seen. For Dorothy the maiden is Kristeva's "third party" occupying the place between the two parental figures of speaker and Jane, a synthesis / child who is both self and other, thesis and antithesis, and as such is in the place of laughter ("Mirthful she is"). Complicating this three-part scenario is that the maiden here is both speaker-self and speaking addressee, both Dorothy and Julia. D. Wordsworth's "And now, dear girl, I hear you ask" allows the maiden entry into the conversational space. The maiden takes shape as both Julia and herself, with the same kind of doubled subjectivity William exploits in "Tintern Abbey," but without the same kind of "speaking for." Julia, too, may write, and so the maiden as present speaker and potential poet both revoices the speaker who had been silenced and revises William's naturalized maiden whose voice is made for inspiration, not dialogue. The silencing mother intrudes three times into the poem, each time marked off by quoted utterances. Bakhtin theorizes that quotations intrude on a discourse in order to show "double-voicedness," or layered voices that allow the speaker to distance herself from what is said. Like the mother, Nature's voice is also integrated into the speaker's narrating voice in "Verses." This slippage merges possible origins for the utterance as well as possible addressees:

> And now, dear girl, I hear you ask
> Is this your lightsome, chearful task?
> You tell us tales of forty years
> Of hopes extinct, of childish fears,
> Why cast among us thoughts of sadness
> When we are asking mirth and gladness?

Both "dear girl" and a storyteller with forty years of tales, the speaker is reproved and trivialized, this time by the maternal as Nature, yet the critique is less straitening than the human mother's ridicule. But the dear girl is also Julia, and the reproof against melancholy is aimed at both maidens for the speaker-maiden's sadness must not transform "the Maid . . . Mirthful she is." The double orientation of the "dear girl" passage reveals Dorothy's awareness of multiple ego centers which can be imaginatively merged in an empathetic competence. The act of being both insider and outsider, both self and other, signals the presence of the maternal: Dorothy as daughter is also Dorothy as mother, experiencing Julia as self, sister-maiden, and child. The alienating presence of the maternal smile in the doubly voiced lines ("'Twill glance on me — and to reprove / Or . . . 'Twill *point* the sting of ridicule") emphasizes the speaker's inability to unite empathetically with that other; these are not words she is willing to own for they recall that

—I *reverenced* the Poet's skill,
And *might have* nursed a mounting Will
To imitate the tender Lays
Of them who sang in Nature's praise.

In a contrast that rehearses the contrast between Jane with her "unshaken truth" and "Mother's heart" and the rejecting maternal smile, the speaker's fusing response in the "dear girl" passage, and the confusion she creates over whose words are whose, indicates a willingness to share words and identities. By mothering Julia, the speaker identifies herself with the tender Jane whose most important characteristics are not her motherhood but her heart and eyes, both sites of poetic vision. At the same time that the speaker aligns herself with Jane against the mocking maternal smile, and twins herself with Julia as maiden, she accomplishes the mothering of herself.

Yet, retaining the positionality of maiden exacts a price of confinement perhaps more limiting than social restriction *because* it is mythic. To attempt escape invites social responses that "stifl[e] ambition," and D. Wordsworth is conflicted over who is to blame for the "natural" order, in the end putting the onus on herself. It was her own "bashfulness," "a struggling shame," fear of "blame," " — Or something worse — a lurking pride," and "fond self-love" which dreaded ridicule, partially exonerating the bad mother. And whereas William's voice of Nature in "Home at Grasmere" leads him to the role of warrior-poet, Dorothy sees herself as still a child/daughter of Nature, open to the mother's reproof. W. Wordsworth's access to an epic plane of endeavor leads him to make a Miltonic ending which trumpets his sublime argument: D. Wordsworth is mired in her admiration of another who needs no reproof, and she ends her poem as a "poor memorial strain" which mourns her own unrealized potential. Melancholy focused on the self is not the pleasing absorption of melancholy in nature. Yet the poem's tag ending validates her mourning, reversing the mother's earlier judgment of her sadness: " — The happiest heart is given to sadness; / The saddest heart feels deepest gladness." The embedded personal message concerning the poetic heart in this couple substantiates the speaker's boundary-transgressing emotions and subjectivity. At the same time, the tag ending gives a generalized authority to the lines, again deferring responsibility for its message which defies and revises Nature's reproof. In contrast to William's direct echo of his poetic father and his willingness to name his ambition, his project, his capability, and his ordination in "Home at Grasmere," D. Wordsworth returns to a communal voice with which to validate and support her rewriting of romantic motherhood *and* poethood.

Dorothy Wordsworth's transgression of binary laws and boundary lines creates a relational weaving that embraces and takes care of Nature as a central figure in her utopian community. But at the same time she valorizes her own standing, not as William's maiden but in the new history of mother–daughter relations. Jane and Dorothy, with their bond of mutual mothering, replay the mutual mothering of Mary and Dorothy for Dora, that daughter who was too much Dorothy's own second self. Jane and Julia carry on this heritage as loving mother and responsive daughter, while Dorothy and Julia continue it as poet and maiden. In the same way, Vološinov's discourse triangles of speaker-addressee-hero, poet-reader-text achieve a new mutation by making a different, nonheroic pastoral in D. Wordsworth's poetry. Whereas William kept strict distances between the three speaking positions, Dorothy takes the triangulating concepts and collapses them: The reader and addressee are the same (Julia, Dora, Edith, D.), and the speaker and poet are both Dorothy in a way that William's speakers are not himself because much more public. The triangles of discourse, then, no longer hover in separate but equal space above the artifact; in D. Wordsworth's poetry, the corners meld and open onto each other, entity entering into entity. With the collapse of disparate function, artifice as artful mastery goes. Dorothy Wordsworth's poems collapse into the personal as she evades sculpting the traditional generic form to fit her thought. She would rather converse and build a form with the aid of someone whose maidenhood can collapse into hers even as a distinctive identity is maintained.

➺ *Transference Love*

Dorothy Wordsworth's preoccupation with maternal love as a way of understanding her circle and her world is in fact an inversion of maiden love. And maiden love, at least as practiced by William Wordsworth, is an interpolation of romantic love: different from but still an integral part of the quest for fusion.

The romantic desire for fusion demonstrated repeatedly in W. Wordsworth's poetry is a symbolic translation of love in the Imaginary's perspectival world. Romantic love depends on the "I/other" dyad as a desire to rest in the other place (the maiden's heart as nest and memory chamber) and to see through the other's eyes. Freudian "transference love" replaces the binary dividing line that can either cleave the two terms to each other or thrust up through them, cutting them violently apart, by a conjoining term: "I with the other."[17] D. Wordsworth's definition of the maternal as "I and/or the other" in "Irregular Verses" lives beside her sibling love of the journals: "Wm and I walked"; "I petted him on the carpet"; "I read aloud the 11th Book of Paradise Lost. We were much impressed and also melted into tears"; "I continued to read to him"; "I slept in Wm's bed, and I slept badly, for my thoughts were full of William."

In romantic love one is in love with, meaning one idealizes rather than loves; what one is in love with resembles a heavenly something, unseen but remembered. "In love with" means that the other sustains memory consciousness, allowing the symbolization of memory in spots of time, in the idealized Lucy, in Emma's heart. It means the affections are ordered quite specifically, since it feeds on the symbolic, a hierarchic stabilizing modality. In transference love, idealization is replaced by self-organization through a permanent back and forth between symbolic (signs) and semiotic (drives). Discourse is necessary to both participants in this form of love; there can be no silent, absented partner because this is a dynamic love that puts off the death of stabilization. It is transference love that W. Wordsworth seeks in his addresses to women, but although he dialogizes the lyric moment, putting off death at least one step, he does not converse with the maiden and therefore does not invite the semiotic into his symbol-ridden field. D. Wordsworth discovers the secret in her sibling love for him; at his side she holds converse ("We had an affecting conversation") and agrees to see the world through his speech as well as through her own eyes: "The full moon (not quite full) was among a company of steady island clouds, and the sky bluer about it than the natural sky blue. William observed that the full moon above a dark fir grove is a fine image of the descent of a superior being. There was a shower" (13 June 1802). William insists on symbolizing and spiritualizing nature as well as love: not only the moon and Lucy but Mary in "She was a Phantom." However, Dorothy describes in a complexity of semiotic and symbolic discourse — such as the repetitious reworkings of moon, sky, and blue — her own remembering, while she renders William's discourse in the symbolic of his utterance and interjects it into her own.

Transference love allows sex to be sorted out from love, leaving the affections to reorganize the Imaginary. To comprehend an intersubjectivity (I with, rather than I/or) gives power to the affections, opening the self up to affect: "Just at the closing in of the Day I heard a cart pass the door, and at the same time the dismal sound of a crying Infant. I went to the window. . . . It was a wild and melancholy sight" (12 February 1802). Poetic melancholy in William's case is the deject's loss of affect that produces the hallucinatory landscape to which the deject has no ties and wanders in exile, disaffected. Dorothy's poetic melancholy is a superabundance of affect, on the other hand, an empathy that dissolves the distance she normatively erects between her station and the scape.

In "Irregular Verses," the speaker's anticipation of the auditor's response shapes the poem, as the speaker expends her energy defending the sadness of her elegy. The anticipation of and response to voices external to the poem as well (Jane's, for instance, and William's) also shape the speaker's thoughts: Her final vindication is the result of an argued defense of her use of the elegy, "The saddest heart feels deepest gladness." Just as W. Wordsworth's defensive posture in *The Prelude* stems from his appropriation of the social epic for the private autobiography, here D. Wordsworth defends her appropriation of the elegy as a tradition-bound vehicle for mourning the beloved or heroic dead to mourn instead her own poetic "death" at the hands of society. Richard Matlak discusses "Tintern Abbey" as a poem structured around its highly self-conscious anticipation of the yet-to-be-uttered response of Dorothy as auditor. His analysis suggests that the maiden in W. Wordsworth's addresses may be textually silenced precisely because her voice is feared for its irruptive possibilities. D. Wordsworth's address to Julia, in contrast, uses the auditor's response to reveal rather than hide its shadow text or covert message. So William's poetry emphasizes the "power" of the sister's mythic relation with Nature for political as well as textual reasons, and while the brother's address form attempts to hide the maiden's real, vocative power, the sister's addresses arrange themselves around an-other's textual inscribed utterance.[18] His assertive romanticism protects the poet from challenges to his vocative power, and Dorothy's rhetorical ploys protect her from the charge of competition even as they insure her romance with melancholy.

We should recall here Nye's interpellation of Kristevan theory, that women's poetry takes the form of either a "euphoric" or a "depressed romanticism," which reverses the masculine-identified narcissistic gratification of the literary tradition. D. Wordsworth's rewriting of William's address-to-women form does, as Nye suggests of women, listen carefully to the male writer's work, returning his artistic narcissism in an attitude of care that translates maiden into mother, speaker into caretaker. D. Wordsworth's subversion is not specifically that of irruptive language so much as that of the resistant woman who values her feminine function over masculinist endeavor. Not a "revolution in poetic language" but a structure of either melancholy or dissent, Dorothy's addresses to women critique the father's rule by embracing transference love.

This reading can work only if we accept the validity of transference love. Homans argues that Dorothy Wordsworth is not a romantic poet because she lets fancy usurp imagination's place, and even then, fancy is devalued in favor of realism (the undecorated truth of "Irregular Verses") and the

literal memory. In her reading of Dorothy's "Holiday at Gwerndovennant: Irregular Stanzas," Homans writes:

> It is the action of the irresponsible fancy, Dorothy says, that would lead her,
> at this point, to believe that she could "travel in one stream" with the
> unreflective play of these children, and their unimaginativeness is the pro-
> jection of her feeling cut off from childhood. . . . Dorothy's fancy tries to
> supply the place of genuine memories of childhood (by causing her to
> dream of playing like a child), but it fails to create a link between child and
> adult because it is not the imagination. [*Women Writers,* 66–67]

Homans's analysis of the impact of the distinction between fancy and
imagination on Dorothy is based on a Coleridgean distinction between
eighteenth-century fancy and the romantic Imagination. "Fully aware,"
Homans writes, "of the Coleridgean value-distinction between fancy and
imagination," Dorothy limits "her definition of the poetic impulse to adolescent fantasy about the future," thereby excluding "the possibility of
poetry's coming naturally at any other period." This poses "a false opposition between poetry and truth" as well as a value-laden opposition of
poetry to prose which is "explicitly free from art" (67–68). Yet how odd
to confine a reading of Dorothy's aesthetics to Coleridge's understanding
of the Imagination as a conceptual nexus for explaining the creative act,
when surely Dorothy would have been even more "fully aware" of William Wordsworth's rather different notion of the fancy and its relationship
to the imagination. To rely on Coleridge as definitive authority, and to
accept his version of Imagination as "that synthetic and magical power,"
causes Homans to write: "In Dorothy's writing there is often a spirit of
fusion, but it is not the same as Coleridge's Imagination" (70). Though
Homans uses this argument to explain Dorothy's minority as a poet, she
could as easily say the same of William's poetry. Further, it is important to
keep in mind the differences between the ideological notions we have
developed—due primarily to Coleridge—concerning romantic Imagination and the creative acts by which we recognize the artistic imagination
at work.

William Wordsworth, in his 1815 Preface, gives a listing of the attributes of the true Poet in which Imagination takes fourth place, in con-

trast to Coleridge's privileging of it above all else. Moreover, Imagination shares its berth with Fancy, and their attributed functions are shared as well: "4thly, Imagination and Fancy, — to modify, to create, and to associate." Whereas Coleridge assigns the powers of association strictly to the fancy, William sees it as being (as in eighteenth-century landscape poetry) an attribute of both. Thus Dorothy's use of "fancy" is not quite so self-derogatory as Homans takes it, and in fact, the first two aspects of the poetical character that William lists are qualities for which Dorothy was renowned in her circle: "The powers . . . of Observation and Description" and "2ndly, Sensibility."

It is the third attribute in William's list, "Reflection," which, Homans argues, causes Dorothy's lack of Imagination, so that her poems are filled with catalogs of memories unmediated by the synthesizing agent. In a fanciful passage, "the metaphors are whimsically selected and disjunctive with one another," reflecting a "fragmentation of identity, resulting from division and evasion of origins" rather than the synthesis of a unified identity unnecessary to Coleridge's "primary Imagination" (*Women Writers,* 71). Homans argues that the fragmenting, self-contradictory myth of origins she sees Dorothy constructing for herself causes this disjunction and "whimsical" selection. In fact, the function of the associative fancy — as well as the Wordsworthian Imagination — is to link memories (especially the spots of time) with whatever calls them up in the speaker's mind. Dorothy's poems are only as free-associative as her purpose allows, and the charge of "whimsicality" is unfounded within the terms of Wordsworthian aesthetics.

A more productive line of argument would be to follow Dorothy's use of the fancy as a response to William's understanding of its place in poetic creativity. Like Blake, W. Wordsworth also created songs of innocence and experience. His "Poems of the Fancy" contrast with the "Poems of the Imagination" in their avoidance of themes dealing with the oedipal rift with the mother, as well as their edenic pastoral settings. His "To the Small Celandine" could easily bear the same criticism Homans gives to Dorothy's poem:[19]

Pansies, lilies, kingcups, daisies,
Let them live upon their praises;

Long as there's a sun that sets,
Primroses will have their glory;
Long as there are violets,
They will have a place in story:
There's a flower that shall be mine,
'Tis the little Celandine.

The poems addressed in this section of William's "cathedral" structure of his collected works do not involve the mythic figures of his "Poems of the Imagination"; instead, they belong to that arcadian world he has banished in "Home at Grasmere."

The importance of the "Poems of the Fancy," in fact, originates in their integral bond with that first aspect of poeticalness, the powers of Observation and Description, and their place in the Beautiful. It is worth positing the following model: that the Beautiful is to the Sublime as the "Poems of the Fancy" are to the "Poems of the Imagination." The one complements the other as Dorothy complements William in his mythic system; thus she would have seen the Fancy as a realm particularly her own. In addition, she would have seen the descriptive, cataloging principles of the associative fancy as a methodology well suited to the expression of her experience in her late poetry. Certainly it is a method we have seen before in journal entries describing landscape vistas. It is intriguing to speculate on the possibilities for collaborative effort in the designing of William's system here, for in addition to Coleridge's conversations with William on the poetic imagination, D. Wordsworth, too, conversed and wrote. And what she wrote specializes not only in catalogs but in that methodology which by 1815 William announces as characterizing the fancy:

> To aggregate and to associate, to evoke and to combine, belong as well to the Imagination as to the Fancy . . . [but] Fancy does not require that the materials which she makes use of should be susceptible of change in their constitution, from her touch; and, where they admit of modification, it is enough for her purpose if it be slight, limited, and evanescent.

Given this content, Homans's argument rings false that in Dorothy's "eccentric poems" literal memory replaces the imaginative act (joy is "merely the experience of a powerful literal memory") whereas for William the imaginative act replaces literal memory (his "memory, where it is most helpful to him, is of his impressions of a place rather than of the place itself" [*Women Writers*, 76]).

It is not the failure of poetic technique, then, but the belief that she is adhering to the principles of Wordsworthian poetics that motivates the structure of Dorothy's poems. And, insofar as she embraces the requisites of the Fancy, she employs those poetic faculties that help her use those principles. William's claim in *The Prelude* is that Dorothy taught him how to truly see nature. Coleridge, too, notes Dorothy's powers of observation:

> Wordsworth and his exquisite sister are with me. She is a woman indeed! in mind I mean, and heart. . . . Her eye watchful in minutest observation of nature; and her taste . . . bends, protrudes, and draws in, at subtlest beauties, and most recondite faults. [quoted in de Selincourt, *Dorothy Wordsworth* 75]

William's version in the rock/breast passage of *The Prelude* claims the importance of Dorothy's eye for the reclamation of his spirit and as a corrective to his tendency to overbalance the importance of sublimity to the detriment of beauty. The literalness of her memory celebrates the act of witnessing nature even from the temporal and spatial distance of an old woman's sickroom, as in her poem "Thoughts on my sick-bed." These memories, in fact, display the power of the imagination in its ability to transform, or transport, not nature but the speaker herself. The critical difference between Dorothy's and William's poetry is not a failure of the imaginative will, as Homans claims, but the failure on Dorothy's part to investigate the male arena of sublime Imagination.

By placing herself in the role of poet while grappling with the issues inextricably bound to the form of the address-to-women, Dorothy Wordsworth works through a revision of the brotherhood and her role in it. That her refinement of her brother's subgenre deals with subtleties of connective tissue rather than of outward form can be read as a feminine tendency that devalues the poet's contribution. But it is precisely this interlacing which holds the key to a female poetics that displaces male romantic notions in D. Wordsworth's work.

Dorothy Wordsworth's displacement of herself from maiden to the role of Poet is not a move easily made; nor do her combined projects of collaboration and taking care allow her to radically dissociate herself from the relational position of women addressed. William's triadic model, in fact, presents Dorothy with severe difficulties as it traces and embodies the male poetic fantasy of simultaneously maintaining individuation and the desire for fusion through the mediating activity of the maiden. D. Wordsworth's version of the triadic model is one that pulls all three positions of speaker-poet, addressee-maiden, and object of the mediation–Nature into the interwoven community of her poetic vision. Nature is no longer solely the object of the gaze; the maiden is no longer the complementarity; the speaker is no longer isolated from the object. Instead, Dorothy transforms both subject and object positions so that neither is alienated from the other, just as she transforms speaker and addressee roles so that neither is subsumed under the other's power. In addition, she forms strands of identity from each of the three positions of poet, maiden, and Nature so as to locate herself via these connective interlacings. Thus she can position herself both in the poet's role and in the maiden's role; and by taking care, or mothering the object as an alternative subjectivity, she is both subject in relation to the mother / Nature and the mother of that mother.

The fluidity that transforms strict roles into an integral community tends to filter out individual voices, and Dorothy's lyrics become at times a kind of communal or choral voicing of the lyric moment, very much in keeping with the consistent communal tonality of the journals. However, Dorothy Wordsworth's struggle with male romantic ideology as well as the problematic of the speaking "I" create conditions in which she at times feels intense isolation from community. It is at these times of a painful experiencing of the subject–object schism that she reaches out through the address form toward the healing nurturance of community and utopian vision.

More than William, Dorothy is obsessed by the address form: Eighteen of the thirty poems Susan Levin has unearthed are addresses. Addresses exist even in the prose: D. Wordsworth's Green Narrative is addressed to Joanna Hutchinson. Like William's oeuvre, a significant proportion of Dorothy's addresses are addresses to women, and several more are addresses to children, a variant form of the subgenre. Dorothy chooses to try her hand first at the time-honored and feminine genre of lullaby and children's story: "To my Niece Dorothy, a sleepless Baby"; "An address to a Child in a high wind"; "The Mother's Return"; "Loving & Liking, Irregular Verses Addressed to a Child —." Her choice is the safety of the domestic sphere. Child rearing is women's work, poems written for children are the natural result of her duties as aunt in William's house, and it is a category of poem William only seldom explores. Her first poems' positive reception is assured: Written to beloved children, they will please the doting parents (William and Mary); written in a traditionally female, trivialized genre, they are not serious bids for attention, pose no real threat, and are included in William's 1815 collected works.[20]

In Dorothy Wordsworth's addresses, particularly a poem such as "Irregular Verses," Dorothy as female poet is not responding simply to what Kristeva characterizes as the artist-as-child (male) model. In the woman artist's dual role as creator and procreator she must adopt both a subordinate and an identificatory relation with the mother object, that which Kristeva argues the artist leans toward and positions himself in relation to. The male artist's desire for annihilating fusion with the Mother / Beloved is replaced in D. Wordsworth's poetry by affective transference that creates the cathectic nexus of chora, choral support, and the unlawful fissure and seaming of boundaries. Dorothy's addresses to young women attempt to imitate her brother's model by using these "Maids" as sister figures, with the result that these figures replace her in William's model as maidens while she replaces William as Poet. The dynamics change radically when the search for the mother becomes a search for the self.

The addresses to children, on the other hand, are spoken in the role of mother and are poems of nurturing or teaching. They are the true love poems even though it is Dorothy's addresses to women that formally enter the love lyric tradition. But it is her love that makes her a mother, which allows her to speak for the mother. To reverse the mother's position from object to subject allows the woman artist to supplement her own authority with that of the mother. Because motherhood socially positions the woman on the threshold where marginality and centrality meet, the speaker as mother can inhabit that complicated space. Poetic language emerges from the chora in the attack of the semiotic on the symbolic monopoly, and again the mother (as possessor of the chora) is the meeting ground, the threshold space. The marginality of the semiotic reaches out against the centrality of the symbolic; their meeting produces the mixture of rebellion, transcendence, and religion that is poetic language, and where it occurs are sites of the located voice.

Though they initiate D. Wordsworth's poetic voice, and establish certain bounds for the addresses she is yet to write, the poems addressing children serve only as a prelude to the introspective addresses to women. These mature poems written in response to the brotherly poems addressing her utilize a set of characteristic moves differing in function and format from those of William's. The moves are: remembering walking in the hills; being able to return to the nests in nature only in or through memory; contrasting the speaker to the maiden addressed; meditating on the self as other.

This formulation of the essential units of Dorothy's addresses to women uses a different apportioning of roles from W. Wordsworth's triadic model. Dorothy Wordsworth's addresses to women are introspective and focus on the self, but this forces a realignment of the model: The object as hero is no longer Nature but a former self, while the auditor as maiden is both a possible role model for the speaker to identify with and a contrast to both her former and her present selves. Thus the model is no longer poet-speaker to object-hero, connected by maiden-auditor, but poet to former self to maiden as second self. This more complex model is actually that of "Tintern Abbey," so that Dorothy is responding to the poem that most deeply implicates her in William's poetic vision of the world.

Like "Irregular Verses," "To D." is an address-to-women in which D. Wordsworth finds connection with the maiden: "A thousand delicate fibers link / My heart in love to thee dear Maid" (1–2). The maiden is free to walk the hills while the confined speaker remembers her own former ability to do so; and while the speaker identifies with the maiden on one level, on the other she distinguishes herself from "D" in more than just age:

Though thine be youth's rejoicing prime
My lively vigour long decayed.
Thou are a native of these hills
. . . *I* hither came in age mature
With thoughtful choice and placid Will.

"Lines to Dora H." also recalls "Irregular Verses," where it is the maiden's request for a poem that initiates and justifies its creation. Again, the maiden is both self (former self) and other, while being both linked to the hero-Nature and separate from her. Again the poem is a vehicle for speaking to the community from which she has been shut off. The other-self as maiden is recalled by the speaker through memory, and it is her voice that revitalizes the feebleness of the ill and aged speaker: "Mine eyes behold the leafy trees, / The skies, the clouds, the gleaming showers, / Crags, lakes and odoriferous flowers," interrupts the plaintive tone of the speaker's elegy with a note of youthful joy at the act of witnessing. This irruption into the misery of illness ("Now age my eyesight oft bedims; / My failing strength, my tottering limbs") has a rhythm and sonorousness missing from the aged speaker's utterance, so that the former self becomes the locus for the entrance of Kristevan poetic language into the text. Again, nature contains the nest that draws the maiden ("And fond affections nestle here"), yet it is also true that the maiden–former self is the space in which the nest is located, for the "here" is ambiguous and refers to nature, memory, and the maiden each. The connection of nature, nest, and maiden to each other reveals a dependence on William's mythic system not found in the *Grasmere Journals*. There Dorothy separates the domestic nest from the nest in nature, seeing the latter as a space foreign to her being and perhaps even dangerous. Here, in contrast, she has linked literal memory with the mother's womblike nest as the choral space in which the maiden as daughter experiences cathexis. Out of this threshold space the joyous poetic language of the semiotic merging with the symbolic irrupts into the painful space of loneliness and isolation from community of the present moment. Homans's argument that Dorothy Wordsworth's poems suffer from a lack of imaginative drive and so celebrate the literal memory over the synthetic (*Women Writers*, 69) fails to explain the contiguous relationship of maid to speaker, as well as the literary references to Dora's album in "Lines intended for my Niece's Album": The album is "in green array," an emblem for the book of Nature, for "'Tis Nature's Choice, her favored hue, / The badge she carries on her front."

The serious project of Dorothy's irregular verses and fragments is to show William just how good a Wordsworthian poet she can be. What her poems more generally inscribe is the complicated response Dorothy has to her brother's address form. Her status as the woman addressed prevents her from attempting the form until she can physically no longer be that maiden, yet clearly she mourns the demise of the mythic vision of her. The discrepancy between being subject-speaker in her own poems while responding to his model of her as object-auditor causes her to embody all the roles of the model at some point in the lyric moment. "Irregular Verses," which provides the fullest articulation of Dorothy's dilemma, shows the speaking "I" inhabiting the role of speaker-poet, hero-object, and auditor-maiden, all within the framework of the poem. The unsettled subjectivity of the "I" equivocates poetic selfhood, creating the opposite effect of William's strong assertions of self. The forceful flow and ebb of the defensive gestures the speaker makes in the poem — toward societal strictures, toward the limitations of William's myth, and toward her own compliance in these restrictions — create the framework of a poem equally structured by the associative meditation characteristic of romantic poetry.

Reading D. and W. Wordsworth's poems intertextually articulates the textual dialogue itself. The different levels of discourse that develop in the texts involve both different voices of the self and others and the different voices the self is anticipating and answering. The awareness of audience is complicated by the writer/reader/audience/reciter interchange (Dorothy copies, reads, recites, and listens to William's poetry), but there is also the awareness of self as audience and a response to the person speaking. When a poem exhibits this second type of audience awareness, then intertextuality as Kristeva more narrowly defines it (that is, as a layering of sign systems within a single text) becomes a more felicitous dialogic method of reading, since it focuses specifically on the text's appropriation of, or response to, a prior text.

The two poems in the Wordsworths' dual canon that offer fertile ground for such a method of reading are W. Wordsworth's daffodil poem, "I wandered lonely as a cloud," and D. Wordsworth's "Thoughts on my sick-bed." The texts these poems respond to are Dorothy's daffodil passage from the *Grasmere Journals* and William's "Tintern Abbey." What is particularly interesting about comparing these two poems is that "I wandered" is an appropriation of a previous text whereas "Thoughts on my sick-bed" is a nonappropriative response to an earlier poem. The comparison, then, allows one to account for the effect of gender on models of intertextual reading and to reread Kristevan intertextuality in order to do so.

William Wordsworth's myth of the poet as deject occurs in the very first line of the daffodil poem: "I wandered lonely as a cloud." His self-reference as Poet in the third stanza confirms his authority in the poem while the nonpoetic self which did in fact also experience the scene, Dorothy, is obliterated from the lyric moment. The message could not be clearer: The poetic experience cannot be shared, even by a twinned sensibility; it is, rather, an experience of the individuated self which can then be related to an(other) or, alternatively, experienced side by side with a passive, silent other.

The passage W. Wordsworth used from the *Grasmere Journals* specifically mentions that the experience was, in fact, collaborative: "We set off after dinner from Eusemere. . . . When we were in the woods beyond Gowbarrow Park we saw a few daffodils close to the water-side" (15 April 1802). Though Dorothy's passage indicates that part of the imaginative transformation of the daffodil scene was a joint venture ("We fancied that the lake had floated the seeds ashore, and that the little colony has so sprung up"), her description breaks down into a nonindividuated account of the Fancy:

> They grew among the mossy stones about and about them; some rested their heads upon these stones as on a pillow for weariness; and the rest tossed and reeled and danced, and seemed as if they verily laughed with the wind, that blew upon them over the lake; they looked so gay, ever glancing, ever changing. This wind blew directly over the lake to them. There was here and there a little knot, and a few stragglers a few yards higher up; but there were so few as not to disturb the simplicity, unity, and life of that one busy highway.

William's poem, in its appropriation of this passage, so transforms it that the appearance of its language as discourse in his poem is divested of its speaking voice. The sign system of Dorothy's passage appears only in reference to William's speaking "I" and is no longer the product of Dorothy's speaking self. Her account emphasizes the communal activity of the flowers as they dance and reel, "ever changing." The flowers are nurtured by other natural objects ("some rested their heads upon these stones as on a pillow for weariness") in a world that reflects her own affinity for taking care. William's account of the incident focuses instead on the echoing action of the lake's waves and the flowers' movement in the wind, so that the rhythm they produce is what stimulates his poetic energies in the choral space of poetic language and is also what he later remembers:

> The waves beside them danced; but they
> Out-did the sparkling waves in glee . . .
>
> And then my heart with pleasure fills,
> And dances with the daffodils.

William's static view conflicts with Dorothy's ever-changing landscape, and his depiction of the scene is one of repetitive movement caught in stasis and encapsulated in his memory. His territorializing gesture of encapsulation is apparent in his description of the move as one of acquisition: "but little thought / What wealth the show to me had brought."

Although Dorothy's sign system can be located in William's poem, a fact substantiated by editors' and readers' recognition of the one text in the other, it has been substantially revised, and her voice does not resonate in his poem. When William does work from Dorothy's journals, it is important for him to distance himself, separating himself from her words as from an actual experience. The voice of another can have a power over William's imagination which silences his own voice, and Dorothy records an instance of her own words as embodying just this kind of power:

> After tea I read to William that account of the little boy belonged to the tall woman, and an unlucky thing it was, for he could not escape from those very words, and so he could not write the poem. He left it unfinished and went to bed. In our walk from Rydale he had got warmed with the subject and had half cast the poem. [13 March 1802]

No wonder that the sister figure as muse in William's addresses to women is silent or, as in "Home at Grasmere," birdlike and wordless in her vocalizations. William's appropriation of Dorothy's voice in the daffodil passage thus transforms her sign system from a feminine way of perceiving the world, and the resulting feminine metaphors of community and nurturing, to masculine imagings of the self.

In reading "Thoughts on my sick-bed," the intertextual dialogue is more complicated than in the daffodil texts. In contrast to the appropriating gestures of William's "I wandered," "Thoughts" offers a responsive reaction to the poem it is in dialogue with. While the tactics apparent in "I wandered" could be traced to the effects of socialization on the male, "Thoughts" can be read as an expression of Dorothy's very different need for community, because of an ego characterized by more fluid boundaries. Her socialization has taught her to seek interdependent relationships as well as to be attentive to the nurturance needs of others. As a result, she has not forgotten the demand to be taken care of by being remembered, expressed in the final lines of "Tintern Abbey": "with what healing thoughts / Of tender joy wilt thou remember me."

Dorothy remembers particularly the darkness of William's prediction and attempts, in her debilitating illness, to answer the poem written in the vitality of his youth. Though "Tintern Abbey" reveals Dorothy's presence only at its conclusion, we can see the effects of that presence throughout the poem as William's utterances are directed toward her, the attentive auditor of his meditation. Dorothy's poem, however, is never a fully acknowledged address to William, revealing the disturbing self-doubt inherent in a project that reciprocates one of William's most masterful poems. Dorothy is unable or unwilling to reverse the male-subject–female-object paradigm which William uses in his address to her as maiden in "Tintern Abbey" and expresses her aversion to the problem by never fully addressing him. Yet "Thoughts on my sick-bed" is the poem most fully directed to William in her oeuvre, just as "Tintern Abbey" is the poem that explicitly delineates and establishes the mythic relationship between them in his.

In her poem, Dorothy Wordsworth stresses the act of remembering as an object of meditation. On her sickbed, memory is the transforming act: "I thought of Nature's loveliest scenes; / And with Memory I was there." Memory is so powerful an agent that it precludes the necessity "of motion, or of strength, / Or even the breathing air." Remembered scenes in nature are described for themselves as whole entities rather than for their effect on the speaker. The speaker's witnessing of natural objects is a caretaking activity as she "welcome[s]" them, "[w]ith busy eyes . . . pierc[ing] the lane / In quest of [them]," and "To all we gave our sympathy." In fact, it is the act of remembering that affects the speaker's consciousness rather than the natural objects, reversing William's use of memory to recall the objects that affect his sense of self in the world. It is memory which, for Dorothy's speaker, makes her feel "a Power unfelt before," resonant of the more mystical "power" or "presence" in "Tintern Abbey" which "impels / All thinking things, all objects of all thought, / And rolls through all things"; here it is a lesser power which is seen only in its individual application as a transporting agent that returns her to the scenes of her youth. The importance of remembering for the speaker is in its ability to waken the inner life "Couchant within this feeble frame," a "hidden life" enriched by unsought-for gifts. It is this hidden quality "in the mind of man" that saves William's speaker when he is " 'mid the din / Of towns and cities," just as it rescues Dorothy's speaker in her sickroom.

D. Wordsworth's speaker at first remembers the self alone in nature but quickly turns to a communal being in nature with the mention of "Our cottage-hearth." The association of domestic nest with collective activity leads her to reverse William's positioning of the younger remembered, solitary self against the present-tense couple: His sister remembers the earlier communal activity against the present-tense pain of solitude. This is especially apparent in her echoing of a lengthy passage early in "Tintern Abbey" where the speaker is "in lonely rooms": "No prisoner in this lonely room, / I *saw* the green Banks of the Wye." William had written

> These beauteous forms,
> Through a long absence, have not been to me
> As is a landscape to a blind man's eye:
> But oft, in lonely rooms, and 'mid the din
> Of towns and cities, I have owned to them,
> In hours of weariness, sensations sweet,
> Felt in the blood, and felt among the heart;
> And passing even into my purer mind,
> With tranquil restoration: — feelings too
> Of unremembered pleasure.

Dorothy's stressing of her active seeing in the memory picks up the stress William's lines place on the importance of how we see the beauteous forms, not as a blind man but as an active observer. Her emphasis of William's point also recalls her own act of witnessing nature in her journals. Her incorporation of his sign system emphasizes the change in their relative positions as well: He is in the lonely room as a young man at the start of his poem; she is in a lonely room as an old woman at the end of hers. Her reversal underscores his placing her in nature as a maiden:

> Therefore let the Mood
> Shine on thee in thy solitary walk. . . .
>   and, in after years . . . when thy mind
> Shall be a mansion for all lovely forms

In her demonstration of the powers of memory to revive her, Dorothy concentrates on both this last passage of William's poem and the "lonely rooms" passage cited above. The temporal setting of William's lonely rooms is between his two visits to the Wye; Dorothy's response to this passage is to stress the clarity of her vision in remembering the present-tense setting of that utterance: as she sees "the green Banks of the Rye." The "feelings / Of unremembered pleasure" echo in her "kindred gifts, / That, undesired, unsought-for, came." William's speaker realizes that the good man's "little, nameless, unremembered, acts / Of kindness and of love" add to "tranquil restoration," while Dorothy focuses not on her own acts of charity but on the nurturance of friends' charitable acts toward her:

> No — then I never felt a bliss
> That might with *that* compare . . .
> When loving Friends an offering brought
> The first flowers of the year
> Culled from the precincts of our home,
> From nooks to Memory dear.

And again, her interest is not in what effect the charitable act had on the well-being of the doer; the friends may well be troubled by their actions instead: "With some sad thoughts the work was done." The weight of

William's passage, however, is chiefly on the metaphysical aspect of "that blessed mood" which he owes to the beauteous forms.

D. Wordsworth, significantly, does not respond to her brother's metaphysics; nor does she, throughout her poem, attempt the sublimity of Nature which is William's sacred ground. Just as her emphasis is on the act of memory and the hidden life it brings forth rather than on the divinity that dwells in all things, so too is her focus on the domesticated nature of the nearby hills: "The primrose a lamp in its fortress rock, / The silent butterfly spreading its wings," the violet, the daffodil, and the thrush. William's visions, by contrast, are of "The sounding cataract / [which] haunted me like a passion: the tall rock, / The mountain, and the deep and gloomy wood." He gains vitality from the "aching joys . . . And all its dizzy raptures," while Dorothy gains a quieter "bliss" from flowers "Culled" from the dear nooks.

W. Wordsworth's address to his sister in the final lines of his poem is three-pronged: his prophecy, the demand to be taken care of, and his exhortations or teachings. Dorothy answers each of these points. She answers the uncanny accuracy with which he predicts her debilitating illness by "Recalling thy prophetic words" and by assuring him that the memories he desired her to treasure do indeed help her escape the pain of lonely rooms. She answers the demand to be remembered throughout the poem; the poem itself is an act of caretaking. Significantly, in the lengthy "living soul" passage, what Dorothy responds to rather than the metaphysical discussion is the troubling doubt William expresses immediately afterward: "If this be but a vain belief." Her project in "Thoughts on my sick-bed" is to assure him that it was never in vain. Finally, the poem is an attempt to prove to William that she has learned his lesson and, in particular, remembered his exhortations. He foresees her memory will "be as a dwelling-place," and she answers, "I thought of Nature's loveliest scenes; / And with Memory I was there."

This chapter explored Dorothy Wordsworth's participation in the mythopoetics of the pastoral valley and her determination of, complicity with, and resistance to her role in the Wordsworthian landscape. Chapter 4 addresses the boundaries of the valley and the difficult terrain surrounding it by focusing on the problematic gendering of the romantic sublime, its geophysical character, and its deep-seated politicopoetic aesthetic.

FOUR

Mountains and Abysses

*But at the same time that immersion gives
him the full power of possessing, if not being,
the bad object that inhabits the maternal body.
Abjection then takes the place of the other, to
the extent of affording him jouissance. . . .
Rarely does a woman tie her desire and her
sexual life to that abjection, which coming to
her from the other, anchors her interiorly in
the Other. When that happens, one notes that
it is through the expedient of writing that she
gets there [to the frontier].*

KRISTEVA, Powers of Horror

*. . . talked much about the mountains, etc,
etc.*

Grasmere Journals

To discuss the topology of Wordsworthian Life solely in terms of
remembered exhortations and memorable pastoral scenes is to
visit the valley without considering its topography. The Lake
District is renowned for both its heights and its abysses, which
still astound with their beauty and still prove fatal to unwary
hikers. In *Pride and Prejudice,* Austen pokes fun at the extraordinary appeal of the Lakes by having Elizabeth exclaim,

> What are men to rocks and mountains? Oh! what hours of trans-
> port we shall spend! And when we *do* return, it shall not be like
> other travellers, without being able to give one accurate idea of
> any thing. We *will* know where we have gone — we *will* recollect
> what we have seen. Lakes, mountains, and rivers, shall not be
> jumbled together in our imaginations [unlike] the generality of
> travellers. [138]

Lizzie's anticipation of a Lakes tour propels her into one kind in a typology of traveler, that of the properly educated tourist. Having done her aesthetic reading — whether Johnson's and Boswell's travel journals, Gilpin's 1786 *Observations on . . . the Mountains and Lakes of Cumberland, and Westmoreland,* or just popular novels like *Ethelinde*[1] — Lizzie is quite ready to have "effusions," but for reasons other than aesthetic. " 'My dear, dear aunt,' she rapturously cried, 'what delight! what felicity! You give me fresh life and vigour. Adieu to disappointment and spleen. What are men to rocks and mountains?" (138). Lizzie wishes to lose herself in visual transport, forgetting herself in the landscape. William Wordsworth, too, seeks this renewal in forgetfulness. But it is Dorothy Wordsworth who, having nothing to forget and even less to evade by transports, loses herself in accurate observation and its remembrance. It is she, more than William, who could echo seriously, "We *will* know where we have gone — we *will* recollect what we have seen."

Oddly, though William is less precise in his observation and even dependent on his sister's keen eye and detail-laden journals, it is he who could answer Lizzie Bennet's impetuous "What are men to rocks and mountains?" Men are poets who write to other men of rocks and mountains, of the sublime. Indeed, William Wordsworth's poetry is by critical consensus one of epical sublimity. Yet it is imperative to recall that during his lifetime he was best known for his volumes of pastoral lyric poetry. And although Dorothy Wordsworth also visited Mont Blanc and also suffered anguish, she is remembered as neither epical nor lyrical but only as pastoralized, a valley maiden whom Elizabeth Bennet might have noted but not spoken to. This chapter will examine the allegorical nature of aesthetic topography and its implications for the differential Wordsworthianism we have been deciphering out of the layers of performative collaboration.

More specifically, the "picturesque" will pose as the Dorothian halfway space between the "sublime" of mountains and epics and the "beautiful" of pastoral lyrics and pastoral valleys. In this sense the picturesque can no longer be considered a discarded aesthetic of Enlightenment self-consciousness or, subsequently, of eighteenth-century sensibility. It must be allowed to ameliorate the aw-ful masculinism of the romantic sublime, the terrible threshold space of its liminality, and the devastating effects it can have for the feminine psyche and the subjective desire for poetic language. I am speaking of a world in which the sublime can be simplistically defined as a masculine privilege that is figured by the female but closed off from her experience. But it is more subtly configured and thus ultimately more dangerous than the reductive model implies, and, in part, this complication is due to the darker romanticization of eighteenth-century theories of taste. To this end, I will differentiate between types and kinds of sublime effect: The principle divisions will be between sentimental melancholy, which is in itself pleasing, romantic "Joy" or liminality, and romantic "Dejection," which is an alienating, masculine melancholy. "Dejection" is a key term, divisible into gendered affects which can be both instrumental and detrimental. To put it another way, besides the alienated melancholic, the Wordsworthian landscape also holds both the male "deject" and the female "abject" as wanderers. The deject is particularly susceptible to visions received by encountering the "feminine sublime," or the sublimation of female figures in the scape. The female subject herself, however, can experience not Joy but only a "natural" fusion with the mother; she is likewise denied masculine melancholy and instead is relegated to the despair of abjection and its accompanying state of objection. In Wordsworthian aesthetics, then, the sublime presents exclusionary and oppositional experiences. The main impulse of this chapter is to trace out the implications and exigencies of William Wordsworth's topographical Imaginary while retaining the overview that it is comprehensively performative. Similarly, this chapter will also explore the ways in which Dorothy Wordsworth is able to acknowledge this aspect of Wordsworthian Life in light of her own experience and to use performance in amending its harsh particulars.

☙ *Sublime Disruption and the Picturesque Defense*

What the picturesque tourist seeks in the pastoral is its ability to close itself off not only from the dirt and grind of everyday life but from the sublime mystery waiting at the threshold. The "hours of transport" Elizabeth Bennet seeks are not a reference to the sublime of Wordsworthian ground, where trauma and fear prevail; indeed, the valley garden locks its gates against the tourist's "disappointment and spleen" as well as the poet's sublime fear. While Lizzie thinks to indulge herself in aesthetic raptures, W. Wordsworth also maps and orders thought so that the unseating sublime cannot enter the pastoral landscape without transgressing borders. Despite his best lyrical efforts, as in the "Poems of the Fancy," for each pastoral delight ("Prophet of delight and mirth, / Ill-requitted upon earth," from "To the Small Celandine") there is always a corresponding "Danish Boy," serene and gentle but also dead. Indeed, the liminal can present itself around each corner ("And in this dell you see / A thing no storm can e'er destroy / The shadow of a Danish Boy"). The harder W. Wordsworth works to fence off the anagogic and aesthetic sublime, with its intrusive presence and its utterly controlling chaos, the more his fences — like Michael's — fall into disrepair, for the sublime is transgressive.

Romantic poets are known for their repeated attempts to seek out sublime experience, but William faces the sublime with reluctance, fully aware of the pain and guilt it will dredge up. Dorothy knows the sublime on a different and more domestic level. And, because of the negative character of both their encounters, neither Wordsworth concedes the sublime a central position in their Life; rather, it is a centralizing preoccupation.

The sublime is gridded apart from the pastoral on William's map as a way to fence it off from daily business, but it overlies the pastoral much as a transparency overlies a graph, and so it achieves a hovering presence. The sublime is thus daily available, for the threshold can discomfortingly be found in the valley itself, in the grove and in hidden places. If the grove locates a protective space in which W. Wordsworth's speaker discovers proper safety in the pastoral grid, then it also houses a liminal space where communion with Nature's essence can occur. Thus, because William understands his charted world as feminine-centered, his pastoral lyrics and narratives perform as centering pieces in his garden plot. At the same time, centerpieces distract attention toward everyday beauty, allowing a necessary gap for the sublime to strike. In that gap, or doorway from here to not-here, the valley dweller exceeds his attention, exceeds his pastoral mandate. He thus becomes a tourist in his own land. But the maiden does not. For though the Wordsworthian valley grounds the female figure, it does not station her but rather places her. She is thus mobile, which is to say, she is not threshold; she (as maiden, as virginal) is differentiated from the maternal and from Mother Nature. And so she is also differentiated from the sublime and cannot achieve it. For the maternal threshold is the portal to the sublime; like a map overlay, the threshold allows an everyday scene to contain a suddenly accessed portal to another map dimension. The maternal is this overlay, and when it appears nature transforms into Mother Nature. It is the precision of epical and lyric delineation, as an almost grammatical parsing of the edges of mental and aesthetic states, that enables Wordsworth to encounter felicitous nature, or the threshold of sublime Nature. The choice is an important one, for true transport robs the subject of his own vital speech through the fusing process, a process the Poet desires and yet fears will incur his self's loss of idiosyncracy and determination in the terrifying power of the subliming Other.

This equation of loss and gain is not all there is to fear from the transgression of boundaries for either Wordsworth. The other side of Joy's transport is the abyss, or what could more accurately be called the "feminized sublime": not liminality but sublimation. Here, too, language ceases to be an effective tool for comprehension in the murkiness of awe and fear or horror, guilt, and self-hate. It is in this sense that the Wordsworthian pastoral can stage sublime departure and entanglement with the Imagination as either an extrasubjective or an abjective experience. In the Wordsworthian valley, the feminized sublime is the grounding of female figures in the maternal landscape, the living death of figures like the Solitary Reaper and other agrarian workers. When sublimation is superimposed on normally subjective women who are then absented—like Joanna Hutchinson in "To Joanna" or Mary Wordsworth in "She was a Phantom of delight"—the feminized sublime has been invoked. The female vagrant figure, such as Margaret, calls forth the other term, abjection.

Abjection is the hallmark of masculine fear of the maternal. It must be stressed here that abjection is a figurative affect of the male Imaginary and implicates not the subjective woman but the objectified female who replaces her in that Imaginary; it is the experience the man expects the woman to be feeling through his own projected distance. It cannot surprise us in the figure of the female vagrant who resonates to that other distressed, deserted, and silenced mother, Annette Vallon. In abjection, the deject self is alienated from its own body, and it projects back on the body disgust and self-hate. This is the fullest extreme of melancholy, where the self has agreed to another's projection of disgust on it and has thereby agreed to feel empty and alienated. Melancholy in its Words-worthian sense is an aestheticized version of this self-disgust, an enact-ment of Werther's sorrows rather than the full fleshing out of disgust, which is abjection. The sublime is thus both the liminality of Joy and melancholy and the anguish of Dejection and abject sublimation.

To aid him in his charting, William draws on the landscape as allegorical convention, purposefully confusing the picturesque with the transgressive qualities of the sublime. The picturesque canvas attempts to bring the scape to a stillpoint, to ease and focus the eye — but also to train the viewer to see himself in the same scape as the last viewer saw himself. This creates an allegorical experience that places the viewer back in the originary Eden and displaces distracting figures who might challenge the view with alter-native stories.[2] Landscape painting, having rejected narrative in favor of the picturesque aesthetic, becomes a form of social control: seeing care-fully composed and possessed by the guide.[3]

William Wordsworth both engages picturesque viewing and, especially in his *Guide to the Lakes,* rails against its desensitizing influence. Yet Doro-thy was quite content with this mode, at least on her own terms and as her own romantic guide. What particularly suited her pastoral role as Virginie is another version of that very literary mode of seeing; this is again a mode of sensibility, but one more open to threshold spaces than the merely picturesque and substantively different from the agony of abjection. This is the melancholy of sensibility, a mode into which Dorothy Wordsworth records frequent lapses when contemplating a scene, and derives from the sympathetic response to external beauty rather than from an internal critique.

William also engages in melancholy but of a different timbre. He learned a more studied and literary melancholy from his Hawkshead mas-ter and poetic supporter, William Taylor. But in passing through the cruci-ble of the French Revolution and his desertion of Annette and Caroline, melancholy became translated into the very detrimental psychodynamic of dejection. Dorothy, on the other hand, preserves her sustaining emo-tional engagement with the scape, with melancholy, and with tears within an equipoise of inner and outer. Her solitary wandering is an exercise in exuberance or endurance, an outdoing of feminine boundaries and laws; William's melancholy, by contrast, is an alienation of self and vision, a disruption of the equilibrium sentimental melancholy should have brought. The differential delineation here between melancholy and dejection is one of thresholds and thus intensities. In this sense an embodied landscape, one that can reach up and embrace the viewer, is a substantially different terrain than the objectivized picturesque scape. Thus William's version of the Wordsworthian terrain is poetry-producing on two levels: when his walks through it harvest its habitation because he sees but does not feel its melancholy; and when his chance encounters with the land's body, its rhythms and ghostly effects, open up a threshold to the sublime.[4] Dorothy's version of the same valley is not productive in either of these senses because she does not view the landscape as embodied but rather sees it as itself a work of poetry which she can, depending on that moment's level of sympathy, read and transcribe. Alternatively, when she is plunged into the abyss of abjection, the scape seems to mirror her despair, but she does not know why it should or the source of its apparent sympathy for her.

These are differential versions of what we reductively call Joy and Dejection, and which we normatively understand as binaries on an emotive scale. Yet melancholy as romantic Dejection is as entwined with its inverse, Joy, as it is with aesthetic pleasure. These states spell two scales rather than one, and their difference is not merely one of degree: Where Joy spells communion, esctasis, and fusion, Dejection is a dis-spelling, a disenchantment, an alienation. And perhaps more importantly, whereas sentimental melancholy depends on visual cues for its apperception of itself, Dejection has a disordered visuality with nonfunctioning or undecipherable cues. And whereas William believes Mother Nature plunges him through the threshold into Dejection, Dorothy's access to abjection is firmly grounded in William's aesthetic map.

There is one additional point to be made. Because viewing is so necessary to William's mapping strategy, the sublime's focus on affect rather than sight offers yet another reason to avoid its embrace. Yet he cannot be an epic poet without vision, and vision — unlike sightedness — is given by sublime interference. He is thus necessarily forced to seek what he would not experience. To this end, his solitary figures are not traditional pastoral inhabitants, for pastures are peopled with shepherd poets engaging in singing contests or lovers sporting in the glen. Nor are they georgic farmer poets or picturesque tourists such as the stranger who so disturbs the Priest of Ennerdale in "The Brothers" ("These Tourists, Heaven preserve us!"). Rather, like the Solitary of *The Excursion,* Wordsworth's solitary is the deject.

We are finally at a point to understand the dangers inherent in the sublime and its liminality between the inspired poetic breath and a failed poetics of insane babble. Worse than the possibility of falling into babble is that of falling into a silence caused by the loss of the self in the fusion with the sublime entity. And alongside this fear is the antipastoral figure, the alienated figure who is condemned to live asocially in order that he might stumble on the access to the sublime and then achieve transport rather than failure. The poet in this dejected state, the deject, is recognizably the knight-errant questing for something he will recognize only when he chances upon it. His fate is therefore tied to a force at once intangible and distancing, and his quest takes him away from the very qualities celebrated in both William's "Home at Grasmere" and Dorothy's *Grasmere Journals.* This is the dark side of the pastoral scape, the heights that capture and entomb the likes of Lucy Gray or the Danish Boy.

The deject lives in a dreamscape of disembodied voices, a world of thetic threshold where the word is still waiting to become meaningfully said. It is an affective state that draws the self outside its own bounds and at the same time empties the self out. The self transcends itself in the sublime, whereas in dejection it is self-alienated and thus can only indulge in a state of self-disgust. Disgust is distaste, a repulsion that alienates the ethos of the Man of Taste, alienates him both from the society he would evaluate and from himself or his body. If W. Wordsworth never goes as far as Coleridge and De Quincey in an embrace of dejection, it is because Wordsworth is drawn against his will into the sublime without being compelled by the addictive despair of the opium users. But more significantly, it is because self-alienation is not the kind of distance and placement William seeks. Although he early acts out the role of Werther as self-afflicted deject, he specifically fences himself off from dejection and from the deject as well through his representative speaker, his "I." This I acts out a distance from the embodied pain he observes, doing so by taking on the role of the melancholy wanderer.

The literary heritage of pastoral melancholy, dejection as a literary trope, can be traced to Virgil's first *Eclogue,* which begins in a state of alienation that continues throughout the *Eclogues*. A tale of exile, despair, disenfranchisement, and death, Virgil's work reveals the unremitting intrusion of the present on utopian dreams. This darkness, which transforms an environment that might otherwise be pastoral into one that cannot be pastoral, is the very grid of dejection, the dreamscape of the thetic function. Within the rules of this scape the self becomes a kind of object, one that is disaffected. In "Home at Grasmere," W. Wordsworth's most extended pastoral, despair is acknowledged but kept at bay by the sister's presence: "But either She . . . was there, / Or not far off." The sister provides stability by metonymically reconstituting the landscape as the object-thing through her own "naturalized" relation to it. Yet the potential for abjection and objectification of the self underlies valley life, which is proclaimed better than that "among the bowers / Of blissful Eden."

In this valley there is both solitude and fellowship, melancholy and bliss, affection and disaffection, and a geography that reaches up to embrace and enclose the poet. Stuart Curran delineates the pastoral tradition as one of doubled vision, a tradition of affection (lovemaking) and disaffection (or at least the foreshadowing of death) that begins with the singing contest of Theocritus (88). "Home" begins before Grasmere is a home, with the speaker recalling a youthful visit when he "sighing said,"

> "What happy fortune were it here to live!
> And if I thought of dying, if a thought
> Of mortal separation could come in
> With paradise before me, here to die."
>   ["Home at Grasmere"]

The valley is "a haunt / Of my affections," the landscape combining both disaffection and affection; it is where the poet conjures up "The vision of humanity, and of God / The Mourner, God the Sufferer," and where "We will be free, and, as we mean to live / In culture of divinity and truth, / Will chuse the noblest Temple that we know." Curran stresses that the Wordsworthian pastoral is less an actual place than a frame of mind, for however much the place itself encloses one it is unclosed by time and mutability: Cottages decay, children die or leave. Indeed, W. Wordsworth's use of temporal frames in his pastoral narratives creates a self-reflexivity that is never far from the doubled time of dejection, that of repressed memory and that of the dreamscape.

Grasmere as pastoral combines the doubled vision and doubled time with a doubled scape, both home and not home. While "this Vale so beautiful / Begins to love us!" as "the bounds of this huge Concave" will "Embrace me," there are also tales of hardship and of feeling estranged. The speaker, then, is also doubled — not in the sense of the sibling couple but in the sense of being a child of nature in one temporality and the object of despair in another. Yet the deject inhabits a land of exile. He is the stray who wanders while he queries the identity of the scape rather than his own. He separates himself from sameness and community and, as Kristeva notes, "therefore *strays* instead of getting his bearings" (*Powers of Horror*, 8). In the dreamscape of dejection — the underside of the blissful edenic scape of the idyll — the deject's unconscious is exteriorized onto the landscape. "A deviser of territories, languages, works, the *deject* never stops demarcating his universe. . . . A tireless builder, the deject is . . . straying on excluded ground" (8). Kristeva's description recalls the tireless walking of both Wordsworths, but even more compelling is the tireless building she associates with world building, colonizing the unknown, construction that is a domesticating of the terrifyingly unbound, unmarked, unsignified. Uncomprehended voices abound in W. Wordsworth's poetry, producing scenes that the poet must draw a line around in order to make them wholes or envisioned spots. These are unstable scapes that move to embrace or to reject. D. Wordsworth's *Grasmere Journals* record their solitary and mutual activities of domestication, planning sites for seats, bowers, alternate homes, cottages.[5]

W. Wordsworth's most alienating dreamscapes are his "spots of time" and the unrepresentational or sublime scapes. But in his pastoral poems the deject can also be present, both as wanderer and as the encountered stray (the rustic, the dislocated soldier or beggar, the vagrant). However, this doubled identity often confounds poetic identity, leading to meditations on the nature of the poetic vocation ("The Leech-gatherer"), or cuts the poet-speaker off from the othered deject whose discourse he now cannot truly or functionally comprehend ("Simon Lee"). To counter the fear of confoundment or lost voice, Wordsworth often projects straying onto the encountered other, thus saving the poet from the pain of disaffection. His voice can then elegize the unfelt but affective other.

Like projected straying, Dorothy's presence also works to prevent William from falling into the horrifying mirror scape of abjection, which would be a falling out of himself. Her presence helps him contain himself just as he also contains her; and the doubled presence of their two selves puts him at ease with death in a more easeful way than the distancing of the graveyard posture. On an April morning in 1802 the Wordsworths walked to John's Grove and lay down on the ground. In an odd foreshadowing of their brother's drowning, William imagines what it would be like to lie in the grave:

> William lay, and I lay in the trench under the fence—he with his eyes shut and listening to the waterfalls and the Birds. . . . William heard me breathing and rustling now and then but we both lay still, and unseen by one another. He thought that it would be as sweet thus to lie so in the grave. [*Grasmere Journals*, 29 April 1802]

The depiction of Dorothy as heard but not seen and heard as part of the natural voice ("There was no one waterfall above another—it was a sound of waters in the air—the voice of the air. William heard me breathing") is a device found repeatedly in William's poetry, though most notably in "Home at Grasmere." William imagines death as living, a quiet resting in the grave with the auditory still operable. Nature's and Dorothy's combined "voice" enables him to find sweetness and peace, "to hear the *peaceful* sounds of the earth," and her emphasis on peace points to its importance to William. What is striking about this entry is that the perceptions are a combination of William's perceiving and of Dorothy's imagining of what William is perceiving, but it is not a record of her own experience in the "grave." It is William's fantasy supported by Dorothy's sympathetic imagination; then the entry returns to recording Dorothy's observations, which include no rumination on death or mourning.

Graveyard poetry heightens the relationship between elegy and the picturesque, without opening the door on the horror of the abject.[6] It recalls prior lives against the currency of the meditator's life similar to the way picturesque tourism derives from the ongoing delineation of a cultural heritage during the eighteenth century: "The longing to discover a Golden Age harmony surviving in remote corners of Britain encouraged the tourists to overlook the realities of pastoral life."[7] Both the horrors of the grave and the dirt of the pasture — and thus the abject — are passed over. Wordsworth would at least aestheticize and displace them. Indeed, while the georgic becomes increasingly unappealing at the end of the eighteenth century with the drive toward retirement and contemplative leisure, William's and Dorothy's participation in the reality of life in Arcadia impels an embrace of the unfashionable georgic values clearly acknowledged in their lived lives but documented only in D. Wordsworth's journals.[8]

The outmoded ideology of the georgic has a clear draw for the Wordsworths' complicated relation to the establishment. Though William's "Letter to Bishop Llandaff" advocates revolutionary acts, he also became successful at sustaining the ancient system of patronage that allowed him to continue his pastoral/georgic lifestyle (unlike his hardworking brothers).[9] Similarly, his poetic relation to rustic figures reveals an attachment to the georgic notion that the gentry labor by directing and watching the workers' labor,[10] while the subsistence economy William and Dorothy practiced partakes of rustic life in its most idealized, Robinson Crusoe form (gaining their food from gardening and fishing but producing no goods to sell except poetry). William's equation of watching with labor in his speakers' postures claims a passive, contemplative existence more in keeping with idyllic pastoral ease than with the reality of the early Grasmere years; his poetry effectively conflates the discord between conflicting ideologies into a bohemian lifestyle that allows him to align neither with the rustic nor with the gentry, yet to belong to the hills as do the rustics and to watch as does the gentry.

The gentle job of watching takes another form when the gentry who watch are tourists seeking out picturesque landscapes. Dorothy and William's attitude toward the picturesque tourist is ambivalent; they themselves toured several times, and in Dorothy's account of William's first trip to the continent written to her friend Jane Pollard, she accentuates the fact that William's encounters with "the sublime scenes of Switzerland" are as a tourist (*EY,* 6 June 1791). Yet when tourists come to Grasmere, there is a tint of pride in Dorothy's journal entry:

> In the morning W. cut down the winter cherry tree. I sowed French Beans
> and weeded. A coronetted Landau went by when we were sitting upon the
> sodded wall. The ladies (evidently Tourists) turned an eye of interest upon
> our little garden and cottage. [9 June 1800]

The entry records that the touristing ladies are given a view of pastoral
ease and of the results of labor already accomplished. What they do not see
is the cottage industry that normally presides, whether it is the improvements Dorothy has been carrying out during William's recent absence or
the reading and writing that consume both brother and sister.

Against the tourists' improper eye, Dorothy poses. But when walking
out she is fully aware of what constitutes proper seeing. And such seeing is
not merely attentive but artistic. Picturesque views may be conceived of as
gazing at a landscape with the intention of framing the scene, that is,
looking with a painterly eye so as to compose the elements of the landscape according to specific aesthetic principles. Consider the following
entry from the *Grasmere Journals*:

> We sent to Frank's field, crawled up the little gien and planned a seat then
> went to Mr Olliff's Hollins and sate there—found a beautiful shell-like
> purple fungus. . . . All the young oak tree leaves are dry as powder. . . .
> After we came in we sate in deep silence at the window—I on a chair and
> William with his hand on my shoulder. We were deep in Silence and Love, a
> blessed hour. [2 June 1802]

This entry evinces two kinds of viewing or, rather, two versions of the
same kind. The first takes place in the landscape but incorporates a con-
structionist viewing that has designs upon the scape ("We . . . planned a
seat"); it also observes acutely while situated within the scape, an active
participation (the fungus, the oak leaves). The second version is no longer
active, and in taking the passive form it frames the landscape (here with
the window frame, although the Wordsworths most often perform this
passive viewing from high vantage points among the surrounding hills).
Framed vistas, with their necessary stationary pose, lend themselves to
meditative gazing, a favorite pastime of the Wordsworths during the
warm months.

What is unusual about this entry is both its juxtaposition of the two forms of viewing and the framed frame: Dorothy does not describe what she and William are gazing at but, rather, depicts herself and William gazing. Clearly, the act of gazing is itself important, for it symbolizes communion both with nature and with each other. Only two months earlier Dorothy writes that she and Coleridge sit and gaze together but William seats himself apart from them to "[feast] with silence"; although the separation does not last long, William has needed isolation for his contemplative gaze. Here he has gazed with her, and the result has been not only the same feasting in deep silence, a consumption of the scape that nourishes, but a communing and benevolent Love as well. This is quite a different notion from the contemplative meander of the Coleridgean conversation poem even as William Wordsworth practiced it. The movement of the gaze from object to object according to, and interwoven with, the "natural" movement of thought produces a landscape through which the gazer/speaker moves. In contrast, framing requires stationary presence, a station or point from which to view the landscape. Dorothy Wordsworth's late poems, and many entries in her journals, employ the station, although this is the only element of Gilpinesque viewing she retains (discarding the use of a foregrounding bough, the necessity for overlapping hills in the background and for rustic figures midground).

W. Wordsworth's narrative double framing, which materially adopts the double plotting of his own mapping, takes a different and less pictorial form than Dorothy's framed framing. In his narrative poetry the doubled frame is a structural device designed to separate out tale-tellers and time sequences (as in "The Ruined Cottage," "Peter Bell," "Simon Lee," etc.); in his epic poetry, however, framing takes another turn. In "Home at Grasmere," which is both the fleshing out of the 1799 "Two-Part Prelude" and the idyllic embryo of the 1805 *Prelude,* there is a framing that warrants attention for its picturesque quality. William Green's watercolor *Overbeck Bridge on Wastwater . . . Cumberland* gives a view of the Lake District that depicts the Wordsworthian speaker's wish, "Embrace me, then, ye Hills, and close me in."[11] Two sloping hills overlap exactly at the center of the painting, while a majestic mountain rises from that crux, and the foreground of the painting pulls the viewer into it in a rhythm of winding paths, stone formations, and water, right into the heart of the hills. The view is reminiscent of the main view from the head of Grasmere Lake as well, and thus this is the stance of the "Home at Grasmere" speaker, a stationing and grounding position. But it is a stillpoint that remains congenial only to Dorothy, whose descriptions, even when she moves through the scape, compose the scene from one positioning stance.

William, on the other hand, develops a roving eye, one that has its literary precedent. Even as the picturesque tourist is indebted to Milton's "L'Allegro" and "Il Penseroso," so, too, is W. Wordsworth recalling Milton with his eye's activity. And whereas Dorothy's affinity is for the quickly moving, keenly sighted eye, William's is the surveying eye of the landscape gardener. The Wordsworthian speaker faces and surveys without confronting and interrogating; even so, the activity of moving through the scape in order to see and judge paradoxically works to achieve stasis. That is, it forestalls the act of becoming because of its highly critical (and therefore symbolic), rather than sympathetic (or sensible), character. To speak for the human condition necessitates dehumanizing oneself, at least one's current self or role, in order to oversee. William's speakers oversee in both senses of the word: They survey, scanning the scape without noticing fine detail; and they see over the literal to the mythic or allegorical, missing what is there for what *should* be there. D. Wordsworth scrutinizes the landscape for that fine detail which is definably present, or takes nature's pulse and temperature for more general reportage: "A sweet mild rainy morning," "still very fine weather," "A very fine morning," "The view exquisitely beautiful." By contrast, William animates the landscape so that it embraces and speaks to him, singles him out, or en-visions him. William's overseeing is not gazing on the landscape in order to see but rather seeing to order.

The larger effect of surveying is that of placing his poems in order (most explicitly with the *Recluse* project), getting his house in order, and ordering his history so as to replace biological family members with mythic ones (mother Nature, brother Coleridge, sisters Sara and Joanna). In addition, nature is also aesthetically ordered: pastoral valleys, sublime mountains, ugly cities. Surveying itself is a necessary skill in landscape architecture; it is the surveying of land, a method of measuring off, counting, and equating which cannot be separated from the survey itself as an enactment of the specular.

Yet the exchange of seeing for surveying requires a spectacular change. In a letter written to Dorothy during his first trip to France and Switzerland with Robert Jones, William writes that he has thought about Dorothy "perpetually" during his trip, so much so that "never have my eyes burst upon a scene of particular loveliness but I have almost instantly wished that you could for a moment be transported to the place where I stood to enjoy it" (6 September 1790). Standing in the same spot, twinning the vision, means that at this point William was interested in the notion of stationing, of attaining a particularized viewpoint. Dorothy has to stand *in his place* in order to share the same view, not *by his side* as she is later depicted in "Tintern Abbey." This twinned gaze denotes a dynamism missing from the survey; it is a gaze employed both in the "Naming of Places" poem written for Mary Hutchinson, an address to Mary spoken by a "we" that shares the same gaze, and in "Home of Grasmere" where Dorothy is represented as so closely at the speaker's shoulder that she is invisible. The twinned gaze inverts Dorothy's framed scene of gazing where she is in front of William and he is at *her* shoulder.

To situate Dorothy representationally if not really at his shoulder, or so close beside him that she is not seen, is to place her beyond surveillance. It is also to contain, or retain, her energy. This containment is analogous to the manner in which both Wordsworths relate to nature: a consumption that is the "feasting with silence," a nourishing rather than blocking absence of words. Dorothy's attitude toward the boundary between nature and domicile, silence and language, indicates that nature is not the holistic power William understands but a community of bodies that are possessable piecemeal. Bringing home wildflowers to plant in the garden can mean bringing flowers from the hills or dug out of someone's yard and brought home to plant ("I went into [Jenny Dockeray's] garden and got white and yellow lillies, perwinkle, etc., which I planted" [28 May 1800]). Nature bountifully gives, but the taking requires labor; so, too, residing in the pastoral home is (naturally) labor-intensive. If Dorothy brings home the flowers as an act of living in nature, William brings Dorothy to make his home in his act of living in the pastoral scape. To do so is a matter of getting his house in order.

Kurt Heinzelman argues that William and Dorothy each forged their own heuristic models of domestic lifestyle in their Grasmere cottage. Certainly William looks for a stasis with which to center him in the pastoral scape, both when he feasts on a scene and when he stations Dorothy behind or beside him. This stationing is in opposition to Dorothy's framed/framing station that places her marginally to the scape. William's stasis is conceptually different from Dorothy's stationing principally because hers allows for attentive gazing whereas his isolates a particular scene in order to turn it to account. The gesture of isolation creates a symbolic scene that is within the pastoral universe but sublime in character. Always for W. Wordsworth there is a process of stasis in change and change in statis: Waterfalls that are frozen in their descent, for instance, delineate the terrible inner essence of the pastoral.[12] William looks for the same stasis in terms of the relational affections. He orders the affections in his cathedral of poetry, ordering them hierarchically according to merit (their relation to nature and to poetry making). He also orders the women in his life (including Nature), placing them in their proper sphere so as to get his house in order. The economics of affectional domesticity aligns disaffection with the solitary poet figure, and domestic affection with the pastoral sibling life exemplified in the Paul and Virginie story. When Dorothy's motherly discourse intrudes on the more usual sibling discourse—"I repeated verses to William while he was in bed—he was soothed and I left him"; "William's head bad after Mr S. was gone. I petted him on the carpet"; "After dinner we made a pillow of my shoulder, I read to him and my Beloved slept"—the journal shifts remarkably from the collaborative tone of "I made pies, tarts, ets. Wm stuck peas" or "We sate reading the poems and I read a little German." The first replicates a maternal nurture that reverses the passiveness of the "Oh my Beloved" phraseology particularly in use in the entries prior to William and Mary's marriage; the second reveals cottage industry and the business of pastoral provision.

∽ *Sublime Acts*

Against such pastoralization, both the sublime and the abject are specifically barred from the cottage or from the sensibility of valley life. They must be fenced out since both dehumanize in egregious ways. After all, the sublime as the romantics received and reworked it was the aestheti-

cization of violence. It gave form and force to the very violence the picturesque embalmed. Philippe Lacoue-Labarthe perceives the sublime as the
essence of classicism which renders the contradictory response of pleasure
in displeasure as a political structure that the romantics continue:

> "Terror" and "pity" are essentially political notions. They are absolutely not
> psychological. Pity refers to what the modern age, under the name of com-
> passion, thinks of as the origin of the social bond (in Rousseau and Burke,
> for example): terror refers to the risk of dissolution of the social bond, and
> the pre-eminent place of that first social bond which is the relation with the
> other. ["Response," 17]

What has divided classical art, which itself represents the sublime for the
romantics, is the aestheticization of the sublime through Burke. Once the
production of the sublime as art became an aesthetic terrain instead of a
rule-bound one, Jean François Lyotard argues, the classical approach was
over.[13] In aestheticization, death enters the field in a more prominent role
than it had held before: The emphasis on terror "presupposes the necessity
of rebuilding the idea of the mind, and of rethinking the importance of
death in life" (Lyotard, 22).

Once aestheticized, the sublime becomes synonymous with the picturesque in the sense of becoming an art form and a stabilized mode of
viewing. The difficult process of hailing and achieving the sublime, however momentary, becomes trivialized for consumerist thrill as yet another
"Catastrophic" landscape by John Matin. The desire to control individual,
unregulated response to the sublime scene as artwork means that transport is reduced to the space of hallucinatory gratification or terror, and the
viewer is turned into Wordsworth's Solitary. Consumerism, the demand
for desirables, implements a process that ironically turns the viewer away
from the space of haunting possibility. But to take the sublime landscape
for the sublime itself is to turn away in the wrong sense; apostrophe, the
marker of sublime presence, is a turning away so that the poet can retain
his integrity, can survive the experience intact. Consuming viewers are
turned away from the very possibility, protected in a manner parodying
Wordsworth's self-protective measures because their turn away insures
they will come back for more. Equally a factor in the new taste for sublime

scenes is the function of sympathy, which is provoked by the experience of and for the solitary questor. The turn away is made even more attractive by the pull toward another human being, and because sympathy is familiar as a key trope in the ethos of sensibility, it feels comfortable and even pleasurable. Adam Smith's *Theory of Moral Sentiments* (1759) posits sympathy as specular: That sentiment which allows us imaginatively to reconstruct the suffering of another operates theatrically. The specular self acts out a morality that was to become socially institutionalized in the aesthetic theatrics of sensibility. If Wordsworth is unable or unwilling to take part in the consumption of landscaped emotions (his early dramas failed and *The Excursion* was misunderstood), he was certainly attuned to the concept of a specular self, as Dorothy was to the concept of sympathy.

Sympathy as a mannered, socially instilled attitude does not figure strongly in the Wordsworthian universe of guilt and sorrow. It does, however, operate within two of the emotive possibilities in the Wordsworthian schema: love (affect) and melancholy (lack of affect). Love comprises, first, sublimity or fusion; second, aesthetic appreciation (the Beautiful); and third, domestic affection. On the other hand, melancholy comprises romantic dejection (an aesthetic sensibility) first, depression (disaffection) second, and abjection (self-hatred or the ugly) third. In the Wordsworthian schema, both number ones are masculine, solitary domains, whereas both domestic affection and abjection become associated with the feminine. Beauty and depression are middle ground between the primary terrain which is William's and the tertiary ground which is Dorothy's; it is on this middle affectional ground that the siblings meet.

Affection is the categorical term missing from any discussion of the romantic quest, and its importance in the Wordsworthian canon is at odds with the professed epic quest of *The Prelude* and the announced *Recluse.* However, there is more than one way to both pursue and evade the sublime, and Wordsworth draws an ambiguous line between his epic and lyric projects: the pastoral vale, cyclical domesticity, and the cathedral structure of his collected works interfusing the one; his great, fragmentary history of solitude, *The Recluse,* exploring the other. Crossing this line is the balancing act between sublime truth and lyrical aesthetics at work in poems that respond to the Coleridgean conversation poem. The prophetic strain of "Tintern Abbey," for example, strives to return to the conversation poem's sublime heritage by compelling an analogy between the mind of man and the "mind" of Nature. It is a feat new only in its positing of Nature's spirit as a "mind" rather than the mirror.[14] Yet the speaker's plea to Nature in "Tintern Abbey" stressing his subjection reinforces the importance not of the human mind's structure but of Nature's matrix, and not of the discourse of introspection but of intercourse with Nature herself. This aligns "Tintern Abbey" with Wordsworth's lyric and not his epic project, though the poem's hybrid genre locates it certainly between the two. If we understand it as lyric in this sense, we can see more clearly why the poem turns to address the woman; her presence facilitates discourse with Nature. Despite the sublime quest initially characterizing the poem's meditation,[15] the resolution addressed to the maiden gives the lyric the last word. Similarly, despite the lyricization of *The Prelude,* its final ascent up the mountain of transcendence claims the supremacy of the sublime, epic voice.

As the final book of *The Prelude* reveals, the sublime poet takes on a public dimension that externalizes his earlier lyric introspections and allows him to speak for and to humankind in his elect or pastor guise.[16] Even as *The Prelude* begins by prophesying to Nature ("To the open fields I told / A prophesy") in a recursive gesture away from a chronological account of the poet's life toward an imaginative reconstruction of the life, so we have the poet's posture immediately as one which "tells *to*" Nature after he has already been taught *by* her.[17] The developmental zigzag from Book I to Book XIII unfolds a story of learning from Nature in order to transcend her, as the poet carries his spots of time with him into the sublime realm. There he may sever his bond with Nature and establish a firmer and more important bond with God. From the Mother's tutelage to the Father's Word, *The Prelude*'s poet makes the oedipal journey of his age: Love of nature teaches him love of mankind, but the search for the Father teaches him that indeed the son transcends the Mother (and sister). Not only can the mind of man find its parallel structure in the mind of Nature, but

> The mind of man becomes
> A thousand times more beautiful than the earth
> On which he dwells . . .
> Of substance and of fabric more divine.

But being more beautiful *and* more divine — stealing all of earth's thunder — has its penalty. For Wordsworth, transcendence as an act of literally standing on Nature as the Mother, in order to achieve alignment with the Father, destabilizes and decontextualizes the Poet, as on Mount Snowdon. The apocalyptic disturbs ordinary sense experience in the Snowdon passage, so that torrents are frozen in time and space, and natural phenomena move upward when they should "naturally" move down. It is the mist, however, which initially alerts us to the son's separation from his mother and his subsequent transport:

> I looked about, and lo . . . on the shore
> I found myself of a huge sea of mist,
> Which meek and silent rested at my feet.
>   . . . a fracture in the vapour,
> A deep and gloomy breathing-place, through which
> Mounted the roar of waters, torrents, streams
> Innumerable, roaring with one voice . . .
> Grand in itself alone, but in that breach
>   . . . had Nature lodged
> The soul, the imagination of the whole.

The mist, passive, silent, and meek, tropes Nature as the nurturing Mother. No longer a source of fear and of the natural sublime, she continues her nurturance of her chosen son by laying at his feet the emblem of her breath / inspiration, thus dissociating those feet from her ground. The mist that separates them, however, still represents her as the essential female to which, silent, he gives voice. "Roaring with one voice," her maternal waters irrupt from her depths through the fracture by which her erstwhile terrifying and engulfing aspect may be known. But, unified, the voice of the multiplicitous waters loses its terror in the interpretive, poetic act, and the constraint the son imposes on her female energies reduces her visionary landscape to "universal spectacle . . . shaped for admiration and delight," the picturesque.

Nature's mind resides in that fracture, the split that identifies the lyric, voiced consciousness, and is represented as that particularly female entity, "[t]he soul, the imagination of the whole." It is the Father whose presence is then realized as "a mighty mind." Concurrently, the poet's silencing of Nature's voice results in his own meditation, which "rose in me that night" of

> The perfect image of a mighty mind,
> Of one that feeds upon infinity,
> That is exalted by an under-presence,
> The sense of God, or whatsoe'er is dim
> Or vast in its own being—above all
> One function of such mind had Nature there
> Exhibited by putting forth, and that
> With circumstance most awful and sublime.

The move from Mother to Father, from the soul of the whole to the mighty mind it supports, involves a move from the realm of the Beautiful, the "spectacle" to be gazed upon, to the realm of the Sublime, "The sense of God, or whatsoe'er is dim / Or vast in its own being." The claim for the poet's superior status is now transferred from being one of Nature's chosen sons and from seeing the human mind mirrored in nature to that of laying claim to a poetic mind,

> By sensible impressions not enthralled,
> But quickened, rouzed, and made thereby more fit
> To hold communion with the invisible world.
> For they are powers. . . .

No longer enthralled or in servitude: such language recalls Nature as the troubadour mistress who insists on the servility of her poet-knight, humbling him with her pride. Overthrown by the epic mode, Nature is displaced, and the poet is no longer threatened with humiliation by the mistress. The poet's communion with the Father allows for severance from the Mother, for the poet no longer has any need for her inspiration, the breath that she lays at his feet; he now has his own power, independent and superior to hers. Rivalry rather than complementation means, at least for the nineteenth century, brothers and not sisters, and the address of epical transcendence is to the brother-poet Coleridge. After a string of odic apostrophes to "O man" and a farewell address to Dorothy, the narrator turns to the brother: "With such a theme / Coleridge — with this my argument — of thee / Shall I be silent?" With the self-empowering address to Coleridge, we understand Nature's as a "secondary grace" compared to "the main essential power — Imagination — up her way sublime."

If William's grasp for the sublime involves the lyric grounding of all his poetry, Dorothy Wordsworth's refusal of the transcendent sublime may expose her resistance to the entirety of her brother's romantic enterprise. His praise of her in *The Prelude* is for her educating him to nonsublime sensibilities, needed both because he had become unbalanced in his quest for the sublime and because he attempted the sublime too soon without first attaining maternal ground to stand on. D. Wordsworth's poetry veers away from such encounters, and even appearances of maternal Nature are in terms of domestic and interpersonal relationships. The poems that come closest to grandeur — "Grasmere — A Fragment," "Lines Addressed to Joanna H.," "A Holiday at Gwerndovennant: Irregular Stanzas," "Irregular Verses" — bind themselves firmly to pastoral themes, scapes, and meters. These poems are more in direct response to Willam's two pastoral epics, "Home at Grasmere," and *The Excursion,* than they are to his grounded lyrics. And *The Excursion* gives Dorothy's taste of poethood a double-edged pain, embodying the epic hopes of the future *Recluse* even as it distressingly redresses the valley as melancholy to the viewer because it is hopeless to the inhabitants. At the same time, *The Excursion* symbolizes the nadir of William's poetic career, and happily he could not see Byron's comment to Thomas Moore, "The people are tolerably tired with me, and not very much enamoured Wordsworth, who has just spawned a quarto of metaphysical blank verse," meaning *The Excursion* (12 August 1814).[18] However William suffered from similar public and private responses to his difficult poem, Dorothy was fully privy to his pain, able both to try it on and to rise to her brother's defense.

Indeed, the Wordsworths' 1814–15 responses to the critical reception of the newly published, epical *Excursion* differ interestingly, particularly as enumerated in their combined letters to Dorothy's close friend Catherine Clarkson. Dorothy's 11 November 1814 letter to Mrs. Clarkson devotes most of its space to giving accounts of family members and her anxieties over the poem's sales. Of the poem's content she writes,

I saw two sections of Hazlitt's Review at Rydale, and did not think them nearly so well written as I should have expected from him — though he praised *more* than I should have expected. His opinion that all the Characters are but one character, I cannot but think utterly false — there seems to me to be an astonishing difference considering that the primary elements are the same — fine Talents and strong imagination.[19]

Although here Dorothy's analytic powers show themselves in full strength, her stress is on the poem's nonsublime aspect. Dorothy's written avoidance of philosophical and sublime themes generally causes her to restrict her discourse to discussions of technicalities, so that she can emphasize readers other than the Byronic: "[Hazlitt] says that the narratives [of Books VI and VII] are a Clog upon the poem. I was not sorry to hear that for I am sure with common Readers those parts of the poem will be by far the most interesting."

Her interest in the common reader contrasts with William's 1798 notion of the common man's language: Dorothy's association here is with reading (as woman and as Maiden) and not speaking (as man and as poet). Though this letter anguishes over the poem's poor sales, she does not continue to stress the common interest and later writes to Mrs. Clarkson that it is the rich and not the common reader they need to attract. "I could be half angry with you for leaving the Excursion with William Smith. Who *is* to buy two guinea Books if not people with such fortunes as his?" (*MY,* 184). Even so, here she defends William's poem in terms of its common appeal, and the villagers' life stories to which she refers are those of everyday rural sorrow which bear the stamp of pastoral life. These tales recount precisely the loss and painful change against which the Maiden protects the Poet in the address-to-women, yet Dorothy sees them as literal testimony to the domestic rather than sublimed histories charged with a "higher" aesthetic.

The next letter to Mrs. Clarkson is written jointly by William and Dorothy; William writes first, and in his sublime mode as prophet-poet:

I am encouraged by finding so much of your letter devoted to the Excursion. I am glad that it has interested you; I expected no less, and I wish from my Soul that it had been a thousand times more deserving of your regard. In respect to its final destiny I have neither care nor anxiety being assured that if it be of God — it must stand; and that if the spirit of truth, "The Vision and the Faculty divine" be not in it, and so do not pervade it, it must perish. So let the wisest and best of the present generation and of Posterity decide the question. [*MY,* 181]

W. Wordsworth is also concerned with the common reader, commenting that "I have a wish for the *sale* of the present Edition, partly to repay the Expense of our Scotch Tour, and still more to place the book within reach of those who can neither purchase nor procure it in its present and expensive shape." But his concern has not the strength of Dorothy's, and his reports of critical reactions far overshadow it.

A third letter to Catherine Clarkson on *The Excursion* written a month later is from William but transcribed by Dorothy and Mary. Again, William's emphasis is on the sublime aspect of the poem, particularly as it is rhetorically manifested.[20] His discussion makes it clear that "teaching mankind" extends to instilling a correct understanding of the versification of prophecy, a theme that leads to an exhortatory meditation of the sublime power of the poet.[21] Shortly before concluding, William notes that "There is one sentence in the Ex[cursio]n ending in 'sublime att[ractions] of the grave' which, — if the poem had contained nothing else that [I valued,] would have made it almost a matter of religion with me to [keep out] of the way of the best stuff which so mean a mind as Mr. [Jeffrey's] could produce in connection with it" (*MY,* 190–91).[22] W. Wordsworth's vehement defense of this one particular line against his critic emphasizes not only the sublime's importance for him but the grave as the site of transcendence rather than a literal sublimation, as well as his continued indebtedness to graveyard poetry.

Much of Wordsworth's poetry emphasizes the connection between lyric, sublime, and death, a connection often associated with either feminized nature or the female figure, as in the Lucy poems. William's vehement response to the woman who dares criticize *The Excursion*'s sublime suggests he is threatened not only by the feminized sublime but also by those women who refuse to be placed within his aesthetic map, women who object. There is a revealing addendum to the letter:

your Friends remarks were so monstrous. To talk of the offense of writing the Ex[cursio]n and the difficulty of forgiving the Author is carrying audacity and presumption to a height of which I did not think any *Woman* was capable. [*MY,* 191]

Clearly, William's message to Mrs. Clarkson, as well as to Dorothy and Mary who transcribed it, is that the sublime is a masculine preserve, ill understood by the female mind. And clearly the women of William's acquaintance skirted audacity and monstrosity as aspects of abjection the best they could or William would not have been so sheltered. Sagacity and monstrosity sit side by side for a woman reader, and Dorothy's earlier critiques of William's poetic style have succumbed over the years to steadfast uncritical support. Ironically, it is these two debasing conditions of monstrosity and of being audacious or out of place that characterize the debilitating physical and mental illness of Dorothy's later years.

⮎   *Gender Politics, Gender Aesthetics*

The question of placement is thus a textual as well as a bodily one. And, as much as Dorothy more or less assents to her place, it increasingly requires an act of the imagination to keep her place at William's side and yet strictly within the bounds of fancy. Yet for both Wordsworths aesthetics necessitates the imaginative act; and both are imperative to the poetic condition because their results are true as physical fact. William Wordsworth's critical and interpretive grappling with the question of romantic aesthetics, a fragmentary essay that we know as "The Sublime and the Beautiful," appropriately follows his *Guide Through the District of the Lakes* in Owen and Smyser's edition of his *Prose Works.* (Although the title of this work varies in its different editions, it is most familiarly known as *Guide to the Lakes.*) While the *Guide* provides a walking tour through the pastoral sublimity of Grasmere (as opposed to the popularized picturesque view of the district that Wordsworth sets out to repudiate),[23] the fragment essay attempts a different purview in answer to Burke's *Philosophical Enquiry into the Origin of Our Ideas of the Sublime and Beautiful.* Significantly, Burke's definition of the sublime was widely accepted, but his definition of the beautiful was not.

For Wordsworth, the principal difference between the beautiful and the transcendent sublime is one of proximity and familiarity. The liminal is a presence that can never be familiarized: "Nay, it is certain that his conceptions of the sublime, far from being dulled or narrowed by commonness or frequency, will be rendered more lively & comprehensive by more accurate observation and by encreasing knowledge" (Owen and Smyser, 2:349). Familiarity itself breeds not contempt but appreciation, particularly for the beautiful. Beauty, in fact, is more necessary to mental health, for the mind is "dependent for its daily well-being upon the love & gentleness which accompany the one, than upon the exaltation or awe which are created by the other" (349). The feminization of the beautiful, not surprisingly, has distinctly maternal overtones; for W. Wordsworth, the object of Nature is to nurture her perceiving children (those who seek the picturesque are mere "tutored spectators") and to encourage true perception through daily contact.

Though the beautiful is feminine, it is the transcendent sublime that seductively overwhelms one's judgment and will: "I have been seduced to treat the subject [of sublimity] more generally than I had at first proposed" (Owens and Smyser, 2:356). Wordsworth makes a corresponding gesture in *The Prelude*, Book VI, when the sublime narrative threatens to seduce him beyond reasonable limits:

> But here I must break off, and quit at once,
> Though loth, the record of these wanderings,
> A theme which may seduce me else beyond
> All reasonable bounds.

Although the seduction is a dangerous one for the poetic voice, in prose it apparently holds no threat for the author.[24] Being seduced in the essay leads to devotion due, and W. Wordsworth spends nearly the entire essay qualifying and characterizing the sublime. The quieter Beauty is given little space except for comparative parallels, yet it is she who nurtures the mind and aids it to appreciate nature's sublime.

Beauty and sublimity can even coexist in the same natural object although the relation between sublime and beautiful encounters depends on the perceiver's receptivity to the object: "I need not observe to persons at all conversant in these speculations that I take for granted that the same object may be both sublime and beautiful" (Owens and Smyser, 2:349). However, the sublime will "strike" first in an aggressive move quite opposed to the gentleness of beauty, for the sublime is primary and "always precedes the beautiful in making us conscious of its presence" (350). At the same time, the transcendent sublime preempts the abject or even sexual, displacing them onto othering terrain. This makes Dorothy's placement of herself somewhat problematic. Mary Jacobus states it more strongly in reading De Quincey's description of D. Wordsworth in his *Recollections of the Lake Poets:*

> Why is Dorothy a virgin? — an absurd question. Ungraceful and even unsexual, De Quincey calls her, while echoing Wordsworth's touching fraternal fiction in *The Prelude* where he attributes to her a feminizing influence that marries the Sublime to the Beautiful. . . . Notice that femininity is a kind of parasite or secondary growth, grafted onto the primary stock of masculinity. [*Romanticism*, 259]

Dorothy is a virgin because she is Virginie, Saint-Pierre's heroine who dies before achieving marital relations, or even the marriage ceremony. And, like Paul, William is one of the brotherhood of poets who can access the sublime because the transcendent is a male province that asserts "the primary stock of masculinity." Thus the brothers can perform the philosophic, divine "marriage" and desemination foretold in the final book of *The Prelude*. And that sublime fusion of mind and nature is, like the fraternal bond between priest and groom in the wedding ceremony, a function of the spiritual realm that precludes women. That the Bluestockings attempt to reverse this gender assignment by making the sublime the focus of their intellectual pursuits is a cause for amusement even for so late a critic as Samuel Monk. However, Monk does see the need to consider seriously the Bluestockings' contribution to the development of the sublime and suggests that W. Wordsworth's poetic experimentation allowed him to go beyond the point where the Blues were blocked in their explorations of the natural sublime.

W. Wordsworth's fragmentary theorizing on the nature of the sublime follows at least a century of speculation, although his major point of departure is Burke's *Enquiry*. Boileau's interpretation of the resurrected Longinus (the *Peri Hupsous*) established an aesthetic discourse, particularly on British ground, which conceived of the sublime as the inarticulatable and unrepresentable. Only a rhetoric whose high style corresponds to the elevated characters of this transcendent concept can communicate something of its essence. As such, the sublime is still an imaginative construct, unconnected with those everyday objects which in themselves can only be of the beautiful.[25]

When Burke's aesthetics of terror deteriorates into sensationalism and the gothic, there is a simultaneous need for the more orderly, rational, legislated picturesque. Wordsworth agonizes over the current fashions which so misread these philosophically and scientifically based arguments. He complains in *The Prelude* that the age is "infected" by the fashionable habit of imposing false aesthetic judgments on any landscape without considering those characteristics necessary for the true picturesque. What he particularly wished to counteract was the domination of the eye over the other human senses which the popularized version of the picturesque endorses and promotes. The sublime, too easily confused with the picturesque by the popular tourists, is to be experienced not by sight but by emotion, through Burkean terror and its resulting pleasure. This aesthetic enjoyment is achieved not through sight but through a sensation whose privileged domain (the first affective category) is the visionary and prophetic. Thus is revolutionary trauma aestheticized and implicated into the culture. What thrills to one's very depths is no longer the self-oriented pain of Wertherian hysterics, or even his introspective dejection.

Yet dejection is still a viable alternative to mind-boggling terror for those who seek extraordinary relation to or departure from their ordinary bodies and selves. Dorothy Wordsworth uses a personalized picturesque aesthetic to displace the treacherous sublime. The picturesque, with its framing and compositional need for observed particularities, allows Dorothy to agree with William's analysis of the beautiful: Gentle and easily taken for granted, it requires careful attention to perceive. When D. Wordsworth practices Gilpin's picturesque she alters the rules so that those particular, discrete elements that work together collectively focus her eye. She thus selects and frames the view which shows a community of natural elements nested within the larger landscape. When her eye picks out a singular form, it is to analyze its isolation and to note whether solitude weakens it.

In William Wordsworth's scheme, the picturesque defines the poet's relation to pastoral nature as the beautiful. The picturesque locates the valley and bower within the larger vista and allows the observer to see them as framed by the landscape. W. Wordsworth differs from other adherents of the picturesque in his desire to be enclosed by the valley and bower and to participate himself in the observed scene instead of viewing from a "station" or vantage point. If William's picturesque belongs to the valley and bower, the sacred grove is where he situates the meeting of the picturesque and the beautiful with the sublime, a meeting that transmutes the feminine into the transcendent and brings the masculine sublimity of mountains home to pasture.

Dorothy's minute detailings of the beautiful or domesticated depictions of so-called sublime landscapes in her journals place her firmly at W. Wordsworth's side in his poetic activity. Because the transcendent sublime represents the masculine arena of aggression and of the competition of fathers and brothers, Dorothy leaves the sublime terrain to William, avoiding a competition that could threaten her dependent status in her brother's family. Avoidance of the sublime also allows her to escape the aggression that destroys community and isolates or orphans the individual. Her choice of the mundane as her specialty, as an aesthetic terrain no man would vie for, gives her eye focus beyond the direction of William's vision. But perhaps more importantly it protects her on a daily basis from those sublime experiences lying in wait for the female subject, experiences that would sublimate her disastrously. Subliming the mundane, however, details the literal plane and so does not entail a high seriousness. Such a lack turns the effort to note detail into fiction (as a lower form of recording) just when poesy metamorphoses into Truth.[26] Dorothy Wordsworth's poems similarly keep her safe by adhering to local subjects and domestic forms, so that she rests properly within the lyric realm of the beautiful even when she experiments with versions of the romantic forms William and Coleridge employed.[27]

D. Wordsworth's response to transcendence would not be surprising simply in terms of Burke's codification of gendered aesthetics.[28] The operational system of Burke's *Enquiry* itself reveals as much: In Part I, the central block of the nineteen sections is given over to a primary unwrapping of the Sublime and of Beauty. The section preceding "Of the Sublime" discourses on "the Passions which belong to Self-preservation," for fear and terror are responses to a power that threatens the integrity of the self: "The passions . . . which are conversant about the preservation of the individual, turn chiefly on *pain* and *danger,* and they are the most powerful of all the passions" (*Enquiry,* 38; emphases are Burke's). These passions are differentiated from "the Passions which belong to society" in the section following "Of the Sublime," but we do not reach a discussion of the Beautiful until after "The final cause of the difference between the Passions belonging to Self-preservation, and those which regard the Society of the Sexes." "Of Beauty" is appropriately followed by "Society and Solitude." Although the function of Part I is only to set the terms of the treatise in motion, Burke makes it clear even here that these terms will be ones of opposition ("Pain and Pleasure," "Joy and Grief," "Society and Solitude") and that these oppositions are founded on gender codes. Beauty here (although Burke later complicates the notion of Beauty) is simply that of sexual attraction and as such is "a social quality": "The object . . . of his mixed passion which we call love, is the *beauty* of the *sex.* Men . . . are attached to particulars by personal *beauty*" (*Enquiry,* 42; emphases are Burke's). Burke consigns love to the social passions but takes care to differentiate the intensities of love from the "positive pain" of the true sublime.[29] He thus rejects the tenet of courtly love that the beloved can raise the lover to spiritual heights through his desire to be worthy of her, definitively segregating love for woman from the sublime quest.

Significantly, Burke's initial discussion of the sublime involves a reference to "the late unfortunate regicide in France," Robert François Damiens. Tortured and executed, Damiens represents for Burke the exquisite pain and terror of the sublime as it conjoins with the oedipal act of supreme patricide, regicide. Burke's sympathy with this quintessential sublime act signals his understanding of the psychological underpinnings of the sublime as a masculine arena of aggression and, as Paul Fry notes, "a drama of power." In rhetorical sublimity, the literary rivalry between the writer and his predecessor involves a struggle for possession; in aesthetic sublimity, the terrain is geophysical, social, and mystical, but the object is the same, getting one's hands on the grail. Once W. Wordsworth achieves a sustained sublimity in the conclusion of *The Prelude,* he has himself superseded not only the Mother but the oedipal Father as well and returns to earth as the Christ-son who will teach man the beauty of his own sublime intellect.

Burke's clear gender demarcations of the earthly versus the divine realms are based on, as David Simpson notes, "a political-theological paradigm already familiar."[30] Sublime vastness, infinitude, and elevation "transport" the male poet over the natural everyday world. This hyperbolic extension of human imaginative resources authorizes sublime discourse, and the authority that supports it is at once paternal, divine, and rhetorical. The leap itself requires a specular as well as an imaginative act, a gazing at the place where one wants to be. How Dorothy responds to William's transported encounter with that romantic symbol of sublimity, Mont Blanc, reveals the gender differences in the specular.[31]

W. Wordsworth's account of his first visit to the emblematic mountain in 1790, fully worked out fifteen years later in the 1805 *Prelude,* expresses terrible disappointment in a landscape whose sight did not elevate and whose barrenness depresses:

> That day we first
> Beheld the summit of Mount Blanc, and grieved
> To have a soulless image on the eye
> Which had usurped upon a living thought . . .

The privileging of imaginative thought over "realities" to which one must be "reconciled," and the depression at the soulless image that occupies the eye but not the vision, elevates the invisible over the visible and implies that the sublime is to be found not in nature but in the human mind — a theme that informs the poem's conclusion. That this grief and usurpation give way to apostrophe is no accident of the composing mood: Apostrophe, the turning aside to receive inspiration and vision, tropes rhetorical sublimity. It is only natural, then, that Wordsworth apostrophizes not the mountain but his own imaginative powers, calling them into being.

The phenomenon is again explored in his essay "The Sublime and the Beautiful":

> I can easily conceive that such a man [a stranger], in his first intercourse with these objects, might be grievously disappointed, &, if that intercourse should be short, might depart without being raised from that depression which such disappointment might reasonably cause. [Owen and Smyser, 2:358]

Such a man was William himself, whose imaginative excess caused expectations which had not prepared him for the reality of Mont Blanc's appearance. When D. Wordsworth saw the alp thirty years later, she had the advantage of knowing intimately William's reaction to the mountain, so that she could prepare for "reasonable disappointment" and resulting dejection.

On encountering the sublime mountain in 1820, Dorothy's expectations are not reversed as were William's in 1790. Her description in *A Tour of the Continent* is sufficiently elevated from her customary journal voice to imply a touch of sublime enthusiasm:

> and, from the brow of the eminence, behold, to our left, the huge form of Mount Blanc — pikes, towers, needles, and wide wastes of everlasting snow, in dazzling brightness. . . . Our station, though on a height so commanding, was on the lowest point of the eminence; and such as I have sketched (but how imperfectly!) was the scene uplifted and outspread before us. The higher parts of the mountain in our neighborhood are sprinkled with brown chalets. So they were thirty years ago, as my Brother well remembered. [*Journals*, 2:282]

The uncharacteristic and stylized "behold" and "but how imperfectly!" reflect the writer's struggle with the sublime's unrepresentability. And, interestingly, Dorothy's response to the romantic alpine set piece alone does not reflect the initial disappointment her traveling party all experience in the face of the natural sublime: "All our party, except myself, were disappointed with Chamouny" (2:283). D. Wordsworth's ability to find each minute detail interesting in her daily walks in Grasmere had prepared her to see beneath the superficial barrenness of the sublime. W. Wordsworth's essay emphasizes that the sublime cannot be directly apperceived "without a preparatory intercourse with that object or with others of the same kind" (Owen and Smyser, 2:359). Perhaps because of her familiarity with the mountains of the Lake District, Dorothy is able to denote with enthusiasm both the "central ravages more dreary" and "the spaces of barren ground," as well as the indications of human habitation William had left out of his description. Whereas William's transport does not occur until the composing moment, Dorothy's occurs on the spot ("behold"). However, the transport itself is of little importance next to her delight in the domestic activity occurring in the valley: "Our walk beside the suburban cottages was altogether new, and very interesting: — a busy scene of preparation for the night!" (*Journals,* 2:283). Next to this bustle, the tale of five people's death on the mountain just three weeks prior raises no expectation of sublime terror and, indeed, shares space in the same sentence with the guide's directions for the next day's travel. As in the *Grasmere Journals,* D. Wordsworth's factual reportage evades confrontation with death by assimilating it to the pastoral life of the valley.

Where Dorothy's journal interacts most explicitly with William's *Prelude* episode, least dialogue takes place; her prose assures him she will not attempt his territory (the disturbing and severe Mont Blanc), except to describe it briefly and accurately. In contrast, the next day's exploration of the Mer de Glace merits her full descriptive powers, with several references to the sublimity, danger, and impossibility of the journey. But where her discourse is most assured is in the nonsublime description of the "busy scene" of human activity. The entry for the Mer de Glace is nearly three pages in length; and although the entry for the day spent climbing Mont Blanc is even longer, only two paragraphs are actually devoted to the scene. *The Prelude*'s language so emphatically claims the scape for its own that the sister journalist responds only as she should to lines such as

> Oh, sorrow for the youth who could have seen
> Unchastened, unsubdues, unawed, unraised
> To patriarchal dignity of mind

And pure simplicity of wish and will,
Those sanctified abodes of peaceful man.
My heart leaped up when first I did look down.

[*Prelude* VI]

What Dorothy Wordsworth knows from such lines is that the sublime
unseats and submerges the pastoral ("My heart leaps up when I behold"),
and at the same time it is the youth who yields to the chastening view of
such abodes and to a resulting "patriarchal dignity of mind." This is no
place for a maiden to set herself, and if Dorothy's relative silence in the face
of the sublime is a cooperation with masculine transcendence, it is also
avoidance of competing on the rhetorical front of the sublime.

⌐ The Rhetorical Sublime and The Lyrical Sublime

William's famous Simplon Pass section of *The Prelude*, which so characterizes his encounter with Mont Blanc, describes in unsublimed disappointment the failure to see or feel anything elevated in the landscape that
submerges him. Such disappointment occasions a retrospective sublime
that occurs by act of imagination as Wordsworth writes about the source
of ordinariness. Hit rhetorically by the transported imagination, struck by
the force of Imagination rather than remembrance, Wordsworth experiences in the solitude of first-draft composition what evaded him all those
years earlier. The rhetorical sublime is to remain the favored locus of safe
placement; this form of the sublime leans less materially on body and on
female body than landscaped sublimity and is therefore a purer and more
distanced form. And, by virtue of physical distance, it is more free to enact
violence on the female body which is not touched.

Longinus is the source for theories of the rhetorical sublime. It is a
source, however, that illustrates rather than explains, as if even in the
realm of language the sublime is inexplicable, untranslatable. Neil Hertz,
in analyzing the Longinian text, discovers that it reveals slippage at the
precise moments we expect explication. Such moments demonstrate the
"sublime turn": The poet, having dismembered or fragmented his material, reabsorbs its energy into himself in a transgressive move that replaces

hero / object with the poet's own consciousness. The rhetorical figure that most explicitly brings on his turn is the apostrophe; in Longinus's view, it is a "figure of conjuration" by which the poet is enabled "to run away with his audience,"[32] but also with himself.

The effects of figuration are twofold: the turn in which divine and dangerous forces through a transformative space become poetic activity; and the function of the beautiful as a mystifier that veils the illusory search for truth. The first of these instances of the rhetorical sublime is structured by an interactive relationship between passive and active states, a Keatsian negative capability. The poet is passive in the face of the negative energies encountered, but this very encounter involves an experience of near death. The violence of the sublime moment of engulfment and self-annihilation transfers into poetic energy, the dynamics of which involve a rhetorical violence equal to the turbulent emotions Burke identifies as terror and fear.

Neil Hertz comments that "what Longinus has allowed us to read is that when figurative language is concealed it may sustain the truthful, the natural, the masterful, and so on; but when it is revealed, it is always revealed as false" (18). Thus the masculine sublime sustains its authoritative truth, which language itself may prove illusory. In his famous invocation to Imagination (*Prelude* VI), Wordsworth first apostrophizes this half-divine, half-human power in a rhetorical gesture which itself breaks the narrative illusion of his alpine story. But the revelation of the first illusion here allows for a fuller belief in the second, for the apostrophe is a "figure of conjuration" which "can do [much] to bring urgency and passion into our words" (Longinus 15.9). Thus we believe the poet is uplifted at the very moment we realize he is not descending the alpine ravine. Lost in the veil of sublime mystification ("I was lost as in a cloud") and resisting the traditionally aggressive character of the sublime ("The mind beneath such banners militant / Thinks not of spoils or trophies, nor of aught / That may attest its prowess"), the poet finds sublime infinitude to be "Strong in itself, and in the access of joy / Which hides it like the overflowing Nile." It is no accident that the traditionally female entity of the Nile suddenly intervenes. The great river that fertilizes the Egyptian land, mind, and culture recalls a culture itself feminized in relation to the masculinist Hellenic cultures. Female, the river hides through joy the sublime's dangerous power now domesticated: "Our destiny, our nature, and our home, / Is with infinitude — and only there." Immediately following this appearance of the veiling and fertilizing river comes the grandeur of the stunningly sublime "immeasurable height / Of woods decayed, never to be decayed," and "the stationary blasts of waterfalls," which perhaps because of their masculinity evoke such sublime terror that the sight is "bewildered and forlorn," and the counterpart to the Nile's functioning as "joy" is a "raving stream" whose "sick sight / And giddy prospect" create such dizziness that the poet achieves a vision of the great apocalypse. The narrative soon resumes, only to be interrupted by a return to the beautiful with an address to Lake Como. The beauty of the sight restores the poet's calm by reversing the transfer of power and making passive again the disturbing activeness of sublime transgression. Once restored by the harmony of the lake scene, the Wordsworthian poet can proceed without that sublime gloom which haunted his impassioned apostrophe. The next verse paragraph beings, "Through those delighted pathways we advanced," as the enabled narrative now continues.

The leap back into the composing moment in this passage, and the final turn to the brother poet, suggests a confluence of the sublime and beautiful as a middle ground. This is the ground of the mother "sweet as love" and of "enduring language," which seems to provide a passive nurturance but not sustained poetic activity. In fact, the quest narrative breaks off just at the point where the maternal mood of this middle ground "withdraws," leaving both participants without creative inspiration.

As if to contradict such loss (and such dependence on middle ground), the gesture of breaking off leads to a question of desire. The seduction of the narrative record the poet must resist is that of an infinite tale "beyond / All reasonable bounds," the same gesture used for Wordsworth's essay on the sublime. Such vastness implies a lack of rhetorical control over one's material, and unreasonable bounds lead to "hollow exultation" and "[h]yperboles of praise comparative." The rhetorical sublime is supremely well suited to the figure of hyperbole, as Longinus himself recognized, but Wordsworth finds great danger in a trope that replicates the move beyond all reasonable bounds. For Longinus, "The important thing to know is how far to push a given hyperbole. . . . I suspect that what we said of the best figures is true of the best hyperboles: they are those which avoid being seen for what they are" (38.1–3). The hyperbole thus makes possible a rhetorical sublime; it is the heightened hyperbolic state that allows the passage of divine and activating powers to the poet, raising him to excited emotional states. Wordsworth finds the hyperbole, however, a threat, a "hollow exultation," once "reasonable bounds" have been transgressed. For Longinus just the reverse is true, since the threat comes not from uncontrollable power but from the collapse of such power through tearing aside the veil of rhetoric's illusion. Once the figure is revealed rather than concealed, the unity of the whole is destroyed. For Wordsworth, the one figure that best tropes the sublime is most likely to disclose its structure, and figurative language "when it is revealed . . . is always revealed as false" (Hertz, 18).

The aesthetic terrain Wordsworth draws for himself makes the classical and conveniently safe claim that the sublime can be powerfully uncovered and made real through rhetorical and imaginative collusion. Yet, as we have seen, the rhetorical sublime contains its own dangers and drains on the poetic spirit. One of Wordsworth's most brilliant moments, as critics have long recognized, was his discovery of the lyrical sublime as a way to claim the potency of anagogic rhetoric while putting off its threat.

The Lucy poems are Wordsworth's clearest example of the lyrical sublime, and they occupy a strange halfway space between the lyrical and the epical in his oeuvre. They also stand between William and Dorothy, at once laying interpretive hands on her and remaining hands-off (Coleridge assumed the lyrics were about her; William denied it even though one final Lucy poem does address her). In any case, they place her so properly that the real Dorothy must look to her own talents in order to write herself out of such grounding.

Clearly songlike, the Lucy lyrics most closely resemble the (sublime) "Intimations" ode in theme and figure. In fact, Lucy allows W. Wordsworth to unfold a doubled temporality, a double plotting, as if it were unified because remembered rather than presently experienced. Lucy-time beyond the poet's sense is monolithic, undisturbed, and silent; her living death disrupts and disturbs the poet at the same time that it gives him peace. Thus he achieves a quietness that is sublime through the swallowing of Lucy by proper time. And Lucy, engulfed by the idea of the whole, embodies threshold energies in a way that Dorothy cannot. Having gone through the dark portals that are both birth and death in the maternal body (earth/nature), she becomes the world beyond liminality. In her isolation Lucy verifies the presence of a sublime that resides in memory rather than the imagination, a Caroline rather than a Dorothy. The problematic of her estranged temporality which aligns itself with both the pleasure of the violet and the confrontation with death unfolds through attention to Thomas Weiskel's analysis of the rhetorical structure of the romantic sublime, and through the positing of that strange space as liminal and integrative, a lyrical sublime.

The founding notion of Weiskel's structuralist work is that transcendence is an integral aspect of language itself, for the sublime occurs not just in figuration but in the lapse between signifier and signified. This deferral tropes the vagueness and unrepresentable aspects of the sublime, presenting a truly allegorical language rather than language about allegory. Lucy, too, is herself allegorical and not an allegory for something else. As they integrate the natural with the supernatural, the beautiful with the sublime, so the Lucy poems attenuate meaning, withholding it even between stanzas. Weiskel's summary of the romantic project helps contextualize their role:

> The Romantic sublime was an attempt to revise the meaning of transcendence. . . . It provided a language for urgent and apparently novel experiences of anxiety and excitement which were in need of legitimation. In largest perspective, it was a major analogy, a massive transportation of transcendence into a naturalistic key; in short, a stunning metaphor. [4]

However, as Weiskel points out, "We cannot conceive of a literal sublime," and thus the metaphor is necessary (4). The beautiful, on the other hand, not only extends a humanizing influence but combats the dualisms that the sublime reinforces. Wordsworth's own integrative system for mapping aesthetic differences struggles to reconcile both these aims, and whereas the addresses to women sublimate the pastoral, Lucy lyricizes the sublime. And in doing so, she tropes a rhetoric of transgression. When transgression is feminized, the male poet can assuage his own aggressive fears by displacing them onto the woman and then letting her take the punishing blow; Lucy's death in the transgressive arena is only "natural" for she exists to protect the poet's spirit by her own sprite.

In Lucy we have a figure whose power is both that of the rhetorical sublime and that of the lyric moment. In Weiskel's formulation she is an excess on the plane of the signifier, placing her in a lyrical rather than "mundane sublime." Lucy is characterized in her poems as lying between the immanent and the transcendent, and it is here we may locate the allegorical moment. A major attribute of immanent sublimation is circularity, undifferentiated being, and the quest for fusion with the mother. Immanence is characterized as passive, female, and "natural" in Western intellectual history, whereas transcendence is active, male, and artistic.[33] As the reified spirit of nature, Lucy embodies the lyrical; she is the *genius loci* who is everywhere sited. As Frances Ferguson notes, "Lucy, that elusive first term, is nowhere and everywhere at once" (183). On the literal level Lucy is absence and loss; she is paradoxically caught in the atemporality of both the pastoral and the sublime, for as the flower she is associated with the fancy and the realm of innocence, while as the earth she is part of the natural sublime and can be comprehended only through the soul sleep in which her speakers dream of her.

"The appropriate business of poetry," Wordsworth writes in the "Essay, Supplementary to the Preface," is to treat of things not as they *are* but as they *appear,* not as they exist in themselves but as they *seem* to exist to the *senses* and to the *passions* (Hayden, 924). If Lucy-love locates her in the realm of the Fancy, what Wordsworth calls "the desires and *demands* of the Imagination" chase her as an object of desire to the realm of the sublime. Lucy is both the spirit of nature and the spirit of poetry — not sprite and muse but the essence of nature, and poetic essence or breath, inspiration. In both cases, she is transcended, powerless, mute — that is to say, dead. Her very passivity invites the poet to assert his own role and function as the knight in quest of a poetics, a knight unencumbered by a demanding and rejecting mistress.[34] Lucy is rather neatly too young, too unclassed, too unknown, too dead, to turn William's chivalric quest to slaveship. Whereas poems of the Fancy present an overarching stability, despite the transient nature of the particular object (the flower, the butterfly), poems of the Imagination seek "the plastic, the pliant, and the indefinite" in an attempt to "incite and to support the eternal [part of our nature]" (1815 Preface).

The multiple addresses to flowers, birds, and other natural objects in the "Poems of the Fancy" do not valorize one particular object over all others of its kind; instead, to address the object is to preserve it, to press its mutable form into the atemporal stasis of the pastoral garden. To thus preserve the object is to allegorize it, making the particular another repetition of the original. The Imagination seeks out Lucy in her fanciful garden, yet finds that she is gone ("and few could know / When Lucy ceased to be"). She is indefiniteness itself, the spirit of the flower or butterfly, the thing each object repeats in an endless transformative cycle.

As de Man notes in "The Rhetoric of Temporality," "the prevalence of allegory always corresponds to the unveiling of an authentically temporal destiny." Yet Wordsworth colonizes and spatializes Lucy rather than grounding her—she is not grounded as in "placed and centred" but grounded as in made into ground, and into background, for she is herself nature as the scene of the meditation.[35] De Man argues that it is the symbol which is of a spatial nature, but despite this, Lucy allegorizes the lyrical sublime, for allegory is writing Otherness as the temporal moment of inexpressibility. Nothing in W. Wordsworth's oeuvre is more alienated than Lucy as she stands representatively, on the one hand, for the Mother as true and inexpressible Other and, on the second, for Love itself. The different but coexistent levels of allegorical meaning in the collision of their meeting cancel each other, forcing us to experience Lucy as silence, absence, death.

As a poetic working out of the inexpressibility of language—a project that places us squarely in the sublime—Lucy functions like the flowers with which she is repeatedly identified. Just as each violet is a repetition of the first, originary violet, Lucy repeats Eve, for the allegorical sign repeats temporally backward, so that the echo replaces the inutterable. For de Man, "[the] relationship between signs necessarily contains a constitutive temporal element; it remains necessary, if there is to be allegory, that the allegorical sign refer to another sign that precedes it" ("Rhetoric," 207). Lucy cannot be pure symbol, for "the symbol postulates the possibility of an identity" (207), and as we have seen, Lucy possesses none; however, she is allegorical in the sense that allegory is the elegiac moment that contains the recognition of death.

The implicit link between allegory and irony which de Man describes in the same essay leads us to Anne Mellor's notions of the interactions of romantic tropes, their transgressions, the Longinian lawlessness of the rhetorical sublime. In both allegory and irony, the sign points to something other than its literal meaning. Mellor theorizes that romantic irony uses a "figural discourse based on the alternation of symbol and metaphor. Both symbolism and allegory, both the rage for order and the rage for freedom, are really authentic modes of human experiences and expression" (*English Romantic Irony,* 186). Although Mellor conflates allegory and metaphor, her understanding of the tension between symbol and allegory as "the hovering between man-made being and ontological becoming" (186) illuminates the dynamic nature and function of the lyrical sublime as not so much Derrida's "analogical displacement of Being" as his "essential weight which anchors discourse" (27). Lucy herself embodies the rage for freedom, as she allegorically and endlessly repeats herself through her name alone; the rage for order finds expression in the insistence on Lucy's death and the suppression of her being. Spirit of nature and of poetry both, she is denied the dangerous female energies of the Mother she represents. The denial comes both from the male poet's conflicted response to the female object of desire and from the deathly status of her "man-made being" which the poet's "ontological becoming" overwhelms.

As figuration for the lyrical sublime Lucy raises again the relation between epic and the address-to-women. It is *The Prelude* as lyricized epic that combines William's two poetic interests, thus leaving Lucy in an odd between-space. Dorothy has resolved this halfway space by assuring the flow of cottage space, making it particular to her own being as well as to her life with William. But William's poetry concedes less in what is for him a powerful issue. Still, if the address-to-women offers a way to step outside lyric monologism, *The Prelude* periodically seeks to leave off the incessant activity of the transcendent quest. Mary Jacobus reads Wordsworth's epic as a retreat from the sublime to the pastoral, finding evidence that Wordsworth consistently replaces his own poetic voice with that of Nature's: "the fiction of a poetry that originates in Nature, like the voice of the Derwent, ensures continuity while providing a safely transsubjective voice in which the poet's own can be merged" (*Romanticism,* 164–65). Whereas the sublime threatens the potential loss of individual identity in the excess of enthusiasm and fervor, the pastoral offers a safe refuge from such annihilation. Jacobus argues that *The Prelude* is "the address of one poet-shepherd to another" (165); the address-to-women allows the poet to speak to the maiden; the Lucy poem only allows him to speak to himself. Jacobus's reading, though it does not account for *The Prelude*'s final access to the sublime, does point out the next logical step beyond the halfway space Lucy represents in the ascent upward to the Father, the poet speaking to brother poet. Weiskel concurs in this progression: "Ultimately, the path of the . . . transcendent sublime leads through the phase of daemonic [or internalized] romance, with its oedipal anxieties, to a symbolic identification with the father" (135). Lucy as sprite, as reabsorbed essence, and as object of the poetic quest does focus anxieties over separation from the mother as death and loss; once the sprite is laid to rest, she is externalized as a fragmented being at one with Nature ("Rolled round . . . With rocks, and stones, and trees"). The brother poet displaces, then, both the maiden and Lucy, and empowers the speaker to assume a Christ-like divinity that rejects maidenly complementation as a thing of the past. Whereas the maiden leaves the poet in awe of the power of the Other and the unknowable, the brother poet gives him license to establish inner vision authoritatively over otherly mystery. *The Excursion*'s structuring brotherhood, with its wandering tribe of shepherd poets, more elaborately figures the last stage in this ascent to join and exceed the Father.

If *The Excursion* demonstrates accurately the effects of extreme brotherhood, then the example of Margaret should reveal the fate of woman—whether character, reader, or poet—in its more fully epic terrain. In a reenvisioning of "The Ruined Cottage," Book I of *The Excursion* is the Wanderer's recounting of Margaret's tale. Initially the Poet is struck by the contrast between Margaret's pain and the Wanderer's seeming diffidence:

But when he ended, there was in his face,
Such easy cheerfulness, a look so mild,
That for a little time it stole away
All recollection; and that simple tale
Passsed from my mind like a forgotten sound. . . .
A heart-felt chillness crept along my veins.

But the Wanderer's reproof reveals that he tells the tale in order to call forth sublime musings on death and loss:

> It were a wantonness . . . if we were men whose hearts
> Could hold vain dalliance with the misery
> Even of the dead . . .
> But we have known that there is often found
> In mournful thoughts, and always might be found
> A power to virtue friendly.

It is the power derived from the dead woman's story, like the uplifting sublimity which Lucy's death enables, that leads the Poet and his Virgilian guide to the ethics of subliming others.

Sublimity, as William Wordsworth's essay on the subject reminds us, resides as much in the viewer's ability to perceive it as in the object itself. Margaret's pain reveals the place of the feminine in a tale of dialogic brotherhood. For Dorothy Wordsworth as sister poet, the tale may reveal more than the Wanderer intends, for Margaret is still clearly the object of the gaze despite her own access to sublime unboundedness. Even as Margaret's "common tale, / An ordinary sorrow of man's life," is a source of sublime emotion, for Margaret herself the story leads to the divine:

> [She], in her worst distress, had ofttimes felt
> The *unbounded might of prayer;* and learned, with soul
> Fixed on the Cross, that consolation springs,
> From sources deeper far than deepest pain,
> For the meek Sufferer.

Tale-telling, unbinding, and the power of prayer connect powerfully for W. Wordsworth. It is perhaps no accident that Book II of *The Excursion* follows this passage by invoking the presence of the wandering rustic poet: "In days of yore how fortunately fared / The Minstrel!" The minstrel's fortune is directly related to his mistress's power; Margaret's powerlessness kills her, her Poet turning from her even as her story structures the epic *Excursion.* Margaret's is the tale of female pain; its relation to the masculine sublime defines the woman's place when men write the story.

Chapter 5 will round out this narrative cartography by providing a reassessment of the previous statement. Underlying its argument will be the question of what happens when a woman rewrites the tale of female pain and its relation to the masculine sublime, and what happens when woman's place is redefined by the woman writing the (male) story. This reassessment can occur because Dorothy Wordsworth literally outlived her role as maiden and complement, and because is that older self she achieved a madness and pain similar to Margaret's, yet did not succumb to either Margaret's futile silence or her early death. Having passed through the crucible of that threshold without falling, she achieved a different vision of Wordsworthianism from that which had mapped out her life.

The Poetics of
Negotiating Charts

In Chapter 4 I discussed William Wordsworth's particular conception of the sublime as grounded in trauma and fear, and his charting of the known world as predicated on the attempt to fence off the different faces of the sublime. Only the lyrical sublime proves safe enough for the Wordsworthian pastoral. To address or apostrophize Lucy and the other female figures who embody difference mediates the terror they affix but translates it into strange and distanced music (as for the Solitary Reaper, Lucy, and a number of other landscaped figures). Certainly, Dorothy Wordsworth strives against such a fate. And however much her brother's exchange of fear for the aesthetic removes the dangerous immediacy of truly sublime experience, to simply domesticate it from ecstasis into pastoral joy, or from dejection into melancholy, does not remove the threat sublimity poses to the woman addressee.

Part of this threat is that the sublime demands a solitude and solitary wandering before an encounter can occur; but the solitude is the speaker's and not the addressee's. *The Recluse,* W. Wordsworth's unfinished epic, indicates by its title that the philosophical solitary will be its subject and its subject-on-trial. Yet all the "pre-epics" that initiate the project — "Home at Grasmere," *The Prelude, The Excursion* — concern the search of the solitary individual *for community* as he learns about "man, nature, and society." It is this epic project that must insure Wordsworth's poetic fame, yet he defers it from 1800 ("Home at Grasmere") to 1805 (the revised *Prelude*) and then to 1808 ("The Tuft of Primroses"). William's continual deferral of philosophy may be due to a resistance to that fame, to true solitude, or to sublime pain and fear.

Dorothy Wordsworth differs from her brother in her refusal to defer the labor expected of her, and she cannot understand his procrastination. Nonetheless, she does agree early on to don the sublimating role assigned her in William's aesthetic map and to thus herself experience fear and pain. The bodily response to these emotions must be abjection as aestheticized self-disgust, and although Dorothy does take on this aspect of the second self, she also discovers in later life a way around sublimation. This chapter argues that the alternative route lies in the thrill of uncharted terrain, the imaginary regions where the older Dorothy Wordsworth quests for signs of self against the ordering and placement of William's mapping. Such questing, I argue, functions recuperatively as a poetic mirroring of William's encounters with uncharted spots of time, minus the terrible fear attendant on his experiences but also certainly long after the fact. Finally, this chapter will show the regenerative capacity of Dorothy Wordsworth's imagination, which shores up the larger fears of William's sublime and sublimating poetic terrain.

➣ Detailing Nature

Like Lucy, Margaret suffers sublimation so that the Wordsworthian speaker can fix his sympathy meaningfully. In D. Wordsworth's own, less divisible comprehension of the world, sympathy crosses all categories. It is what allows her to step easily into the shoes of another person, and it also

allows her to study nature's intricacies: "The Stirring, the Still, the Lo-
quacious, the Mute — / To all we gave our sympathy" ("Thoughts on my
sick-bed"). Sympathy binds the affects together, an act Dorothy replicates
bodily when she conceives her heart as the bonding place that holds her
brothers together.[1] Nor does it necessarily disappear in the negating
moods. Dorothy's understanding of melancholy differs from William's
because for her it does not spell affectional dissociation or loss of sympathetic powers.

For the male romantic, melancholy is a poetic disposition characterized
by specular display of disturbance, of a tearing away of the self and a
questing. D. Wordsworth translates this sensibility into melancholy as an
excess of affect, an overburden of pleasure that brings tears. But the tears
distilled by a glorious landscape are aesthetic tears, not dis-pleasure but a
distillation of pleasure, not an essentializing of nature as object but an
essentializing of emotion as self. Beneath the aesthetic mood, however,
lies the melancholy of emptiness and despair characterized by a distressed
reaching out for the sympathy of others, a request to be mothered oneself.
Thus D. Wordsworth details her ills and sorrows in the journals more fully
than her pleasures. And beneath this sorrow lies the self-negation of abjection — not the masculine grotesque which is the maternal body but an
abjecting of the bodily self, a disgust for one's own body. Self-disgust must
relocate the body as the place to begin making meaning anew, here where
the self is interred two levels beneath the normal signifying field. If the
Man of Taste represents the opposite pole of experience from that of self-
disgust, taste itself might be less the antipode of disgust than is gusto or
the visibility of life force in the viewed object. Hazlitt writes that gusto "is
power or passion defining any object. . . . There is a gusto in the colour-
ing of Titian. Not only do his heads seem to think — his bodies seem to
feel . . . not merely to have the look and texture of flesh, but the feeling
in itself."[2] Melancholic or joyous moods witness the in-forming and de-
forming of the self as that self inhabits different places and levels within
the Wordsworthian chart of affective terrain. The progress through different stages of self-making, then, produces an unraveling or de-forming
of the signifying self. The differentiations possible from the love that
hovers above and the melancholy that hovers below the pastoral valley

mean that the formation and deformation of the subject is choosable and performative. Yet the Wordsworths did divide up and chart these emotive possibilities into appropriate and appropriable roles.

D. Wordsworth's partition of the universe, for instance, posits love and care as normative; William sees love as superlative. If for W. Wordsworth love suffuses the positive, ascendant sublime while the valley is the site of domestic and communal affection, for Dorothy melancholy provides the only safe role among William's sublime possibilities. Like Milton's Adam and Eve, William looks at the sky while Dorothy looks at the ground.[3] The assigned possibilities in William's universe for Dorothy, then, are the feminized sublime (Lucy-death, which is Lucy-love) and abjection (the abject death of Margaret).

These are, of course, both male-determined ways of sublimating the female, and to call this last "feminized" is to ascribe to it not women's ways of perceiving themselves but women's perception following the dictates of male gazing. It is important to call attention to these constraints on Dorothy's self-aestheticization because they confront her on the plane of taste, forcing her to take an oppositional role to the aestheticized man, the Man of Taste, but also to deny her own characteristic gusto and enthusiasm for life at large. Within the limits set by construing oneself as a viewed object with, as Hazlitt writes on Correggio's figures, "exquisite sensibility without energy of will . . . what a soul is there, full of sweetness and grace," Dorothy seeks out two other emotive possibilities in William's affective charts ("On Gusto," 202). Both act as protectively disabling but not disgusting roles: the sublime of detailism (the literal or mundane) and the melancholic as a pseudosublime, a heightened sensibility that for Dorothy allows her to keep her feet on the ground. Both entail sympathy and a reaching out to others that oppose William's self-isolating gesture toward ascent and ecstatic self-possession, for they are domesticated versions of the sublime: pocket editions.

Naomi Schor comments that the eighteenth century's contribution to aesthetics was the "departicularization" of the scene or object: "The censure of the particular is one of the enabling gestures of neo-classicism, which recycled into the modern age the classical equation of the Ideal with the absence of all particularity" (3). To ascribe to the awful stillness of Burke's sublime is to partake of the romantic sensibility's division of nature into the calmness of pastoral beauty (the everyday countryside) and the aphasia of mountainous terrain (scapes difficult to arrive at, seen for the first time). Both of these deny the particular in favor of the larger impact that can invert time and senses when detailism would lock the emoting self into place. For D. Wordsworth to then fix her own gaze on the detail is to draw perspective away from aphasia (which in the feminized sublime would compromise *her*) and onto the localized or mundane. What William's schema changes in the neoclassical rejection of detailism is to view the detail as grounding the sublime or, rather, to view Dorothy's ability to perceive finely as the ground for his aphasia.

To put the particular within Dorothy's coordinates on his map is to acknowledge the detail as feminine and yet important or portending. The current of detailism had always been undervalued and suspect, denoting lack of true intellectual vigor, effeminacy, surface play without depth, domesticity, femininity. Even when W. Wordsworth writes lyrically of the valley, his Margarets and shepherds are symbolic figures that detail the landscape, not literal inhabitants. But when William looks through Dorothy's eyes by way of her fine notations, he accords her valorization of detailism a substantive place in his aesthetic terrain. Critics, however, rarely assess D. Wordsworth's descriptive precision except by association with William's work, and her descriptions of villagers and their conversations draw critical silence, for here she enters the mundane and is dismissed. Her sickroom poetry also engages the domestic mundane as an aesthetic orbit that touches on the alterior sublimity of abjection, but again she is dismissed as debilitated and pitiful.

For D. Wordsworth, to focus on the mundane is to tell the story from the perspective of the particular, and as Schor notes, this "is inevitably to tell *another* story" (4). Arguably this different story can derive from different ways of seeing, not in the sense art critics like John Berger intend but in the differentiating perspectives of both genre and project. The writing project itself partially determines how one sees. D. Wordsworth records how nature looks and what strikes her, but knowing that she is impressing the scene on her memory so that she can write the details down later (perhaps several days later) determines her perception. In order to replicate something striking about the same scene one has already and repeatedly detailed, the viewer must force herself to negotiate fine differences in shade and tint, alterations in placement, the birth and death of things.

In contrast, William Wordsworth's project is to study not nature but the human experience of being in nature. Consequently, the object he needs to keep a steady eye on is not the natural object but himself. The act of walking through nature for William and Dorothy, even when side by side, is a fundamentally different act, then. To walk in nature for William means to concentrate on one's inner meditation — to see inwardly while feeling the pressure of nature's presence on one's psyche. It is a behavior determined by William's writing act. Dorothy Wordsworth, on the other hand, cannot afford to walk regard-less through nature for her study must be outward-directed. Instead, she must walk thought-less where William is thought-ful, so that she can be attentive to (attendant on) the scene. Her collection of details and words, impressions, and rhythms feeds William's imagination; when he rereads the journals, the literal helps him imagine what Dorothy saw in his absence or what he did not notice. He then turns the literal into the abstract, for the poet's task is to see the inner, not the outer truth of things. The writing project informs not only how one sees but how one envisions: seeing the literal landscape and composing a psychoaesthetic schematic vision in which to encompass that scape.

To understand this underlying difference in composition of the self, the scene, and the text, we must see the Wordsworths' conception of the writing act in relation to other writers. The importance of twinship as a functional concept in D. Wordsworth's relationship with her brother leads naturally to their collaborative activity. Collaboration is best recorded in the journals in the years of most intense cooperative effort in the home ground of Grasmere. One strain in particular that recurs in this collaboration is that of almsgiving followed by a story of misfortune. Sometimes only a few words, these entries can expand to lengthy passages that give detailed versions of the beggars' tales or descriptions of their appearance. In fact, appearance and tale become equated through detailism as embodiments of the beggar-personage who is a stranger to the community, a wanderer in the valley, a poetic patch. But, as if to keep in her place, Dorothy's sublimity of detailism accrues to this representation and not to its description, which is written matter-of-factly, in the discourse of the mundane. The mundane dispels poetry and takes on the distanced, clinical voice Dorothy reserves for those parts of the journal she writes for William as raw material. Unlike the generalities that her own poems will later validate, these journal entries are disturbingly particular and oddly objective. The entries engage gender-appropriate versions of the sublime that become sites for disowning, for objectivity, and thus for a kind of objection or disturbance in the sibling community. At the same time that Dorothy is uncomfortable with the object relations in sublimity-cum-sublimation, she produces prose that will become William's poetry, her words sublated into his. Overcoming disturbance in the community for William has meant projecting that discomfort onto female figures, but Dorothy finds that discomfort pushes her toward melioration and toward the ground for collaborative merging, for the doubling of voices and the twinship of minds.

Dorothy Wordsworth's interest in beggars seems to stem from a desire "to please William," as her first entry indicates about the *Grasmere Journals* in general. Her almsgiving is always followed by a recorded story of misfortune; yet only once is it made clear how or why these stories are told. Most often we receive a complexly detailed description of the beggar's appearance, but the entry only notes the beggar's tale briefly, chronicling it in the style of parish records or some other public document. One incident, however, reveals that it is a matter of methodology rather than social custom to receive the story in return for coin. During the period when William was working on "The Pedlar," he and Dorothy encountered a beggar on a daily walk. Oddly, Dorothy decided against stopping for the beggar: "From a half laziness, half indifference, and a wanting to *try* him, if he would speak, I let him pass. He said nothing and my heart smote me" (22 December 1801). Dorothy's guilt, it becomes apparent, is from two counts: She has ignored someone in need (a sympathetic failing), and she has ignored a chance as collaborator to gather material for William. She then turns back to ask the beggar his story, recording the event in her journal so as to include the back-and-forth rhythm of the exchange (important to William's "encounter" poems), the motivation (both hers and the beggar's), and incidentally, how she actually gathers these stories of misfortune. "I turned back and said, 'You are begging?' 'Ay,' says he." What is unusual here, apart from the fact that it appears at all in the entry, is the inclusion of self ("I" and the two action verbs relating to self, "turned" and "said"), as well as the inclusion of another's voice. Dorothy's entries concerning beggars and itinerant workers generally take the form of abbreviated stories told in a dispassionate voice that appropriates the beggar's story and voice without any intrusion by herself. Yet here there are several quotations of the beggar's words, plus an interacting "I." The guilty act of ignoring the collaborative mission is atoned for by a full account that exceeds the length of the preceding entry by five times and the successive entry by six times. Encountering the beggar, moreover, assumes more importance in the entry than does the beggar's tale, reflecting William's way of viewing the experience: Her account presents all the information William would need even years later for the creation of a poem. The entries concerning beggars are puzzling in their dispassionate sympathy and excessive detailing used normally for landscapes and must be read specifically as data for William.

But they also have another function. According to Richard Wollheim, the artist must engage several perspectives or seeing-roles simultaneously: "An artist must fill the role of agent, but he must also fill the role of spectator [so that] [i]nside each artist is a spectator upon whom the artist, the artist as agent, is dependent" (101). Although Dorothy's detailed landscape descriptions articulate this complex relation between visuality and production, her descriptions of persons who are dispossessed and thus made strange disallow her artistic sensibility from making poetic use of the art object. She leaves this task of double vision turned into art to her sublimely competent brother. And she does so not simply for his pleasure, as she well knows: Composition is always for William a disturbing, even sickening process.[4] Yet, however discomposing the multiple levels of seeing are for William, he does not contend with the further effects of gender-authorized seeing. Dorothy's objectivity in her descriptions of the dispossessed allows her to abstain from turning these estranged people into objects. That is, her prepossession leaves the act of objectification to William as the sublimer.

After some notes about the day's events, the entry continues with a sudden recursion to the beggar's red nose, and Dorothy speculates on his earlier days and drinking habits.[5] She moves immediately from that thought to a poetic passage about a rock she saw, the "cushion of snow" conceit that recurs in at least two of her later poems. The sudden intrusion of landscape allows her to retreat into poetry; but then her thoughts return to the beggar for a third time as she remembers a story she was told two days previous about a woman who became alcoholic because of her unloving and adulterous husband. As in the rest of the journal, the connections between the three meditations on the beggar are not sketched in. The abutments of information leave the reader to make his own conclusions, and Dorothy's structuring thoughts concerning human downfall as a product of not being cared for by others (a theme that informs much of her writing) are invisible, objective, and nearly absent.

William, of course, is the reader of such entries. The poem William has been working on for weeks is "The Pedlar," a work which eventually becomes part of the epic-length *Excursion*. It concerns an itinerant peddler who carried goods in a manner similar to this beggar's "two bags hanging over his shoulder." Particularly during this period, when William is also involved with "The Ruined Cottage," Dorothy collects any stories having to do with wanderers, itinerants, beggars, and displaced or dispossessed families. Her absorption of William's interests and obsessions does not deflect her own acute understanding of each incident, and her interest is as sharp as if the obsession were her own. After several recordings of these stories, Dorothy makes the move typical of her own thought process, despite its implications for her poetic sensibility, wondering how it would feel to be in the shoes of another, a very different question from the sort of "What difference does this encounter make to me?" question underlying all of William's verse. Her questioning thought is, "When the woman was gone, I could not help thinking that we are not half thankful enough that we are placed in that condition of life in which we are"; and again, concerning a letter carrier, "I could not help comparing lots with him. . . . He seems mechanized to labour" (12, 8 February 1802).[6]

The collaborative effort that distances artistic production for Dorothy and enhances it for William is not solely relegated to her provision of raw material. Her roles as critic and as amanuensis were the duties Dorothy most cherished in her life with William. In addition, the maiden myth William constructed around her fed his poetic vision to such an extent that she fitted herself and her memories of her earlier self to this myth. The entries surrounding the composition of "To a Butterfly" relate how Dorothy's childhood memory inspires William to composition. Next, they record daydreams about butterflies but are silent on the fact that she is thinking about what William needs to think about: "The moon was a good height above the mountains. She seemed far and distant in the sky; there were two stars beside her, that twinkled in and out, and seemed almost like butterflies in motion and lightness. They looked to be far nearer to us than the moon" (16 March 1802). And one month later William does write another poem on butterflies (also called "To a Butterfly"). Throughout the journals, when William is working on a particular poem, his sister's eye is turned in that direction. To be as close as possible to her brother's thoughts, Dorothy thinks about the same subjects, sprinkles her journals and letters with quotes from his poems, and reads his poems alongside Milton. Rather than record her thoughts and interpretations of the poems, typically she decenters the self and allows the quoted voice to replace hers. His lines are substitutes for her own thoughts, so that his voice momentarily overpowers hers. Or she gives him voice, so that their two voices interlock in the same lyric moment as a willed collaboration.

The rock that "looked soft as velvet," with snow that "looked soft as a down cushion" and a flower blooming beside it, "a young Foxglove, like a star in the Centre," is a poetic patch embedded in the beggar story of 22 December 1801 that fully implicates the sorrows of the beggar, Coleridge's real tragedy ("We were very sad about Coleridge"), and Lamb's literary one (*John Woodvill*) in the metaphorical power of nature. The 22 December passage is a prose poem that unlocks one more aspect of collaboration in the journals. Just as this patch occurs while William is deep into "The Pedlar," another quietly vibrant passage occurs (amid several flat entries that record only the greyest aspects of daily life) in the first entry in which Dorothy notes that William is working on "his poem to Coleridge," most probably his epic reworking of the "Two-Part Prelude":

Mary went into the house, and Wm and I went up to Tom Dawson's to speak about his Grandchild, the rain went off and we walked to Rydale. It was very pleasant—Grasmere Lake a beautiful image of stillness, clear as glass, reflecting all things, the wind was up, and the waters sounding. The lake of a rich purple, the fields a soft yellow, the island yellowish-green, the copses red-brown, the mountains purple. The Church and buildings, how quiet they were! . . . Wm wrote part of the poem to Coleridge. [26 December 1801]

Like the prose poem in the beggar entry, these poetic flashes often occur when William is engaged with a difficult or long poem; the flashes are written as if Dorothy is trying her hand at the *sensation* that lies behind creating an arduous work.

D. Wordsworth's desire for twinship, then, apart from any discussion of William's own desire for union, consists of repeated efforts to come as close as possible to the creating poet as William. This is the self that surveys the normative level of the aesthetic terrain, awaiting threshold encounters to the ascendant realm but avoiding possible descent into the mordant levels. The discipline of selving hails that part of Dorothy's imagination in rebellion against maidenhood and the resrictions of aesthetic placement. So seduced, she attempts to think William's thoughts too, busies herself with his obsessions,[7] and imitates what she thinks are his very sensations in order to insert herself into the poetic moment. But this is a dangerous and secondhand process; pursuing such ends opens up the threat detailed by objectification and sublimation; and the result of such imitative efforts can only lead her to devalue her own work, to discount the genius of the journals. Within the worlding of Wordsworthian life, poetry making is the only creative product Dorothy can validate, and she attempts her own verses by imitating William's very method of composition: As she writes to Lady Beaumont, "I have often tried when I have been walking alone (muttering to myself as is my Brother's custom) to express my feeling in verse" (*MY*, 24–25, 20 April 1806). The sense of failure derives from being unable to imitate the end product, despite her endeavors to imitate each step of the process ("but prose and rhyme and blank verse were jumbled together and nothing ever came of it," the letter continues). Her failure to practice art as her brother does leads her to denigrate her own talent and to remark to Lady Beaumont, "looking into my mind I find nothing there, even if I had the gift of language and numbers" (*MY*, 20 April 1806). In Dorothy's case, the desire to be twinned with William's poethood causes her to submerge her self and her achievement in the fullness of *his* mind and his poetry. Such submersion deflects the pain and danger of objectification on William; as Poet, William is authorized to see double and to objectify, which is to make abject. Working collaboratively through her brother allows Dorothy to conceive of what she dare not.

Submersion, however, refigures twinship. It also looks distressingly like sublimation and abjection, an emptying out rather than a gaining of self. In her one thoroughly reworked journal, *Recollections of a Tour in Scotland,* Dorothy locates a communal act of composition which reverses the collaborative process while still leaving poetic authority to William. Revised four times at friends' encouragement and the express interest of Samuel Rogers, who hoped to help publish it, Dorothy's Scottish journal is condemned by de Selincourt in its fourth version for being overwritten, against her normally "unstudied prose." But the original genius that de Selincourt values is also what devalues her writing and makes it count only in its being coined in William's poetry. The Scottish travelogue contrasts with her domestic journals by sustaining a narrative, one that is surprisingly full of poetic patches. By her second version of the journal, Dorothy has incorporated those poems of William's which resulted from the tour, so that the *Recollections* become a collaborative textual effort. Such revision resees the travel narrative as novelistic in the fashion of Ann Radcliffe, through the interlacing of poetry with prose to represent more fully the effusion or melancholy of the narrated moment. Dorothy's emulation of this device, practiced to extreme by several sentimental writers, still in 1820 provides her with a way to instill community in the writing moment while heightening emotion and legitimacy through her brother's recognizable voice.

William, too, used Dorothy's voice, although for different purposes: After a tour of Ullswater, Dorothy wrote a journal of the trip which William edited and appended along with another of her narratives ("Scafell Pike") to his *Guide to the Lakes.* The difference, however, between the two is that of appropriation versus community: Dorothy incorporates William's poems as an additional voice and vantage point into her own, nestling his poems as fully separate entities into her surrounding prose; William recasts, appropriates, suppresses her voice, while at the same time isolating it from the textual purity of his own voice by appending it to his work.

Although the mix of prose and poetry is not a startling achievement, D. Wordsworth's use of the amalgam to produce a formal equivalent to the subjectively experienced landscape reproduces William's voice as one that sings from its nests. She differs in her equipoise of narrative and poetic, female and male voice from the literary examples available to her — specifically the sentimental novels of Charlotte Smith, Mrs. Hervey, and others, who frequently interpolated their own poetry as effusions into the narratives.[8]

In de Selincourt's edition of Dorothy's *Journals,* the *Recollections* is quite long (209 pages) and includes many of William's poems from the tour, as well as several other lines of his and of other poets too. And as is her habit, she attends to distinctive voices, noting unusual ways of speaking and idiomatic phrases; here she is also careful to capture William's speech with strangers. Nestled within these other voices are the three actual travelers: Dorothy, William, and Coleridge. Her inclusion of other voices, with her own voice acting as the communal or choral voice between them, allows Dorothy to experience herself as a nonindividuated self whose identity is a part of the corporate body: Her need for relative self-positionings includes the need to be actually a part of another's self, as well as to take care of that other. D. Wordsworth thus poses her narrative voice as a closeting form that creates space for others to speak in creative discourse or pre-staged converse (that which is not yet romantic "conversation"). Like the pastoral, the closet can come with you; like the nest, it can be found anywhere Nature holds state.

Driven by aesthetic notions of the self, William experiences his originating myth of continuity within division as allowing him access to that absent presence which is the site of poetic vocalization.[9] It also causes him to understand collaboration as the crossing of divides, an uncomfortable straying from the gridded spaces of his chart. Yet his fascination with the sublime means that collaboration *must* become sublimation, whether it is the dis-acknowledgment of Coleridge's influence or the appropriating of Dorothy's perceptions and language use. Just as the artist loses himself in the Divine at the moment of ecstasis, fusing the self with a higher Self, so the collaborative effort of poet and complement becomes the sublimation of the alternate self into the prime agent. The disparity between these two visions of the collaborative effort is that of centrality for the complementary self as a freeing agent despite the accompanying relegation to the margins, and of centrality as the swallowing up of the territorialized complement.

The address-to-women problematizes the sublime for Dorothy Wordsworth because its specific structure enables the male poet to transcend by mediating between the beautiful and a sublime she cannot access. The Maiden facilitates the Poet's transport but is herself constrained when the real-life maiden, Dorothy, tries her hand at poetry. Although D. Wordsworth does explore ascendantly sublime terrain through prose, particularly in her 1820 *Journal of a Tour on the Continent,* she describes the romantic Mont Blanc and its environs as inhabited, and she avoids rhetorical transport by addressing the reader rather than apostrophizing the muse when excited. In poetry, Dorothy Wordsworth avoids the rhetorical sublime altogether, and her revision of the address-to-women form dislocates its sublime character. For instance, her conversation poem "Thoughts on my sick-bed" retreats from odic sublimity, and the earlier "Grasmere — A Fragment" adopts an odic thought pattern at the same time that it carefully differentiates the speaker from "a wanderer's mind." The masculine or transcendent sublime, then, opposes the lyrical, pastoral realm in form and telos; its propensity is to appropriate others and otherness. Its counterpart within the male poet's universe is the feminized sublime or grotesque, a male construct inscribing masculine needs and desires on the female body. Dorothy revises the poet's and the maiden's roles in her poems so as to escape either alternative, yet in her journals she records experiencing abjection. But more often she projects a sublime of her own making that establishes community through a detailism that enters deeply into the everyday. This version of the sublime can recall neither the hyperbolics of Longinus, or the lyrical sublime, nor the absolutes of the Burkean sublime. But it does effectively stave off the feminine sublime, an affective state so horrible precisely because it houses the abjection associated with bodily horror.

⮑ The Feminine Sublime

Burke's notion of the sublime as pleasure derived from pain, Fredric Jameson comments, allows us to see sublimity as

> some fitfully or only intermittently visible force which, enormous and systematized, reduces the individual to helplessness or to that ontological mar-

ginalization . . . a "decentering" where the ego becomes little more than an "effect of structure." But it is no longer necessary to evoke the deity to grasp what such a transindividual system might be. [262]

Jameson's language reveals another aspect of Burke's theory. The sublime replicates for men what religious authority signifies for women; "enormous and systematized," it "reduces the individual to helplessness." This "transindividual system" results in dejection for the male ego and submission, the very opposite of the empowerment sought. But the fear of submersion in unsystematized vastness is always also a statement of seductive longing; submission is paradoxically transport, dejection is transcendence.

Mythically, this much is possible and admissible, but submission as a necessary forfeiture in the metaphysical economy becomes distasteful in the material realm of aestheticized emotion. For submission is the result of subjection, and subjection is characteristic of the feminized sublime. If the maiden is complicit in her own mythicization because she is hailed, addressed, and subjected, then it is important to note who hails her. Evocation of the deity, as a specifically male act, imposes subjection not on those who summon it but on those it calls and names.

For the socially constructed female ego, subordination through hailing can demand a decentering of the ego and a resulting loss of individual selfhood. This is a worse fate than the male ego's, which only suffers humiliation when defeated by a rival: W. Wordsworth's warning to the maiden in the final lines of "To a Young Lady who had been reproached" concerning the possibility of "melancholy slaveship" in old age recognizes the woman's peculiar danger. In the dialectic of male humiliation and female abjection, male dejection and female slaveship, the main construct of a feminine sublime provides the aesthetics of Otherness. The feminized sublime exists in a dark realm of dejection and revulsion at the body, in counterposition to the heavenly realm in which woman is angel.

If male visions of the sublime entail paternal authority, terror, and transcendence, the feminized sublime (as viewed through the male poet's lens) necessarily comprises maternal power, horror, and abjection.[10] Abjection and humiliation are both posited by Longinus and Wordsworth as inappropriate responses to or versions of sublimity. Distinctly echoing Longinian discourse, Wordsworth writes in his essay on the sublime.

> Power awakens the sublime either when it . . . calls upon the mind to grasp at something towards which it can make approaches but which it is incapable of attaining . . . or, 2dly, by producing a humiliation or prostration of the mind before some external agency [in] which it . . . is absorbed in the contemplation of the might in the external power . . . so that, in both cases, the head & the front of the sensation is intense unity. [Owen and Smyser, 2:354]

The difference between a positive, "egotistical," and transcendent response to the sublime and a negative and nonelevating one is that, in the second response, fear for self-preservation outweighs transcendent excitation, so that, "the feeling of the self being still predominant, the condition of the mind would be mean & abject" (354). Abjection here has reference to "a humiliation or prostration of the mind," as in the reverence due a deity by his subject or a mistress by her courtly lover. The master–slave relationship between lovers can invert at any point that the lover perceives his beloved as not angel but whore or demon, not pure but grossly sensual. Sensuality is the physical sense of the female aesthetic, beautiful body as simply body. For the male subject, abjection necessarily reverts to the maternal body and to a disgust at the site of physical generation. And as much as Dorothy Wordsworth interposes alternate forms of the sublime between herself and the alienated self that gazes at its own abjectness, she cannot escape the sensuality of the feminine as long as she consents to remain embedded in William's aesthetic chart.

Bodily abjection, then, is the woman's humiliation and is opposed to the deject's hallucinatory landscape as externalized body. It has to do with subordination and slaveship rather than rivalry and defeat, with sublimation rather than sublimity. Within a masculinist aesthetic terrain, however, abjection itself is a sublime response for it causes as full an introspective exploration of the soul as does transcendent sublimity. The feminized sublime, which finds its full realization in the grotesque, internalizes the power of demonic force expressed as aesthetic, sensory excess.[11] The lyric is a sacred mode and strives for the masculinist, egotistical sublime rather than the feminized; such sacredness is that of the virgin angel (Dante's Beatrice) and not the sublime's demon — which may not be Milton's Lucifer, after all, but Homer's Circe, Milton's Sin. Sandra Gilbert and Susan

Gubar discuss Mary Shelley's dread of the masculinist assumptions behind a feminized sublime in a chapter of *Madwoman in the Attic* entitled "Horror's Twin: Mary Shelley's Monstrous Eve" (213–47) and read *Frankenstein* through the metaphor of childbirth, the monstrous operation of maternal power. For Kristeva, childbirth is perceived by male eyes to be "the dark portals of life, that is, the emanation of the interiorized daemon" (*Powers of Horror*, 160). The chora, too, is a portal or threshold space, one that gives rise to poetic language. And while "dark portals of life" offer a way out of engulfment, an e-merging, they also represent the interiorizing process of the feminized sublime, the demonization of the soul. Threshold operates dynamically, and the terror is that one can go either way. Threshold, too, as the liminal provides access to the transcendent sublime, a barrier to traverse, a boundary to transgress.

The masculinist or transcendent sublime offers inner knowledge through escape from the self, transport from the body. Introspection comes by way of ecstasis. In the greater romantic lyric, as M. H. Abrams characterizes it, the poet-speaker also reaches out to the liminal but is prevented from the move into the sublime by a return to the self. The end result of this circuitous (rather than ascending) movement is questioning, doubt, and prayer rather than epic certitude. Both the conversation poem and the address-to-women connect William's Wordsworthian lyric project to a feminized sublime through sequestering the masculinist sublime in its own quadrant. Necessary to this bodily relation, however, is the absence of a true, rather than represented or silenced, female subjectivity. Dorothy Wordsworth's attempt to supply this last deficit through her own addresses to women comes very near to the space of female pain reproduced in Margaret's tale in *The Excursion*. The epic as an expression of the transcendent sublime exploits such pain because the male project defines female experience as narrative matter and as alterity. The Wanderer must distance himself from Margaret's death because the aesthetic effect of her story outweighs what she herself felt; it is an effect, however, which depends heavily on Margaret's silence, or on the silencing of Margaret. The Poet's initial lyric response is to accept the cheerfulness of the tale-teller, and "that simple tale / Passed from my mind like a forgotten sound" (*Excursion* I). The barrenness and hurt of the woman's story, however, reveal its sublime nature, and the Poet-auditor resists what he hears, overturning the Wanderer's authoritative dismissal of a tale that threatens to involve him in its pain and disrupt "the calm of nature." The auditor resists by embracing the tale's sublimity:

> In my own despite,
> I thought of that poor Woman as of one
> Whom I had known and loved . . . I rose.

His rise is both literal and figural, for his oedipal uprising repeats the emotional experience of sublime accession. The relation between his rise / sublimity and the woman's death/sublimation finds its link not only in her silence but in her repression or disappearance. The story of epic sublimation returns us, with Margaret's abject poverty, to abjection and the question of self-knowledge built on the ground of female silence. But when the woman is a voiced subject, not a character but a living subject-on-trial, abjection produces self-knowledge of a different sort.

If transcendence is the leap up, abjection as the feminized sublime involves a turning inward to close introspection. This is not Burke's self-critical examination, not a moral or behavioral testing. It is instead always structured by another's perception, the eyes following what another has disgustedly seen, and it is localized by that male gaze. The disgust Kristeva finds at the site of the mother's body by the male viewer ("those who fear decay and death at the touch of feminine" [*Powers of Horror*, 159]) is directly linked with the visible and the immanent, thus turning the maternal body into maternal earth, a bodyscape. This scape occupies the space of the female grotesque, a counterpart aesthetic to the picturesque. As the picturesque and masculine sublime are philosophically and aesthetically linked, so too are the negative quadrants of the aesthetic map. And where the feminine grounds the picturesque landscape, with its sublimation producing the site of the sublime, the female abject and grotesque cannot exist without the defining gesture of the male viewer. Female ugliness, Milton's Sin, reveals horror not as awe of a supreme power but as the horrible, the true "powers of horror." Self-knowledge thus achieved is not Truth but resignation and surrender to a man-made map of female being.

Within such a charting of how the female should be, the question of subjectivity and who feels what becomes paramount to the representation of such experience. At the same time, sexuality as an analogue to and insight into aesthetic experience becomes gendered and privileged. Ex-stasis characterizes masculine sexual climax, a transcendence of body that paradoxically occurs during the interpenetration and fusion of two bodies. The spiritualization of bodily drives allows for the transference of immer-sion ecstasy from bodily consciousness to sheer consciousness, that is, to the aestheticized self. Sexual intercourse allegorizes mystical experience, which is itself transferred onto the sublime landscape and subsequently reexperienced as a solitary venture. Female sexuality contains no such code of referents. Ecstasy as a sublime gusto is a transcendent experience for men and a grounding one for women. Gusto or exuberance itself is dis-turbing when exhibited by women, for it signals a self-sufficient disposi-tion that is at once "wild" and gypsyish and in control of the outer scene as a stage-managed aesthetic. Thus, if knowledge on the master's or dic-tator's side desupposes knowledge on the slave's side, then abject self-knowledge is nonknowledge. Even if abjection is a feminized sublime expressed through demonic sensuality, there is still no transcendent self-knowledge, for as one master puts it, "what is her *jouissance* from? it is clear that the essential testimony of the mystics is that they are experiencing it but know nothing about it."[12] The same can be said of Margaret's pain.

Dorothy Wordsworth, however, clearly identifies as a subject-on-trial. The fall into the feminized sublime or the grotesque is most seductive when she is outside the collaborative project, empty of William's presence and therefore deprived of twinship. Abjection requires silence even of the experiencing subject; to sustain voice, Dorothy must replace the feminine sublime with her picturesque aesthetic by writing herself into detail. She thus keeps the gaze off herself and on the scape; in doing so, she sacrifices beauty for the Beautiful as everyday, or the mundane.[13] The mundane neutralizes aesthetic experience: Even as the scape is no longer pleasur-able, it is also not painful or inward-turning.

This is not to say that D. Wordsworth does not consider herself capable of aesthetic heights — the hallmark of the romantic writer and thinker. In several passages of her *Journal of a Tour on the Continent* (1820), her encounter with a mountain other than the masculinist symbol of Mont Blanc shows her finding alternative visions of the transcendent terrain.

One month prior to the 1820 visit to Mont Blanc, the Wordsworths and their friends toured a different grouping of alpine mountains. Two journal entries in particular dwell on a mountain that is conceptually more accessible because identified with the maiden figure: "the Jung-frau (the Virgin) burst upon our view . . . the Maiden Mountain" (*Journals,* 2:110). Dorothy's account of the Jungfrau contrasts with the Mont Blanc passage most significantly in tone: Phrases such as "Our mirth," "awe struck yet delighted," "we were as gay as larks" sustain a mood that undercuts the expectation of high seriousness. Her mirth is a deflation of romantic Joy, domesticated and familiarizing the isolated self-absorption necessary to joy. The entries' overarching effect is both to undercut William's *Prelude* Mont Blanc and to anticipate Dorothy's own experience of Mont Blanc the next month. The result is an experiment in a sublimed mundane intermixed with elements of the picturesque and a joy that balances and subdues the debilitating abjection of the feminine sublime. Mirth transmutes dejection into a tolerable melancholy Dorothy defines as "connected with social life."

The Jungfrau's maidenly identity allows D. Wordsworth to rewrite both the masculine mountain and the masculine sublime, but like William's figuration of the maiden, Dorothy's Jungfrau is enclosed, textually framed by the sublime. Her first brief description of the mountain pays homage to traditional notions of the sublime while her parting gesture returns to this homage:

> [T]he Jung-frau (the Virgin) burst upon our view, dazzling in brightness, which seemed rather heightened than diminished by a mantle of white clouds, floating over the bosom of the mountain. The effect was indescribable. We had before seen the snow of the Alps at a distance, propped, as I may say, against the sky, or blending with, and often indistinguishable from it. [*Journals,* 2:110]

> The gloomy grandeur of this spectacle harmonised with the melancholy of the vale; yet it was *heavenly* glory that hung over those cold mountains. [123]

These two complex gestures accord with W. Wordsworth's aesthetics, yet they frame six pages of description that continually undercut the masculine sublime (110, 119–23). The "indescribable" effect is rejected for a thoroughly describable landscape which reveals itself repeatedly as an antidote to the sublime. The alp blends with the sky and snow as D. Wordsworth redefines the landscape as picturesque and domestic both, providing a collective of natural elements that clothe and prop the Maiden mountain, caring for and enclosing her. In treating another traditionally sublime phenomenon, D. Wordsworth unveils sublime mystery:

> [S]uddenly we heard a tremendous noise — loud like thunder; and all stood still. It was the most awful sound which had ever struck upon our ears. . . . We could not *believe* that such mighty tumult had proceeded from a little rill . . . and I suspect we were loth to have the mystery explained. [120–21]

The "I suspect" intrudes everyday common sense into the "tumult," while the worn cliché of thunder defigures what William might have made of the scene if he were recording. Mixing rhetorics and vocabularies in general lawlessness, Dorothy discomposes sublime terrain, placing the avalanche in proper proportion. The picturesque demands that no single element overwhelm the others, and she carries this over from stationary objects to motion itself. D. Wordsworth next juxtaposes a domesticizing description of a rude cottage nestled in the mountainside with a water source she refers to as "the *household* spring (so let me call it)." Slippages from the literal, like the earlier Grasmere bower and Windsor fairy coach, are literally "flights of fancy," ascents to the realm of Fancy where William locates her and she feels at home. Within this domesticating act further avalanches lose any transcendent quality and become an interesting exercise in language play:

> Again we heard the thunder of avalanches, and saw them bursting out, fresh foaming springs. The sound is loud as thunder; but more metallic and musical. It also may be likened to the rattling of innumerable chariots passing over rocky places. [121]

D. Wordsworth interweaves the sublime ascent and subsequent deflations of it with her own maidenly concerns, as she attends to detailing the alp's pastoral and sublime aspects. Also on record are a full account of meals, notations on daily mountain life, and a portrayal of her own family as a group.

But there is also a wish to relive the trip W. Wordsworth and Robert Jones took all those years before; and she climbs the Jungfrau with Mary Wordsworth as a substitute venture ("Mary and I resolved to set out together"). But whereas ascent should correlate with solitude and transport, Dorothy preserves the "we" which is Mary, herself, and their own guide and then transforms her group in telling of how they wait for the rest of the party to join them. The women's ascent occurs in a bright sunlight that unmasks all mystery and opposes the disappointments of William's soulless image; even the group that joins them is "a gallant cavalcade!" as Dorothy jokes to relieve the somberness of poetic ascent. In addition to mirth, Dorothy uses the picturesque mode to balance the effects of a sublime landscape: "As I have said when I first saw this vale from a point sufficiently near to distinguish the objects . . ." Vantage points become keys to unlocking the sublime, pointing out its deceptive character as well as noting that the scene is, in fact, a mix of sublime elements with the picturesque, the pastoral, the domestic. The perspective gained from a station reveals the disorienting space of the sublime as actually and physically realizable and recognizes the deception inherent in sublime vastness: "It is indeed astonishing how *far* one must travel in the Alps to reach an object that has appeared close at hand" (122).

As the address-to-women only allows a partial transcendence to William's maiden figure, so Dorothy's ascent ends halfway up the mountain. What interests her instead is the descent into inhabited domain: "*We* had not further ascent. The Jung-frau Hollow seemed to have been a passage to a *peopled* region" (emphases are DW's). The descent is more arduous than the climb has been, and in a reversal of sublime expectations the group has to pass through a scene of death, "this ghastly forest," before reaching the human community: "We descend to a blasted pine-forest . . . sometimes the whole form of the tree a skeleton." D. Wordsworth's aversion to the sublime and the subsequent encounter with death reverses her earlier mirth to a seriousness recalling romantic dejection. The "melancholy vale" and the "fears . . . from the tremendous powers of nature" stem from the shock of the skeleton trees and their grove of death. Reversing the sublime allows Dorothy to encounter the dark side of the address-to-women's sacred grove and the danger the Maiden faces when the Poet leads her there. "Passing the last stragglers of this ghastly forest," however, "we come to green-headed living trees . . . and here the children brought us their offerings": Passing through death leads to life, rebirth in the next generation, and reunion with the human community.

The descent by a "steep stony track" remains difficult, and the "descent became so precipitous that all were obliged to walk." Although the climb down continues the journey into dejection, it is "a sense of melancholy . . . no desolation, or dreariness . . . but connected with social life in loneliness" (123). Significantly, D. Wordsworth chooses to characterize this part of the descent with apocalyptic imagery: "The [cold] blast seemed as if its birth-place was in the icy cavern, and thence issuing, it would be fed with indestructible power." The sun no longer illuminates the scene, and "the impressions were very melancholy." However, throughout her descent into a revised sublime, D. Wordsworth interjects maidenly associations which buffer her from extreme despair. These gestures are intriguing because they reserve the function of William's maiden, who herself protects the Poet from the dark sublime.

Dorothy Wordsworth's maidenly mixture of pastoral and transcendent description is apparent in this passage:

> The Vale of Grindelwald first opens on the view in [the] form of a large deep basin, at the upper side of which a Glacier appears to be lying upon a gentle declivity at the base of a mountain. . . . The first notice we had of our actual approach to Grindelwald (long seen as I have described) was a flower-garden beside a large comfortable wooden house, upon a slope at a little distance from the road. A girl came tripping over the grass with a dish of starveling cherries and bunch of flowers in one hand, and in the other a wooden bowl of handsome fir apples. [122–23]

The cottage, the flower garden with its feminine associations, and the maiden bearing fruit are a welcome relief. The maid's gifts are emblematic of her function: fruit to nourish and give life and flowers to redeem the stony barrenness. But Dorothy's mention of the cottage precedes the maid's appearance, illustrating that her connection to domesticity and fam-

ily nurture outweighs the girl's other significance. The maiden is not forgotten after this incident and reappears by association after more descent:

> Soon the vale lay before us with its two glaciers, and, as it might seem, its
> *thousand* cabins sown upon the steeps. The descent became so precipitous
> that all were obliged to walk: deep we go into the broad cradle valley; every
> cottage we passed had its small garden, and cherry-trees sprinkled with
> leaves, bearing half-grown, half-ripe fruit. [123; emphasis is DW's]

The flower-cottages, particularly as they are cradled by the valley, suggest
a fertility and family life among the glaciers which make bearable the
remaining climb down. The Jungfrau passage ends similarly, with the
"*heavenly* glory that hung over those cold mountains," immediately superseded by "[w]e found the Inn comfortable."

Dorothy Wordsworth's revision of the masculine sublime does not follow the maidenly mediation William had assigned to her function. In the
passage between Dorothy's first brief view of the Jungfrau and the lengthier entry is an interlude in which William is absent and cannot address the
maiden. "[H]aving given up all hope of being hailed by Wm. and M.,"
Dorothy's own seriousness is lightened by "minstrel peasants" who exchange their plaintive songs for "bursts of merriment" (155). Her subsequent happiness jars with her textual moves in this passage; William's
absence is replaced with one of his poems, which she cites in whole and
nestles within her own prose. With a gesture unusual for her, Dorothy
comments on the poem, arranging the literal scene not only spatially but
also by feminizing the minstrels so that they are now singing maidens.

William's absence in this instance from Dorothy's experience reorgan-
izes the courtly poet formulation; now it is the poet who is not present, and
the woman sings his song by including it in her story. Though she waits for
him to do so, he does not hail her and so does not implicate her in his text;
instead, she embraces poetry on her own terms through a double-voiced
inclusion. The song itself is about maidens singing, and the woman writer
refers to these singers as troubadour minstrels. In his song, the poet has imposed transcendence on the maidens; angelic, they are "Pupils of Heaven,"
dispensing the "gracious aid" of their heavenly inspiration with "influence
display'd." Like the maiden figure of the address-to-women, these singers

commune with divine powers in order to aid the poet who stands away and observes. Yet in her story the woman stresses that the poet has "transported" the maidens and describes the minstrels as "singing *plaintive* ditties . . . but with bursts of merriment they rowed lustily away."

The difference between poetry and prose that remains true to the scene is that poetry engages a more powerful, transformative rhetoric, as well as a more compelling ideology. Textually, even within the lyric, it inscribes the sublime in a more threatening and disabling fashion for the woman writer. William's maiden transcends to commune with Nature and to fuse with her by becoming thinglike. Dorothy's vision averts such transport because it is not true, and her aesthetics of the detailed everyday demands truth as it already is in nature or in the experience. The same demand for accuracy leads her to include references to her illness in her poems, or to sign a poem addressed to a young woman. "D. Wordsworth Old Poetess, October 7th 1836." Similarly, one poem is entitled "Lines written (rather than *begun*) on the morning of Sunday April 6th, the third approach of Spring-time since my illness began. It was a morning of surpassing beauty" (emphasis is DW's). The exactitude of the title imposes truth on poetry: Even the romantic myth of spontaneous composition is belied with "written (rather than *begun*)."

W. Wordsworth feels himself inspired through the semiotic energies evoked by the maiden's presence in his pastoralized scapes and lyric forms. His poethood depends on his hail of the maiden whose evocation allows him to vanquish doubt. His sister feels the rhythms of poetic language but neither hails nor subjects others. William sees the beautiful as lulling him to a sleeplike meditation where he need not observe nature and can instead turn to poetic vision. It cannot be sloughed off, however, and its pastoral valleys must be traversed before achieving the "heaven-imparted truth" of the sublime Alps (1850 *Prelude* VI). Dorothy finds truth in nature and not the deceptive sublime; poetic vision cannot replace accuracy of active seeing, and imagination works to formulate comforting memories rather than to create new realms. More than the search for a poetics of accuracy and regard, D. Wordsworth values dialogue and an interactive economy. Collaboration, which cannot take place in the sublime even between brother poets, leads Dorothy to value the poetic realm, which does partake of community and shared voices.

It is unsurprising that D. Wordsworth's body of extant poems evades the sublime and explores instead the pastoral order. To embrace the Fancy is to hold onto the poetic voice achieved through collaborative writing with William and through the intercourse of the address-to-women form she carefully explores in her own poetry. She is thus able to avoid both the feminine sublime and the male sublimation of female figures like Margaret. Sublimation of the intercourse (rather than the mere desire for it) becomes in her poetry an insertion of self in other and other in self. Her revision of William's lyric and epic enterprise into a protection *against* transcendence allows her to rewrite the Eden myth as home economics — not an exchange of voices but the production of a collective good.

D. Wordsworth's address to Julia, "Irregular Verses," further revises Eden by recounting her adolescent utopian dream where she and Jane "wish[ed] for aught beyond the dell" and "still repaid / Frank confidence with unshaken truth." A community of women deposes the problem of sexual connivance in Coleridge's cot ("Eolian Harp"), and of despair and death in Margaret's ("The Ruined Cottage"), by ridding the dell of sublimating agents. The dell is a "faery ground," and "A belt of hills must wrap it round, / Not stern or mountainous, or bare." Only pastoral elements will encompass the "verdant dell," and it will not be adorned even by the women with "works of Art," for it remains (figuratively and literally) in the Fancy. "Jingling rhyme" must not turn the dell to account, for its economy is one of frankness and truth, given and repaid like the mosses and plants Dorothy culled from nature for Dove Cottage's bower. Dorothy's domestic negotiation replaces William's isolating and sublimating politics, and she will not let poetic production turn "guileless dreams" into inner vision or the silencing of dialogue. However, certain events do threaten that production.

⁐ Thresholds as Commonplace

If in 1802 Dove Cottage received a new mistress, which rendered problematic the Wordsworthian collaboration, in the 1830s another woman besides Mary threatens to displace Dorothy Wordsworth from the pastoral landscape. As her namesake Dora becomes William's new travel companion (to the Scottish Highlands to see Walter Scott, to Cambridge, and to the Rhineland with Coleridge), Dorothy stays behind with Sara or keeps house for her nephew. And throughout this period she keeps a book that re-creates the familial community of those gone. In an unpublished manuscript notebook (DCMS 120), Dorothy played with poethood, collaboration, death, fantastically extended life, fame, maps and graphs and plans. This is the notebook in which Susan Levin discovered most of D. Wordsworth's extant poems, but true to Wordsworthian poetic production this was a commonplace book, open to the family to read and write in collaborative as a circle of friends.

Yet this notebook does have two sides to it, a public and a private; in other words, it is its own closet and its own outing. It presents a kind of visual textuality, of having a quality of being visually crafted to represent life in the Wordsworthian drama. And the community it locates is described within a reversion of William's early schema, one that places the affect of sympathy and the structure of community within all quadrants of the aesthetic chart. But it also provides, perhaps for the first time, an alternative to the safety of detailism and melancholy as domesticated sublimes. For Dorothy finds in this notebook a way to escape the delineations of William's grid lines. What she discovers — a sublime all her own — allows her to give over categories of being to the notebook while she takes the enabling of outage and selving to heart or to mind; that is, role playing for her own determination finally overcomes playing roles in William's scheme. She thus discovers a new form of sublimity to inhabit, one which is buried within William's schema but remains untouched by him — the transport across boundaries and over thresholds, rather than the move untenably upward. It is illness, but one that allows new roles to be put on and does not concede to bodily abjection of the feminine sublime.

It is important to realize that although Dorothy's poetry meanders across notebooks, scrawled hatchwise against a journal page or over an earlier fair copy of another poem, her prose is carefully organized into notebooks: journals, travel journals, reading notebooks, commonplace books. Although the commonplace book is the most apt to be used for incidentals — including domestic records — Dorothy's notebooks have a clear purpose.[14]

By placing categories on the notebook, D. Wordsworth produces a domesticated version of William's schematized verses, and the book collects and pursues specific classes of things: death, long life, illness, pastoral poems. Commonplace books historically sorted commonplaces or quoted passages under general headings. Dorothy's arrangement is more haphazard than William's careful organization of his works, but her notebook does demonstrate clear interest in the same topics under which William has organized his poems in his collected works. And just as William collects verses by family members and publishes them under the headings for his own poems, Dorothy's notebook contains poems by different friends and family members and copied by various hands.

The commonplace format under D. Wordsworth's management avoids the kind of swallowing that verses by family members undergo in William's mapping arrangement. Dorothy could have chosen to follow the more usual commonplace arrangement in which verses and epigraphs by famous writers are carefully copied into a notebook kept by one person only. This style swallows the words of others in the same manner that William's collected works do, and Dorothy had experienced the effect of such swallowing and placing. One friend, Henry Hutchinson or "the Ancient Mariner," finds his way into both William's and Dorothy's books. In a note to a verse by Henry which he included apparently without Henry's knowledge, William confides that the lyric "falls easily into its place" in the "Itinerary Poems of 1833": "I hope, as it falls so easily into its place, that both the writer and the reader will excuse its appearance here." Dorothy's book places the poem of the brother of her sister-in-law in a different way: Henry's poem in his hand is simply pasted into the book on the page next to a newspaper clipping containing a poem that celebrates the recovery from illness of Dorothy's younger brother, "the Rev. Dr. Wordsworth, Master of Trinity College." Henry, the "Ancient Mariner," replaces not Coleridge but another brother who was not recovered, the dead sailor John Wordsworth. Putting both "brothers" next to each other in a metonymy that we have seen before in Dorothy's spatial placement gives Christopher back his brother.

A more substantial difference between brother's and sister's representative mapping strategies is that, whereas William organizes and places verses to flesh out the sectors and quadrants on his map in an increasingly detailed vision dating back to 1798, the older D. Wordsworth gives over trying to make her place in that map and begins to cross boundaries and take uncharted imaginative trips. The "Commonplace Book" and her reading notebooks of this period are filled with extracts from travelogues to Africa and China, making her an armchair traveler. One entry, for instance, is entitled "Route Copied from Mrs. Elwood's overland Journey to India from Geneva to Paris (1830), noting the towns and postilion charges."[15] Indeed, the notebook itself is the result of travel, probably bought in Paris during the 1820 trip to the continent.

Travel of a different kind occurs in the illness of her late years, when barely legible pencil scrawls repeat lines from her own poems on various pages, sometimes writing over other writing. The slide into madness is a different kind of uncharted travel into regions of the mind William had not theorized. The ill body was itself so little charted that Dorothy's disease was a transgression of proper placement that wrote itself corporeally on her. This literalization of William's sublimating map of Mother Earth's body, or of the abjection of the feminine sublime, finds little voice in the notebook, and unlike her earlier years she now does not give in to such a self-perception. Instead, her explorations have an excitement similar to the sublime quest of William's youthful trips to the continent, looking for something analogous to those few difficult-to-locate passes through alpine mountains. If the threshold in the domestic grave is under the auspices of younger maidens — poets' daughters rather than their sisters — then the unfamiliar thresholds of unmapped reaches are finally approachable if only in imagination. And both in illness and in health, D. Wordsworth began exploring the dimensions of the literary page as uncharted territory too. Indeed, the book itself becomes an exploration in renegotiating charts, since it is started from both ends (one side inverted) to produce two sides but one book, a transgression of normal editorial order.

Just inside the notebook cover, the front verso endpage is covered with bits of verses in Dorothy's hand but from different periods. Centered on the page is a newspaper etching of "The Pitt Press," with no other printed or handwritten legend. Below that is pasted a notion for "The Life and Travels of the Apostle Paul illustrated by a Comprehensive Map," which "promises by its 'pleasing narrative' that [the reader's] feelings [of pleasure and instruction] must be increased tenfold." Paul, the patron of travelers, begins the journey taken in this book.[16] Several verses are arranged around the press and notice, and they concern the heart, the wind, village minstrelsy, and the affections, all of which are strong themes in D. Wordsworth's poetry.

The opposite inside cover, which initiates the inverted half of the book, contains two verses and a newspaper clipping on "The Last Moments of Lord Sydenham" affixed with candlewax, some of which covers penciled words. The most legible lines of the first verse are "Small service is here, service while it lasts / Of Friends however humble I thank [w]" (last word made illegible by an overlying line). None of the other lines is completely legible, but the words that recur are typical of D. Wordsworth's poetic lexicon: friendship, bird, sunshine, love, quiet, daily, dewdrop, mirth, like. Together these endpapers provide a self-articulating discourse of life and death, village song and service, which frames and comments on the interior entries.

Throughout the notebook, entries are grouped by theme or by some connective thread. For instance, collected on one page are the following entries: "Epitaph on Lord Rolle," possibly in Sara Coleridge's hand; "Epitaph in a country Churchyard in Devon" and "Copied from Melrose Churchyard—no name no date," both in Dorothy Wordsworth's hand; a poem written by Mary Barker in 1816, "On the Birth of Mr. Littleton's eldest child—a Son." Life and death, epitaphs, and no name or date.

The book begins with a poem dated "26 June 1830 Sunday Evening Dictated by William Wordsworth to DWordsworth Senr" ("In this fair Vale hath many a tree") [fig. 1]. The next page contains a copy of "Dr. Schoeffer's Prescriptions for & experience in the cure of the cholera morbus—Vienna," and above this title is written "N.B. For Jew's prescription—see the other end of Book—printed paper," a reference to the extract from "An Effectual Cure for the Cholera" at the opposite end. "Copy of Mr. Carr's Statement for Dr. W. Phillip, 28 July 1824—the account of an illness with particular attention to the condition of the tongue" follows and may attest to the Wordsworths' ongoing interest in the new developments in medical knowledge as well as to the state of their own health. But the focus on definable symptoms may also refer to the copier's illness, which she is probably researching on her own. In addition, her interest in fatal illness is strongly answered by the multiple entries on four other pages of tombstone epitaphs and obituary notices for extraordinarily long-lived people. One of these entries is D. Wordsworth's reading notes from *Taylor's Annals* on a sixteenth-century man who lived 209 years, but her handwriting indicates she is quite ill; next to it in an equally ill hand are two verses from "Loving and Liking," her pedagogic poem on appropriate emotional relations with nature. The strategy she creates by juxtaposing a refrain that gives her life philosophy to her interest in the mysteries of death is one she repeats with the physicians' statements. Following those notes is the single couplet: "By liking a friendship may grow out of strife; / But love is the sunshine & starlight of life," written in the same hand and sepia ink as the copied accounts of cholera.

Dorothy Wordsworth's interest in mortality is not idiosyncratic: William's collected poems have by this time long contained a section entitled "Epitaphs and Elegiac Poems," as well as the 1810 "Essay upon Epitaphs" written for Coleridge's significantly named *The Friend,* and the 1814 and 1815 essays. And while William is more concerned with the "Monument" itself, and its "awful language," he asserts in the first essay that "Man could never have had awakened in him the desire to live in the remembrance of his fellows: mere love, or the yearning of kind towards kind, could not have produced it" without the addition of Reason, a sense of immortality, and the development of social feelings (Hutchinson and de Selincourt, 728). Certainly, Dorothy's "Loving & Liking" is a detailed illustration of this assertion of life over death. But then William's discussion of the church and graveyard as belonging at the very center of the human community unveils the necessary connection between the entries on life and death in the commonplace book. Copying epitaphs and obituaries of strangers and friends pulls them into the human community of the notebook and cross-pollinates them with the community's law: friendship and love.

Oddly, a page near the beginning of the notebook is entitled "Copy of a poem written by William Wordsworth as a school exercise. He was then fourteen years old." William's poems are typically copied into this notebook to aid his drafting process (as in Fig. 2, a version of "Chatsworth"), but here the more usual commonplace function of keeping what is precious comes to bear. It takes four pages to complete the transcription, which in its very act of republishing is a commemoration to earlier days when anything was possible. William's "Poems Referring to the Period

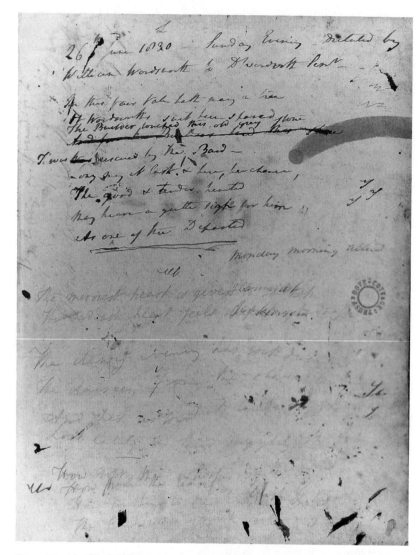

Fig. 1. Dorothy Wordsworth, "Commonplace Book," p. 89ᵛ, DCMS 120, Wordsworth Trust. Because the archival pagination for this manuscript is from back to front, this "first page" is numbered as the final page.

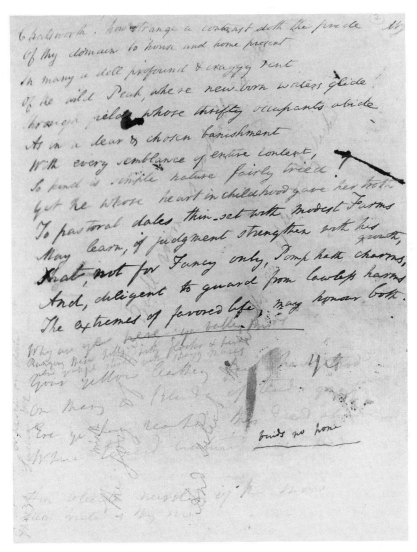

Fig. 2. Dorothy Wordsworth, "Commonplace Book," p. 2ʳ, DCMS 120, Wordsworth Trust

of Childhood" often recall earlier moments or achievements in order to make something of them in adult thought, but several of Dorothy's own poems which also recall earlier moments do so in order to compare how the youthful dream is unfulfillable. Here, however, the poem seems without commentary, a monument to William's youthful potential.

Soon after come notes for a production of William's years of fame, written for the man who helped make that fame possible: "For a Monument to be placed on the grounds of Coleorton Hall Leicestershire to the Memory of the late Sir George Howland Beaumont." On the following page Dorothy has written "Sir G.B. ordered that no Inscription but the common one of Name, age, time of decease, &c — should be placed over his tomb; but desired that the following words might be inscribed on his coffin 'Enter not into judgement with thy / Servant, O Lord!' " Evidently, brother and sister did not agree as to how Beaumont's wishes should be followed, or, it may be that simply a reminder of his wishes was felt necessary.

Nearby are copied extracts from the *Commonplace Book of Isabella Countess of Glencairn.* Under the last few lines is the note, "From the mouth of the Countess of Glencairn — written down by Miss Barker (Mrs. Slade Smith) & copied from her Scrap Book." This is followed by a three-page biographical sketch of Lord Erskine, also copied from Miss Barker's scrapbook and ending in two short anecdotes about impoverished but silly Frenchmen. All of these entries explore the melancholy and pleasure in traveling that part of the continent that Dorothy had seen, but all through the eyes of her inexhaustible and adventure-loving friend.[17] The commonplace book of the exiled Countess of Glencairn is doubly intriguing then, both for the space allotted for its transcription and for the exotic melancholy of an unhappy and unfortuned woman. This is the dejected princess figure who so claimed Dorothy's youthful imagination in *Clarissa;* most delightful is the notion that her remembrance constitutes a commonplace book, an analogue to the very book Dorothy copies her into. If the anecdotal Frenchmen are common in their silly poverty, Isabella is analogous in her commonplace; that is, she and Dorothy can speak the same tongue, at least in a fanciful register.

Not surprisingly, then, the next group contains poems, most of them

Dorothy's own. It begins with a transition poem by Mary Barker, a three-page poem on the birth of Mr. Littleton's son, "January 6th, 1816 — copied by DW." Next to this is a second copy of William's poem copied in the first page of the book. After this comes the lengthy section of Dorothy's own poems, some of them much reworked right on the page.

"Blair's Grave," a poem by [Thomas?] Campbell written apparently from memory or recitation, is followed by several sonnets by Henry Hutchinson. Another poem signed "Rydal Mount JH June 21st 1832" bemoans the speaker's absence at the death of the addressee, who died on 2 May. In addition, two poems have been copied from Christopher Cookson's "Forget Me Not" and are followed by a biographical notice (Cookson was a cousin to the Wordsworths). Curiously, part of this group is "Imitation of Horace, book 2nd. . . . By Warren Keslings made in 1783 during his voyage from India, & addressed to his fellow-passenger John Shaw, now Lord Feignmouth." This is followed by a pasted-in page entitled "Coniston Lake: Sonnet Dedicated to Miss Wordsworth" and signed "the Ancient Mariner." Following that is an obituary of a local couple, more verses signed by the Ancient Mariner, and a sonnet clipped from the paper, "On hearing of the recovery of the Rev. Dr. Wordsworth." This group weaves together family and friends living and dead, in Dorothy's and in their hands, copied in and pasted in. It is what we might expect of Dorothy Wordsworth, given her *Grasmere Journals* and her letters.

All of these organizational clusters look like the raw material for a domesticated, even parlor edition of William's schemata. The uncharted passage I suggest D. Wordsworth makes in this book is best exemplified in the endpages, which are overwritten along all the margins (as in the front) or covered over with pasted-on news clippings of death (as in the back), all illegible or incomprehensible from any head-on, charting perspective. However, one particular group of entries begins the move into uncharted terrain by suggesting that boundary transgression can occur on the literary page. Near the inverted end of the book is a variant of William's sonnet "Chatsworth! how strange a contrast doth the pride / Of thy domain to house and home present." The fair copy of "Chatsworth!" is in ink; however, in pencil and overlapping its last two lines and continuing down is another poem I have not been able to attribute but which is clearly a draft:

Why are ye here; ye valley Birds
Ranging these hills with flocks & herds
And youthful steeds with shagy (*sic*) manes
Your yellow leathery feet have trod

On many a Blade of tender grass
Ere ye have reached this Dread abode
Where timid creature ["never" crossed out in ink and replaced by "finds no
home"]
Then delicate nursling of the snow
Stern winter is thy [home?]

This page, then, contains two poems, one of a stately human home and
one of the natural but dread abode in the hills. Written diagonally across
both poems on the page is a large, loose scrawl in pencil of a couplet,
which reads, "The joy of the Ball room is instantly checked / And silent
the walls so splendidly decked." What the orthographic cross-hatching
suggests is that, whatever has silenced the gaiety and splendid walls of a
manor like Chatsworth, the manor itself represents that to which Dorothy
is marginal. And, indeed, Chatsworth is a mansion William visited alone
on his way to join Mary and Dora for a trip to London while Dorothy and
Sara, the two sisters at the heart of the family, were left in charge of the
Wordsworth house. Thus centered as mistress of the house, the sister is
ironically also edged out, defamiliarized, unseated.

For Dorothy, there is no voice at the center; only the conversant margin
yields the sister's tale. And so the last stanza of a variant verse from "Loving & Liking" spills onto this scene from the facing page. This marginal
verse also concerns a human home in which a bird transgresses the house's
boundary and creates a unity between the natural and the domestic within
the parameters of affection, a domestic sublime:

And when driven in by nipping air
From leafless woods & pastures bare
Bold Robin shews his starlit breast
No beggar but a parlour guest
Withal a prime ventriloquist

Who seen by glimpses now — now missed
Puzzles the listener with a doubt
Of the soft voice he throws about
Coming from within doors or without

Whether the Bird flits here or there
O'er table bed or perch on chair
Though Susan &c.

Levin does not note this variation for "Loving & Liking," and it is perhaps more important as a fragment here than as yet another version for a poem written out elsewhere. Here the fragment is centered on this double spread and yet occupies the space between the visually more important texts: the fair-copy poems, the newspaper clippings, or even the pasted-in "Loving and Liking." Isabella Fenwick dates "Loving & Liking" as finished in 1832 (noted in Levin, *Dorothy Wordsworth*, 213); but the placement of this fragment here is important because William's very similar poems, "The Redbreast (Suggested in a Westmoreland Cottage)," which he writes to amuse his ill sister, was written in 1834 but not entered in the "Commonplace Book":

Driven in by Autumn's sharpening air
From half-stripped woods and pastures bare,
Brisk Robin seeks a kindlier home;
Not like a beggar he is come,
But enters as a looked-for guest,
Confiding in his ruddy breast
As if it were a natural shield
Charged with a blazon on the field,
Due to that good and pious deed
Of which we in the Ballad read.
But pensive fancies putting by,
And, caught by glimpses now — now missed
Puzzles the listener with a doubt
If the soft voice he throws about
Comes from within doors or without!

Was ever such a sweet confusion,
Sustained by delicate illusion?

The final "Loving & Liking" verse, on the other hand, retains none of
what William borrowed:

And when the Bird with scarlet breast
Hops round the carpet, a bold guest
Though Susan make an angry stir
To scare him as a trespasser
Do you step forth and take his part
Encouraged by a loving heart.

The significance of these two transfigurings of the centered yet marginal
fragment is two-part: The fragment transgresses the room of the page just
as the transgressive robin enters the parlor; and, where Dorothy delit-
eralized the story as a general allusion to instruct the addressed child,
William's version embroiders the tale to make it deeply literary. William's
transformation of literal tale to balladry, with the knightly bird's "natural
shield / Charged with a blazon on the field," changes the parent who sings
the tale from a caretaker into a self-absorbed troubadour singing of manly
honor. Similarly, the listener's inability to locate the true voice is now
valued more than the bird's illusory song. In a more questionable transgression than that of the commonplace page, William redresses with his
barely rewritten lines and gives no indication in his own note or the
Isabella Fenwick note of Dorothy's authorship. By revoicing Dorothy's
lines, William reenacts the troubadour as he sings to the loved one, and
like the troubadour he thus silences his muse. William Wordsworth seeks
out troubadour or courtly themes in his later poetry as a way to understand relations; Dorothy Wordsworth, however, continually assesses the
inadequacy of these themes, as her final choice for the robin verse shows.

Transgressive writing occurs even earlier in the inverted half of the
book, as early as the first page. This leaf is an official beginning to a record
discontinued immediately afterward. The entry is effaced by several other
later entries, but officially it begins in very light ink.

Dorothy Wordsworth

Journal

Bright sunshine — cold air — bitter wind
[harsh?] sea — paved roads — Fine cauliflowers in October.
Grapes seven sous the pound in the boullivards — 3 sous under
Montmartre — 4 sous the green — Cheeses of Neufchatel

Over this entry is a stanza from "Loving and Liking" written in darker ink
and a different nib but in Dorothy's hand. Underneath both are two
medicinal recipes written in sepia ink, one for Miss Barker's white salve
and one for Dorothy's own: "Drawing Salve" to be used with the first.
Across all of this, lengthwise and in a loose pencil scrawl, are lines probably from a later ill period that rework the most significant sentiments of
"Loving and Liking": "While is the death-bed of strife vanishes [grief?] /
But like this love is the solace & pleasure of life / To like is [——] / By
liking a friendship may grow out of strife / But love is the pleasure &
solace of life." And at the extreme right margin Dorothy has inserted, "By
liking [——] may grow out of strife" and, penciled above "strife" in the
top corner, "watchful heart."

To capture essence in surface minutiae is not William Wordsworth's
"seeing into the heart of things" but instead feeds his endeavor to sublime
the everyday as a pastoral vision. This kind of seeing, this fine detailing
and close perception at the center of things, has been Dorothy Wordsworth's trademark characteristic in its regenerative capacity to install love
in the gap William recurrently imagines as the death of Lucy, or of other
young maidens. In it she remains centered, rather than marginalized as
not-maiden or as abjectly ill. It is the watchful heart, she seems to claim,
that can see more than that which *sees into* the heart. Finally, her sightedness and resilience consistently underlie her brother's survey and prophecy, giving proof and pleasure to the Life they dreamed and made happen.

Notes

Introduction

1. For a use of the performative in Wordsworth as a purely textual feature, see Cynthia Chase's essay, "Monument and Inscriptions: Wordsworth's 'Lines,'" in a special issue of *Diacritics* entitled "Wordsworth and the Production of Poetry," ed. Chase and Andrzej Warminski (*Diacritics* 17, no. 4 [Winter 1987]: 65–77; rpt. in Johnston et. al., *Romantic Revolutions,* 50–77). Chase argues for the linguistic performative in William Wordsworth's inscriptions. Wordsworth uses the particular form of the inscription, Chase argues, to play with a poem's textuality *as* historiography — poetically accounting for its own origin and status — in order to transform history (as determination of the text's limits) into "the *in*determination of the text's limits and origin" (Johnston et. al., 55). Such a move recalls the general character of Wordsworth's work, which is the "irreducibility, in Wordsworth, of the material to the cognitive dimension of language, mark[ing] the shift from a cognitive to a performative model of the text" (52). That performative, relative to what it performs which Chase names "history," sits against those formal and cognitive models in which tropes are

nonreferential and not themselves material or performative. Though Chase's analysis clarifies the problem of inscription in a manner congenial to later sections of *Becoming Wordsworthian,* her understanding of the performative is linguistic, purely textual. By contrast, I am using the term to describe the text as a historiographic account of how poetic composition is conceived, imagined, discussed, revised, played out, redressed, and responded to. Not just inscriptions but all of the Wordsworths' texts record this activity, I argue. And, most importantly in this comparison, it is not the texts but the Life as it is lived collaboratively which is performative. I am indebted to Orrin Wang for drawing my attention to this issue of *Diacritics* and for reminding me of Chase's essay.

2. Critics such as William Galperin, Gayatri Spivak, and Mary Jacobus have used a variety of critical methods to question the gendered base of W. Wordsworth's authority.

3. Despite his paternalistic attitude, Hardwicke Drummond Rawnsley's recording, in the dialect of Grasmere residents, provides an intriguing account of W. Wordsworth as invariably solemn and holding himself apart: "Why, why, Wudsworth nevver said much to t' fowk. . . . He was distant, ye may saay, verra distant"; "Wudsworth . . . for a' he had nea pride nor nowt, was a man who was quite one to hissel, ye kna"; "But he was a lonely man, fond o' goin' out wi' his family, and saying nowt to noan of 'em . . . many's a time I've seed him a takkin' his family out in a string, and never geein' the dreariest bit of notice to 'em . . . —a desolate-minded man, ye kna." *Reminiscences of Wordsworth among the Peasantry of Westmoreland* (London: Dillon's, 1968).

4. The 1805 *Prelude,* ed. J. Wordsworth, Abrams, and Gill, from the Norton edition, will be cited throughout, unless otherwise indicated.

5. Coleridge modulated this form from the classical odic dance of strope and antistrope to capture the structure of human meditation. See Abrams's analysis in "Structure and Style."

6. The Wordsworth library contained a copy of Agostino Isola's translation of Italian verse (1778); Isola was W. Wordsworth's Italian tutor at Cambridge, and William kept for years his earlier copy of Isola's translations (used in tutoring sessions).

7. See Easthope's discussion of courtly love in *Poetry and Phantasy,* particularly 68–71.

8. Vološinov would describe this as class consciousness (becoming conscious of others' perceptions of one as object): "Any motivation of one's behavior, any instance of self-awareness (for self-awareness is always verbal . . .) is an act of gauging oneself against some social norm, social evaluation—is, so to speak, the socialization of oneself and one's behavior . . . *self-consciousness* in the final analysis, always leads us to *class consciousness*" (86–87).

9. For a thorough discussion, see Jacques Lacan, "A Love Letter," in *Feminine Sexuality,* 137–61.

10. Easthope writes that "it is only when discourse appears transparent that an addresser can communicate a message to an addressee. . . . human beings can only become subjects by entering a system of signifiers which relates to each other independently of the subject. So there is no discourse without subjectivity and no subjectivity without discourse. On this basis the Lacanian conception seeks to show how subjectivity is always constituted in relation to discourse, how the split in the subject between conscious and unconscious is brought about in and through discourse" (*Poetry as Discourse*, 32).

ꙮ Chapter 1. The Wordsworthian Performative

1. All references to Dorothy Wordsworth's journals will be to de Selincourt's *Journals of Dorothy Wordsworth*. The epigraph is from 1:58.

2. The term "self-completing universe" is John Holloway's and is borrowed by Liu to described the totalizing effect of the "dome of labor" he sees as structuring the *Grasmere Journals* (Liu, "Autobiographical Present," 117).

3. Kurt Heinzelman's essay on Dorothy and William's domesticity, for instance, reads the Wordsworths in domestic partnership and points out the difference between the romantic and Victorian phases of Wordsworthian domesticity.

4. Ian Jack notes that Charlotte Smith, the Reverend Mr. Bowles, and his friend Coleridge were the dominant influences on Lamb's early poetry as well; his *Rosamund Gray* is particularly indebted to the sentimental movement (*English Literature, 1815–1832*, in the Oxford History of English Literature series [Oxford: Clarendon Press, 1963], 282).

5. Pamela Woof notes that Wordsworth, then at Cambridge, had subscribed to the fifth edition of Smith's *Elegiac Sonnets* in 1789. Smith was at Brighton when Wordsworth visited her, but Williams was not at Paris when he arrived there. The admiration for both poets continued throughout Wordsworth's lifetime, and Woof notes that even forty years later, in 1830, he wanted Alexander Dyce to include Smith's "I love thee, mournful, sober-suited night" in a collection he was compiling. This sonnet is no. xxxix of her *Elegiac Sonnets*. See Woof, *Grasmere Journals*, 255 n.

6. Burke was of the Liberal party in Parliament, yet he believed in the importance of a ruling hereditary aristocracy; both his work against the monarchical bid for greater powers and his attempts to correct the corrupt governance of India attest to his liberal leanings. Rather than a Rousseauistic philosophy of the social contract, Burke supported the doctrine of the Law of Nature, predicated on a universal ordering by which moral precepts can be adduced. Before his years in office he belonged to a literary and artistic circle that included Dr. Johnson, Goldsmith, Reynolds, and Garrick; his credentials for this circle rested on his *Enquiry,* which treats the physiological and social origins of how we conceive the sublime

and the beautiful; his credentials for authorship are that of the Man of Taste. The treatise, which already reveals an interest in social custom, grew out of his wanderings in England and France after leaving the Middle Temple in dissatisfaction.

7. See McGann, *Beauty of Inflections,* 267–68.

8. All references to the Wordsworths' letters are from Shaver, Moorman, and Hill, eds., *The Letters of William and Dorothy Wordsworth,* rev. ed. Vol. 1, *The Early Years, 1787–1805,* will be cited in text as *EY*; Vol. 2, *The Middle Years, 1806–1820,* will be cited in text as *MY.*

9. William's first published poem, "An Evening Walk" (1793), subtitled "An Epistle; in Verse. Addressed to a Young Lady, from the Lakes of the North of England," begins with an address to the sister-maiden as a framework for the narrative: "Far from my dearest friend, 'tis mine to rove / Thro' bare grey dell, high wood, and pastoral cove." "Evening Walk" contains many of the elements Wordsworth is soon to codify into the address-to-women form: the woman addressed, the grove, the speaker's interpretive meditation, and Nature as the object of his regard. What Wordsworth has not yet incorporated is the immediacy of the meditative interaction, the collaborative quality of the maiden's copresence, and his desire for both participation in and transcendence of Nature's presence.

10. These poetic dates are, in fact, the terms of Chandler's political and philosophical division of Wordsworth's career (3–30).

11. Richard Holmes, in his recent biography of Coleridge, repeatedly refers to the poet's "self-dramatisation" (236) and role playing. See, for instance, p. 259: "Like a flock of starlings, each scheme appeared to expand or contract, according to Coleridge's correspondent, faithfully reflecting what each one wished to hear." Or, p. 96: Peter Vandyke's portrait of Coleridge reveals a "bright top-coat and high white silk stock . . . in the latest fashion of the French Directory, and the radiant face of the young lecturer, with parted lips, glows with 'sensibility' and inspiration. The patrons seem to have got their money's worth." The self-consciousness of these dramatics is revealed in Coleridge's youthful expedition to Wales, where his "favourite device was to adopt some Romantic pose, and then explode it with laughter. . . . This was play-acting at being the poet, like the Pantisocrat" (67). Likewise, in their exhibition catalog of Byron memorabilia, Anthony Burton and John Murdoch note aspects of Byron's propensity for roles: He liked to imitate his great-uncle's legend "to an often rather frightened audience"; on being called "Gaby" after a literary character, Byron felt he was "[g]iven a role to play" and so "found his confidence"; he dieted violently to "ma[k]e himself thin and fascinating"; on drinking from the skull cup he had made for his masquerades at Newstead Abbey, he would declaim, " 'I shall go mad,' but Scrope Davies deflated him by saying 'Much more like silliness than madness.' " *Byron: An exhibition to commemorate the 150th anniversary of his death in the Greek War of Liberation, 19 April 1824* (London: Victoria and Albert Museum, 1974).

12. The gendering of nature as a psychological as well as social phenomenon

among the romantics is discussed by scholars such as Richard J. Onorato and Barbara Schapiro.

13. For instance, Smith's narrator describes Ethelinde's first approach to Grasmere Lake: "and passing between two enormous fells, one of which descended, cloathed with wood, almost perpendicularly to the lake, while the other hung over it in masses of staring rock, they turned round a sharp point formed by the root of the latter, and entering a lawn, the abbey, embosomed among the hills, and half concealed by old elms, which seemed coeval with the building, appeared with its gothic windows, and long pointed roof of a pale grey stone, bearing every where the marks of great antiquity." Here the description is of another lake than Grasmere, as is the description of the abbey as being between the lake and a steep fell. Although Smith is correct to describe the abbey as built of grey stone, both that detail and the characteristic stone footbridge from which Ethelinde gazes at the stream are to be found in pictorial guides to the Lakes. Even her description of the evening star being "reflected in the bosom of the lake, now perfectly still and unruffled," has a painterly sense to it that points to the water's depth, a perspective not so clear from the lake shore (*Ethelinde*, 1:23, 31–32).

14. *Sir Walter Scott on Novelists and Fiction*, ed. Ioan Williams (New York: Barnes and Noble, 1968), 184–90. Scott's review was first published in his *Miscellaneous Prose Works*, vol. 4 (1827).

15. The 1793 *Annual Register*, subtitled "or, A View of the History, Politics, and Literature for the year 1793," divides its narrative of the year into "The History of Europe," "The Chronicle," "Appendix to the Chronicle" (a section containing graphs and charts), "State Papers," "Characters," "Natural History," "Useful Projects" (reporting recent inventions), "Antiquities," "Miscellaneous Essays," "Poetry" (including occasional pieces by Pye, the current poet laureate, and other representative poets), and an "Account of Books" (a highly selective review, mostly of historical material) (London: John Nichols and Son; rpt., London: Baldwin, Cradock, and Joy, 1821).

16. Burke frequently broke into tears in Parliament, he blindly aided his relatives' enrichment, and his inconstancy forced Thomas Paine, Thomas Jefferson, and others to question his principles. See L. G. Mitchell's introduction to *The Writings and Speeches of Edmund Burke*, vol. 8. This volume includes *Reflections on the Revolution in France* and speeches and letters concerning the French state from 1790 to 1794. General editor, Paul Langford. 9 vols. (Oxford: Clarendon Press, 1981–1991).

17. Except for *The Prelude*, all references to W. Wordsworth's lyrics will be from Hutchinson and de Selincourt, eds., *Poetical Works*; all references to Dorothy Wordsworth's poetry will be from Levin, *Dorothy Wordsworth and Romanticism*, App. 1. For Dorothy Wordsworth's narrative of the Green family, see de Selincourt, ed., *George and Sarah Green*.

18. Dorothy Wordsworth believed her brother to be touring with Jones in the

Vale of Clwyd during this period, and after she knew the extent of his mental anguish she became as reluctant as he was to discuss it. See Gittings and Manton, 40–41.

19. See Kristeva's *Revolution in Poetic Language,* esp. "The Semiotic and the Symbolic," 19–106.

20. W. Wordsworth's interest in gardens and landscaping, classical Arcadia, and the picturesque is well documented. His *Guides to the Lakes* alone shows he has read Capability Brown, Reynolds, Gilpin, West, and others. His library holdings at his death include twelve editions of Milton, a volume of Tasso's *Gerusalemme liberata,* three editions of *Paul et Virginie, Emile* and *Le Contrat social,* all testifying to his interest in the mythic and social force of gardens.

21. "This degradation": i.e., "this decline of imaginative responsiveness." Degradation is, however, both a literal decline and a humiliation of the spirit through creative dearth and anticipated creative death.

22. In the general model, the triadic ratio of speaker to object to listener operates interrelationally, with each element shifting alliance with changes in content and form. Vološinov comments that the utterance can either "dote upon" the object or denigrate it, depending on the auditor's accord with the speaker's intentions: "Nothing is more perilous for aesthetics than to ignore the autonomous role of the listener" (112). The poet cannot speak to the air, the field, or the blank page alone; he depends on the answer to his word for, as Bakhtin notes, "every word is directed toward an *answer* and cannot escape the profound influence of the answering word that it anticipates" ("Discourse in the Novel" in *The Dialogic Imagination,* 280).

23. Kristeva posits her theory as a way of understanding the heterogeneity of language, particularly poetic language. Positing the theoretical status of the chora rather than asserting its absolute existence is necessary for Kristeva, since the chora is "unnameable, improbable, hybrid, anterior to naming, to the One, to the father, and consequently maternally connoted" (*Desire,* 133).

24. See particularly Homans's discussion of the speaker's self-conflict in the face of a maternal Nature in "A Winter's Ramble in Grasmere Vale," in *Women Writers,* 49–53.

25. For instance, when William requests that Dorothy note down a story about a turtledove, from which he composed "The Poet and the caged Turtledove," she provides only the outline, devoid of any descriptive language or interpretation (*Grasmere Journals,* 30 January 1802).

26. *Desire,* 250. Kristeva's discussion of the sacred conversation sheds light on romantic conversation, its intent, and its intentionality.

27. Empson, 6, 11–31.

28. See Bruce Graver's edition of Wordsworth's *Aeneid* for *The Cornell Wordsworth* (series ed., Jared Curtis), forthcoming.

29. "Wordsworth, New Literary Histories, and the Constitution of Literature," in Johnston et al., 417.

30. John Singer Sargent notes regarding his 1878 painting *Capri* of a local peasant girl, Rosina Ferrara, that she is "a magnificent type, about seventeen years of age, her complexion a rich nut-brown, with a mass of blue-black hair, very beautiful" (exhibition notes, Museum of Fine Arts, Boston). In *Mill on the Floss* (1860), George Eliot gives her heroine nut-brown skin and draws explicit comparisons between her appearance and that of witches and gypsies. While Maggie Tulliver's cousin comments that "A painter would think Maggie's complexion beautiful," her uncle says, "Though there was a song about the 'Nut-brown Maid,' too; I think she was crazy — crazy Kate" (*Mill on the Floss* [Oxford: Oxford University Press, 1990], 383–84).

31. *EY,* DW to JP, 27 January 1788.

32. See Lynn Hunt, *Politics, Culture, and Class in the French Revolution* (Berkeley and Los Angeles: University of California Press, 1984), and Joan B. Landes, *Women and the Public Sphere in the Age of the French Revolution* (Ithaca: Cornell University Press, 1988).

33. For two lively introductions to novels of sensibility and pathos, see Janet Todd, *Sensibility* (London: Methuen, 1986), and Kate Ferguson Ellis, *The Contested Castle* (Urbana: University of Illinois Press, 1989). Although I am thinking more particularly of novels like Saint-Pierre's *Paul et Virginie,* discussed below, eighteenth-century novels of sensibility often depended on the double-hero and double-heroine device (same-sex sibling pairs) which Jane Austen draws on for *Sense and Sensibility* and *Pride and Prejudice.*

34. Homans specifically poses what I am calling Dorothy Wordsworth's project as William Wordsworth's: "The role of handmaiden was indeed taken up by those [women] who were quite literally the first readers of romantic poetry. . . . Dorothy Wordsworth largely accepts and literalizes this romantic role, allowing her writing to be appropriated by it" (*Bearing the Word,* 40).

35. In W. Wordsworth's mythic biography, *The Prelude,* the "Vaudracour and Julia" episode displaces the story of William's revolutionary love affair, occupying precisely the moment in the biography when Annette should have made her appearance.

36. D. Wordsworth's early letters repeatedly record the pain of the years spent with her grandparents. See *EY,* particularly the adolescent letters to Jane Pollard, 1–108 passim.

37. See Shaver and Shaver, *Wordsworth's Library.* Gittings and Manton note that *Paul et Virginie* was clearly a favorite read of W. Wordsworth's, and "when taxed by Hazlitt with borrowing ideas from it, William, though denying the borrowing, showed . . . a clear knowledge of the novel" (101).

38. "I have certainly spent some enviable hours at inns . . . at a little inn on the borders of Wales, where there happened to be hanging some of Westall's drawings, which I compared triumphantly . . . with the figure of a girl who had ferried me over the Severn, standing up in the boat between me and the fading twilight — at

other times I might mention luxuriating in books, with a peculiar interest in this way, as I remember sitting up half the night to read Paul and Virginia . . . and at the same place I got through two volumes of Madame D'Arblay's Camilla" (William Hazlitt, "On Going a Journey," in *Selected Writings,* ed. Ronald Blythe (Hamondsworth: Penguin, 1970).

39. Claire Clairmont records for 8 November 1814, "Read Paul & Virginia — in the Evening. I admire the descriptions [of] this beautiful Country." The novel is "in itself trifling & uninteresting [*sic*] — the speeches and Characters are inflated & unnatural" (Stocking, 59). Erasmus Darwin includes the novel in his reading list for *A Plan for the Conduct of Female Education in Boarding Schools* (1797).

40. For the obvious similarities between Rousseau's early life and W. Wordsworth's youthful wanderings through France, see P. D. Jimack's introduction to Rousseau's *Emile*. Of course, the relation between preromanticism and the romantics has been thoroughly documented from Joseph Texte's 1895 *Jean-Jacques Rousseau et les origines du cosmopolitanisme littéraire* to the writings of Paul de Man and Jacques Derrida; however, it is a topic that continues to demand attention.

41. The primary text in Rousseau's own *Emile; or, On Education.* Also see "The Pedagogical Imperative: Teaching as a Literary Genre," *Yale French Studies* 63.

42. Interestingly, the conflux between Rousseau and Smith in the Wordsworthian terrain is ongoing: Smith translated Isabelle de Montolieu's *Corisande de Beauvilliers; anecdote française du 16ᵉ siécle* (Paris 1806), giving it the English title of *The Letters of a Solitary Wanderer.*

43. La Curne de Sainte-Palaye, ed. Claude François Xavier Millot, 3 vols. (Paris, 1774). See Shaver and Shaver, *Wordsworth's Library.*

➤ Chapter 2. The Charted Valley

1. Gayatri Spivak uses the term "worlding" to denote the colonizing attitude of those invested in the politics of imperialism: "the notion of textuality should be related to the notion of the worlding of a world on a supposedly uninscribed territory. . . . Now this worlding actually is also a texting, textualising, a making into art, a making into an object to be understood" (*Post-Colonial Critic,* p. 1).

2. Published in the quarto of 1793, "An Evening Walk" later became an object of Wordsworth's intensive revisionary scrutiny which produced the successive editions after 1820. However, the lines discussed here are original to the 1793 version.

3. Frances Ferguson treats the quest element in "Nutting" in *Wordsworth: Language as Counter-Spirit;* Marjorie Levinson's chapter on "Nutting" in *The Romantic Fragment Poem* treats the poem as a spot of time belonging implicitly to a longer work. Levinson notes the interesting absence of any discussion of the maiden in Geoffrey Hartman's treatment of "Nutting" in his *Wordsworth's Poetry.*

4. Feminist anthropology is indebted to Mary Douglas's work on purity and

pollution for understanding women's sexual relation to culture (*Purity and Danger*). For more recent discussions of inculturated sexual constraint, see Cixous and Clément, *The Newly Born Woman;* Foucault, *The History of Sexuality,* vol. 1; Jacobus, *Reading Woman;* Kristeva, *Powers of Horror;* Lerner, *The Creation of Patriarchy;* and Ortner and Whitehead, *Sexual Meanings.*

5. "Lines left upon a Seat in a Yew-tree," "Lines written in Early Spring," and "Lines written a few miles above Tintern Abbey" are the earliest of this eventually abandoned genre.

6. Although Basil Montague lived with the Wordsworths for only a few years, he came to them during the crucial Alfoxden period, when brother and sister were constructing a working relationship for both their art and their domestic needs. Basil was their "little boy," taken in to board for extra income, and Dorothy in particular took charge of his Rousseauian or "natural" education. When Tom Wedgwood visited Alfoxden in 1797 to invite Wordsworth to head his plan for an academy run by Godwinian philosophers, Wordsworth declined. The poet clearly distinguishes what he considers a proper or natural education from that conducted by scientific theory in his *Prelude* passage on the prodigal child. (See Gill's *William Wordsworth,* 130–31, for Wedgwood's plan.)

7. See Herrick, *Poetical Works.* The sister is called to nature not for the carpe diem's fertility rites but for the poet's priestly celebration of the benevolent goddess mother: "There is a blessing in the air." Like Corinna, the sister is associated with natural elements and spring's rebirth: Corinna must "Rise, and put on your foliage, and be seen / To come forth like the springtime, fresh and green, / And sweet as Flora," while the sister is exhorted, "Then come, my sister! come, I pray, / With speed put on your woodland dress." Corinna's speaker desires her to rise because he believes her lazy, associating her with the indolence of the young poet of "Nutting": "Then up I rose." However, the sister desires to read industriously with "toiling reason," a labor reflecting Matthew's "toil and trouble" over "barren leaves" in another poem of 1798 ("The Tables Turned").

8. This study will not exhaust the number of addresses to women in Wordsworth's canon, nor will it attempt to take into account his intent in the poems to male addressees and the addresses to natural entities.

9. Kristeva reads Vološinov believing him to be Bakhtin writing under a pseudonym. See "Discourse in Life and Discourse in Art (Concerning Sociological Poetics)," App. 1 to Vološinov, *Freudianism,* 93–116.

10. W. Wordsworth's visualizing takes on a mythic dimension in his sister's records of their walks that reveals the same process he used to rewrite Dorothy's journal entries into poems pregnant with poetic license. A minor example of this impulse is Dorothy's entry for 23 April 1802: "It was very grand when we looked up very stony, here and there a budding tree. William observed that the umbrella Yew tree that breasts the wind had lost its character as a tree and had become something like to solid wood" (Moorman, *Journals,* 115).

11. Seward successfully (in the economic sense) transfigured her lesbian longings into sentimental verse, a highly dramatic love for a married choirmaster (Mr. Saville), and intense sentimental attachments to several younger women whom she attempted to dissuade from marriage. The best known of these, Seward's foster-sister Honora Sneyd, became the wife of Richard Lovell Edgeworth.

12. Compare Dorothy's hasty accounts mixed with the other business of the day to Robinson Crusoe's careful businessman's accounting. When Dorothy attempts to keep track of household finances, Crusoe sets out methodically to take stock. Dorothy's records of household labor, on the other hand, are meticulous in comparison. But it is not until Mary Hutchinson joins them as mistress of the house that household accounts as ledgered records begin to appear.

13. See Bialostosky's *Making Tales* for his distinction of the dialogic encounter.

14. Both Boswell's *Life* and Mrs. Thrale's desire to have her correspondence published as a literary artifact attest to the interest the "Life" genre held for London's literati earlier.

15. Saint-Pierre's novel was declared a masterpiece at its publication in France; it was translated and reissued repeatedly in England, Holland, Italy, Spain, and Portugal and was translated into Greek, Armenian, Hungarian, and Russian.

16. Gittings and Manton cite D. Wordsworth's adolescent reading of *Clarissa* as creating a mere habit of language which she continued to use in adulthood: "She is simply using the vocabulary in which her tastes were formed" (16).

17. "Social phantasy" refers to an agreed-upon social fiction which answers a particular historical need, such as a romantic love. See Easthope, *Poetry and Phantasy*. Easthope's concept will be referred to throughout as "social fantasy" for purposes of clarity.

18. John Murdoch discusses the signifying landscape in "The Landscape of Labor" (see esp. 186).

19. Stephen Gill's biography of W. Wordsworth notes that William Mason's *Poems of Mr. Gray: To which are Prefixed Memoirs of his Life and Writings* (York, 1775) contained Gray's journal of his 1769 visit to the Lake District. Mason's edition was reprinted several times; Wordsworth owned the 1776 edition. Gill also notes that the young Wordsworth was paraphrasing Gray in his letters to Dorothy from his visit to the Alps with Robert Jones (*William Wordsworth*, 432 n., 48).

20. Stuart Curran, commenting on Southey's *Eclogues*, writes that pastoral is a state of mind "foreign to the structures of modern civilization and not to be discovered in a nostalgic veneration for lost traditions" (98). Southey saw the pastoral as a politically locatable genre: Botany Bay as well as England, but always in the real present rather than the mythical past. Curran notes that Southey's *Eclogues* on England were highly influential for both Coleridge and Wordsworth.

21. For further discussion of chapbooks, see Klancher, 21.

22. See de Selincourt, *Dorothy Wordsworth*, 111.

23. The romantic cult of the child, too, developed from the pastoral. Bryan Loughrey notes that "Post-Romantic conceptions of childhood as a state of natural innocence, joy and wisdom, corrupted by entry into the adult world, allowed the child to usurp the traditional role of the shepherd" (21). Loughrey also notes that, with childhood as an arcadian existence, nostalgia becomes "the emotional core of most pastoral literature" (21).

24. Call ye these appearances,
   Which I beheld of shepherds in my youth,
   This sanctity of Nature given to man,
   A shadow, a delusion? . . .
   But when that first poetic faculty
   Of plain imagination and severe . . .
   Began to have some promptings to put on
   A visible shape, and to the works of art
   The notions and the images of books,
   Did knowingly conform itself. . . .
   There came among these shapes of human life
   A wilfulness of fancy and conceit
   Which gave them new importance to the mind.
   [*Prelude* VIII.428–31, 511–12, 515–18, 520–22]

25. Like Shakespeare and Chaucer, Milton incorporates both pastoral and epic visions in his mythopoetic narratives; these are, in fact, the three favorite readings of both Wordsworths, according to D. Wordsworth's log of reading activity.

26. "Home at Grasmere" is one of the few poems in which the language of shepherds dismays William: "That Shepherd's voice . . . / Debased and under profanation, made / An organ for the sounds articulate / Of ribaldry and blasphemy and wrath / Where drunkenness hath kindled senseless frays" (423–27).

27. From Dorothy Wordsworth's reading notes of an unattributed narrative of travels in Africa, DCMS 26: "There is another species of Hottentots who have got the name of Boshies-men from their dwelling in woody or mountainous places. These . . . are sworn enemies to the pastoral life . . . & are ignorant of agriculture."

28. De Quincey, in his romantic enthusiasm, describes the Wordsworths' cottage as having "a perfect and unpretending cottage window with little diamond panes, embowered at almost every season of the year with roses," and so very much the picture of the pastoral cot (*Recollections of the Lakes,* 128).

29. By contrast, in the male grove of Wordsworth's poem "Yew-Trees," with its "fraternal Four" yews, the "solemn and capacious grove" shelters "ghostly Shapes . . . Death the Skeleton / And Time the Shadow," rather than the poet.

30. In "The Cult of Domesticity," Kurt Heinzelman argues that "[t]he most significant social act of the early Grasmere years became the assimilation of Mary Hutchinson into the household as William's wife" (52). Heinzelman is interested

in characterizing the early Grasmere years as ones of assimilation, however; in terms of the current discussion, Mary's entrance into the household is more pertinent as a divider between premarriage and postmarriage relations in the family.

31. Bruce Graver has studied the large ledgers where the Wordsworths had begun this enormous task. Manuscripts are in possession of the Wordsworth Library and Trustees of Dove Cottage.

32. Mellor explains German romantic irony, particularly as developed by Schlegel, as a fundamentally chaotic world view that involves a dynamic process of unending disruption and restructuring, an open-ended "never-ending becoming" (*English Romantic Irony*).

33. De Quincey, *Recollections of the Lakes*, 120. De Quincey also refers to neighboring Easedale, the valley in which the tragic Green family lived, as "a closet within a chamber—a chapel within a cathedral" (251). While De Quincey reveals here his sympathy with Wordsworthian geo-aesthetics, this passage is located, ironically, in his reappropriation from Dorothy Wordsworth of the Green narrative.

34. See Erich Neumann's discussion of the Mother Goddess and her consort in relation to the Freudian notion of the phallic mother (*The Origins and History of Consciousness*, foreword by C. G. Jung, trans. R. F. C. Hull [1954; Princeton: Princeton University Press, 1970], 16–63.

35. Michael Cooke develops the concept of the romantic will as a force that shapes poetry and lives. However, insofar as the matter of will is a masculinist concept, it is unhelpful in determining the interaction of forces in Dorothy Wordsworth's work (*Romantic Will*).

36. Dorothy associates herself with wildflowers but stops at any metonymy of body with flower, and for good reason. Saint-Pierre's Virginie is associated with wildflower seeds and large restful rocks in image clusters similar to those W. Wordsworth uses to describe Lucy as a violet beside a mossy rock. Both heroines are love objects who are beloved precisely because of their uncultivated, natural identifications. Less dangerous is the notion that the valley nest can embody a resting place. In *Paul et Virginie*, this spot is marked by two trees planted by each of the mothers at the birth of her child; these trees, which "constituted all the archives" of the group, stand at the foot of the rock called "La Découverte de l'Amitié," on which the family sits at night employing all their senses to "enjoy in silence the freshness of the air, the fragrance of the flowers, the murmurs of the fountains and the last harmonies of light and shade" (36–37).

37. In Saint-Pierre's tale, Virginie's propensity for her bower recalls her mother's earlier seeking out of this secluded valley: Madame de la Tour had decided to live in obscurity, in "some hidden nook where she could live alone and unknown . . . where she retired as if to a nest" (3).

38. Alan Richardson's article, "Romanticism and the Colonization of the Feminine," in Mellor, *Romanticism and Feminism*, 13–25, offers an intriguing analysis of sexual colonization in the romantic imagination.

39. "It was an April Morning." "Emma" and "Emmeline" are William's poetic names for Dorothy.

40. Both Margaret Homans and Susan Levin discuss the swallow section of the *Grasmere Journals* in terms of the impending marriage of Mary and William; their readings, however, are much more biographically and psychologically based. See *Bearing the Word*, 59, and *Dorothy Wordsworth and Romanticism*, 27–29.

∽ Chapter 3. Authoring Selves, Traversing Ground

1. See Mavor, *The Ladies of Llangollen*. Wordsworth visited Lady Butler and Sarah Ponsonby in 1824 and wrote a poem about their "cottage," Plas Newydd. The Ladies referred to one another as "beloved," although it was particularly Sarah's term for the older Eleanor. Mavor writes of their relationship that "There are clues here and there, some dropped unawares. They share everything. Their bound books are gold-lettered, E.B. on the front, S.P. on the back; so with their china and with nearly every possession they have. Their letters are signed jointly, the initials of the Beloved followed by the full name of the writer of the letter. In speech they always use the collective 'We.' They call one another 'Beloved' always" (95).

2. "Ideology and Ideological State Apparatuses," in *Lenin and Philosophy*, 182. Although Althusser posits a static subjectivity, his concept of the hail is essential to understanding D. Wordsworth's reaction to her brother's addresses.

3. The mirror image, which the child recognizes as himself and yet not-himself, provides a peculiar basis for the reception of the hail through a recognition of the self as hailed. W. Wordsworth's deliberate suppression of visual over auditory power in his poetry causes him to represent Dorothy as pure voice. He does not wish her to function as a mirror in which he actually sees his image reflected, for she is to be *his* specular ego. That is, as complement and second self (something like Lacan's *salutary imago*), she is not her own subject-self but his own mirrored self. The Subject's interlocutor-interpellates recognize themselves as "his *mirrors*, his *reflections*" (Althusser, 179). Yet the subject's mirroring back to the Subject reproduces the interpellation so that he is made a subject-Subject: "This mirror duplication is constitutive of ideology and ensures its functioning" (Althusser, 180). See Jacques Lacan, "The mirror stage as formative of the function of the I as revealed in psychoanalytic experience," in *Ecrits*, 1–7.

4. De Quincey comments that he thought it strange Mary Wordsworth was not more conversational, given the "daily society of her husband and his sister, not only hearing the best parts of English literature daily read, or quoted by short fragments, but also hearing them very often critically discussed in a style of great originality and truth, and by the light of strong poetic feeling" (*Recollections of the Lakes*, 129).

5. To base a reading of D. Wordsworth's oeuvre on Abrams's and Wasserman's keystone theories in the field of romanticism, as does Homans and to some extent Levin, would be to misread her entirely. Abrams and Wasserman theorize on the nature of the romantic creative process based on the evidence garnered from works by the romantic brotherhood (Abrams, "Structure and Style"; Wasserman, "English Romantics").

6. W. Wordsworth's discussion of fraternity and its moral character in relation to the natural world belongs to the 1800 text of the Preface and was edited out in later revisions. It is part of a larger discussion of one of William's poetic tenets: "that the feeling therein developed gives importance to the action and situation, and not the action and situation to the feeling" (Owen and Smyser, 1:128).

7. See, for instance, Homans's treatment of the muse–poet problem for women poets such as Emily Brontë and Emily Dickinson in *Women Writers and Poetic Identity*.

8. Anne Cookson Wordsworth died when D. Wordsworth was six years old, and at her wish, Dorothy was sent to live with an unmarried cousin, Elizabeth Threlkeld, who was caring for orphaned nieces and nephews of her own. For nine years Dorothy lived within a large social circle filled with female cousins and friends; this happiness was broken when she was sent to live with her maternal grandparents where she was the only nonadult in the house.

9. It is interesting to see how close D. Wordsworth's poetic responses are to those of Keats, though she shared none of Keats's sense of himself as a major poet. In visiting the Lake District, Keats's experience at Ambleside Falls leads him to an ecstasis of being: "I cannot think with Hazlitt that these scenes make man appear little. I never forgot my stature so completely — I live in the eye; and my imagination, surpassed, is at rest" (to Tom Keats, 25–27 June 1818, in Gittings, *Letters of John Keats*). Keats senses being in nature as "liv[ing] in the eye," much as Dorothy acts as witness to it; both contrast with William's self-positioning when he writes, "I have at all times endeavoured to look steadily at my subject" (Preface to *Lyrical Ballads*, 1802). William's statement valorizes the ego-self whereas both Dorothy Wordsworth and Keats wish to achieve a state in which the ego's "imagination, surpassed, is at rest." And thus her work is more truly "in the eye" than is Keats's, who confesses his desire to write poetry as "the abstract endeavor of being able to add a mite to that mass of beauty which is harvested from these grand materials" (to Tom Keats, 25–27 June 1818). Even Keats's act of "harvesting" nature and his conception of nature as "material" align him, in this sense, more with the male romantic project than with Dorothy's project of taking care. And his reaction to the falls, unlike Dorothy's journal writing, is noticeably self-reflexive and self-aware. His sense of poethood and of his ability to create beauty causes him, like W. Wordsworth, to position the self over the object. Yet William owns the object as he looks steadily at "my subject," whereas Keats owns only himself ("my stature," "my imagination"). However, in Keats's notion of negative capability he and Dorothy

find common ground, for each recognizes that a passivity of the imagination is necessary to being receptive. It is that negative state of absence which for Keats feeds passion but which for Dorothy pays tribute to the presence of the other.

10. In 1800 Dorothy records reading "Midsummer Night's Dream" (17 May), "Timon of Athens" (18 May), "Macbeth" (25 May), "King John" (29 May), and "Richard II" (3 June); and in 1802 rereading "Midsummer Night's Dream" and reading "As You Like It" (22 June). This was not her first encounter with the Bard; Dorothy had requested Richard to send her a volume of Shakespeare when she was isolated from her brothers in Penrith.

11. Though she often practiced critical analysis in her epistolary discussions of literature with Jane, her first sustained exercise in criticism was directed at William's first published poetry, and she undertook it with Christopher. In a letter to Jane she asks how Jane's own critical analysis proceeded: "By this time, you have doubtless seen my Brother Williams Poems, and they have already suffered the lash of your criticisms. I should be very glad if you would give me your opinion of them with the same frankness with which I am going to give you mine. The scenes which he describes have been viewed with a Poet's eye and are pourtrayed with a Poet's pencil; and the Poems contain many passages exquisitely beautiful, but they also contain many faults, the chief of which are obscurity, and a too frequent use of some particular expressions and uncommon words, for instance *moveless* . . . it is a very beautiful epithet but ought to have been cautiously used, he ought, at any rate, only to have hazarded it once, instead of which it occurs three or four times. The word *viewless,* also, is introduced far too often. . . . I regret exceedingly that he did not submit the works to the inspection of some Friend before their Publication. . . . Their faults are such as a young Poet was most likely to fall into and least likely to discover. . . . My Brother Kitt and I, while he was at Forncett, amused ourselves by analysing every line and prepared a very bulky criticism" (*EY,* DW to JP, 16 February 1793).

12. Pamela Woof points out the use of this phrase in her article "Dorothy Wordsworth, Writer."

13. de Selincourt, *Dorothy Wordsworth,* 84. Coleridge's contribution to the 1798 *Lyrical Ballads* becomes a questionable and then absent presence in the subsequent editions that bear William's name. Nonetheless, Coleridge as brother is powerfully visible, named, and present in that collaboration in a way Dorothy as sister and maiden can never be.

14. In the letter of 16 February 1793, Dorothy also told Jane Pollard, "I look forward with full confidence to receiving you in my little Parsonage, I hope you will spend at least a year with me. I have laid the particular scheme of happiness for each Season. When I think of winter I hasten to furnish our little Parlour, I close the Shutters, set out the tea-table, brighten the Fire. When our Refreshment is ended I produce our Work, and William brings his book to our Table and contributes at once to our instruction and amusement, and at intervals we lay aside the

Book and each hazard our observations upon what has been read without the fear of ridicule or Censure. We talk over past days, we do not sigh for any Pleasure beyond our humble Habitation 'The central point of all our Joys.'" The register of dependency that colors the adult letters is missing in these letters when Dorothy is most dependent. The acknowledgment of censure and humility, however, is clearly there.

15. David Erdman raised this point at the 1986 meeting of the English Institute, Cambridge, Mass.

16. De Selincourt notes that Dorothy as a child may well have been like her niece Dora; such a characterization supports the notion that Dorothy's feminine gentleness was in large part socialized behavior and that the self-history she offers William is a fiction. Dora is "a mixture of wildness and elegance . . . wayward and difficult to subdue, not a little, may we say it? like what aunt Dorothy must have been at her age" (*Dorothy Wordsworth*, 242).

17. Transference love compels countertransference love, the other's responsive moment of identification with the subject, "[t]emporary and yet effective mergings" (Kristeva, *Tales of Love*, 11).

18. For instance, "Irregular Verses" begins, "Ah Julia! ask a Christmas rhyme / Of *me*[?]; "Lines intended for my Niece's Album" is propelled by Dora's utterance, "When thou gavest the word . . . / 'My Book shall appear in green array'"; "Loving and Liking" has the line, "Say not you *love* a roasted fowl"; "Thoughts on my sick-bed" uses an alternate self who asks, "And has the remnant of my life / Been pilfered of this sunny Spring?" to which the speaker answers (herself), "Ah! say not so—"; and "Lines to Dora H." is initiated by the Maiden's textually incorporated request for a poem to be written in her book.

19. It is interesting that while William casts his eye downward to the small wildflower Dorothy is looking skyward as if to reject what is normally her realm while William is in it: "I sowed the flowers, William helped me. We then went and sate in the orchard till dinner time. It was very hot. William wrote *The Celandine*. . . . After Dinner . . . [w]e first lay under a holly, where we saw nothing but the holly tree, and a budding elm, and the sky above our heads. . . . We walked towards King's, and backwards and forwards. The sky was perfectly cloudless. N.B. Is it often so? Three solitary stars in the middle of the blue vault, one or two on the points of the high hills. Wm wrote *The Celandine*, 2nd part, tonight" (*Grasmere Journals*, 1 May 1802).

20. The composition dates for three of Dorothy's most explicit addresses to children are "The Cottager to her Infant," 1805; "An address to a Child," 1806; and "Loving & Liking, Irregular Verses Addressed to a Child," 1832. It is interesting that the first two of these poems were written so early yet remained unpublished until 1815. For W. Wordsworth to include them at all indicated his acknowledgment of and investment in their collective literary activity. But what does it mean for a poem to remain for ten years unpublished yet unforgotten? In her last years,

Dorothy repeated her favorites of her own poems to herself when she was particularly ill; she cherished her own poetic works as symbols of what she could and could not attain. "Loving and Liking," the third address, was written twenty-seven years after the first and, according to William, "belongs to the same unassuming class of compositions" as "An address to a Child" (William's note to the poem in William Knight's edition of his works, 7:308).

ᔫ *Chapter 4. Mountains and Abysses*

1. The first three are the suggestions of James Kinsley and Frank Bradbrook, while *Ethelinde* is R. W. Chapman's as cited by Kinsley and Bradbrook (Austen, *Pride and Prejudice,* 138 n.). Similarly, according to books Austen is known to have read, Lizzie might be referring to William Combe's *Tour of Dr. Syntax in Search of the Picturesque* (1812); however, numerous examples of travel literature on the picturesque focus on the Lake District and surrounding areas as loci for aesthetic landscapes.

2. Alan Liu analyzes the development of picturesque landscape painting, which praises and stabilizes the pastoral and finds that it comes to eschew narrative in favor of form, exchanging active story for rest (*Wordsworth,* 84).

3. The picturesque painting becomes in aesthetics what Liu calls a "counter-institution": "Fixed in a ritual posture of religiosity named repose, back turned to the world, and eyes adoring . . . the picturesque tourist stood in worship" (*Wordsworth,* 87). The tourist is incapable of experiencing the sublime for, as in the Catholic tradition, only the priest may speak to God. To keep the tourist from Nature's gates, her violent aspect is contained in the form of institutional ruins (ruined abbeys and castles), and the tamed scape becomes a canvas for unowned vistas appropriable to the eye alone (92).

4. For full-length studies of the relation of language to the sublime, see Longinus, Hertz's *End of the Line,* and Weiskel's *Romantic Sublime.*

5. One of their earliest activities is to name specific sites, as do Paul and Virginie in Saint-Pierre's novel. Though the Wordsworths early append names to objects in their new environs — most of the naming poems as well as "Home at Grasmere" are written in their first year of residence — usually doing so on the occasion of a single event, the family of Paul and Virginie name places only gradually as significance begins to accrue to objects that gain status through repetitive acts. The novel's tale-teller remarks that the family bestowed tender names to spots of ground or a group of trees that to all but themselves were indifferent objects, so that the very act of loving and naming creates meaning in the object. Everyone participated in the commemorative and edenic act of naming, including the two slaves (who had married each other, replicating by their act the bonding that is envisioned at every level of this "family"). Place-names preserve living memory,

and the Wordsworth circle enlarged this notion beyond tying events to places to tying persons to places: "John's Grove," for instance, brings John to life each time any of them visit it.

6. Thomas Gray, famed for his graveyard poetics, also delved into explorations of the sublime in his Pindaric odes, "The Progress of Poesy" and "The Bard." His *Journal in the Lakes* (1769) recounts his tour of the Lake District (see Gosse).

7. Andrews, *Search for the Picturesque,* 5.

8. James Thomson's *Seasons,* a great favorite with nearly all the romantics (and which Dorothy records Mary Hutchinson as reading during a visit), is the "quintessential Georgic poem" (Murdoch, "Landscape of Labor," 189).

9. Richard Wordsworth complains in an early letter to William that he might have retired to the country but for William's hesitancy in choosing a lucrative vocation. That Richard wishes to leave his London law practice in order to play the gentleman farmer — just as John wishes later to leave the seafaring life and retire to Grasmere — shows how strong a compulsion the pastoral is. See Gill's reading of Richard's letter in his biography of William (*William Wordsworth,* 89).

10. Adam Smith advocated "head-work" as the way in which the ruling class can labor side by side with the working class to produce a united land. The war with France and the threat of invasion brought fears of Republican insurgence; it was necessary to position the laborer ideologically, and the pastoral with its prehistorical, prefactual state and picturesque inactivity proved an effective fixative. John Murdoch notes: "Through the Picturesque, Labor returns to the landscape: the Picturesque landscape is peopled, it is . . . made up of people, the habitations and the marks that they make over the lanscape . . . in uncorrupt simplicity and without the corrupting influences of Taste or Self-Consciousness — at the level of subsistence. At this point, the landscape of Labor is being transformed into the landscape of Nature. Labor, provided it is Mindless, is equated with Nature" ("Landscape of Labor," 191–92).

11. Green was an Ambleside artist whom W. Wordsworth encouraged and promoted. When the Reverend Joseph Wilkinson asked Wordsworth to introduce Wilkinson's own prints of Lake District views (*Select Views in Cumberland, Westmoreland, and Lancashire*), William feared unnecessary competition for Green's work and hesitated before agreeing. This anonymous introduction became Wordsworth's *Guide to the Lakes* (1810), subsequently revised and retitled for various editions.

12. See Paul de Man's discussion of *The Prelude*'s stationary waterfall passage in *Blindness and Insight,* 196–99.

13. Lacoue-Labarthe's argument concerning terror and pity, the two central terms in any discussion of the sublime, is part of a dialogue on the sublime by Lyotard and Lacoue-Labarthe published in the ICA volume on postmodernism. Lyotard's differentiation between art and aesthetics constitutes what I take to be the central point of his reply (Lacoue-Labarthe, 15).

14. The classic analyses are Abrams, *The Mirror and the Lamp,* and Richard Rorty, *Philosophy and the Mirror of Nature* (Princeton: Princeton University Press, 1979).

15. See Marjorie Levinson's exploration of the political implications of "Tintern Abbey"'s opening meditation in *Wordsworth's Great Period Poems,* 14–18.

16. Stuart Curran points out the interrelation between pastoral poet and pastor in Wordsworthian poetics (106).

17. My understanding of this concept comes from dialogue with Marlon B. Ross and from his "Naturalizing Gender." Mary Jacobus also argues this in " 'Behold the Parent Hen': Pedagogy and *The Prelude,*" in *Romanticism, Writing, and Sexual Difference,* 235–66.

18. Peter Quennell, ed., *Byron, A Self-Portrait: Letters and Diaries, 1798 to 1824* (Oxford: Oxford University Press, 1990).

19. Shaver, Moorman, and Hill, *The Letters of William and Dorothy Wordsworth,* vol. 2, *The Middle Years,* 165.

20. In the same letter William writes, "To you I will whisper, that the Excursion has one merit if it has no other, a versification to which for *variety* of musical effect no Poem in the language furnishes a parallel" (*MY,* 187).

21. William insists to Mrs. Clarkson, in answer to the "Lady" who has criticized him ("she talks of my being a worshipper of Nature"), that nature and God are differentiated. This distinction is necessary to his apprehension of the sublime, and his defense is not only against "the Ladys errors of opinion" but in order to state that "I have transfused into that Poem from the Bible of the Universe" (*MY,* 188). That is, he has performed the proper duty of the Miltonic poet.

22. *Excursion* IV. 237–38.

23. Wordsworth's essay on the sublime ends with "Oh, says one of these tutored spectators, 'what a scene should we have before us here upon the shores of Windermere, if we could but strike out those pikes of Langdale by which it is terminated; they are so intensely *picturesque*' " (Owen and Smyser, 2:360).

24. Mary Jacobus explores the threat of the sublime for the poetic voice in "Apostrophe and Lyric Voice in *The Prelude,*" in Hošek and Parker, 167–81, rpt. in a longer version in *Romanticism, Writing and Sexual Difference,* 159–83.

25. As more voices entered this theoretical discourse, the sublime took on more definitive characteristics: It was known by its vastness, limitlessness, lawlessness, passion, and its association with the pathetic. John Dennis founded the sublime on enthusiasm as an aesthetic emotion differentiated from emotions of practical reality, that is, a higher plane of feeling (*The Advancement and Reformation of Modern Poetry* [1701], and *The Grounds of Criticism in Poetry* [1704]). His contribution is additionally important for locating the psychological underpinnings of the sublime in Longinus, thereby establishing an authoritative ground for the movement toward David Hartley's full-blown associationism. Dennis also points out that nearly all of Longinus's illustrations of the sublime are based on religion

and religious emotion. Thus Dennis establishes a complex schema involving a psychological basis for a sublime aesthetic; enthusiasm (which later became romantic passion) as the perceiver's necessary emotional state; and religion as the basis for faith in an invisible presence. Such a matrix provides the link for associating the grandeur of the sublime with the greatness of the human soul. The sublime is defined as masculine from its origin, since invisibility and unity of the elect in thought and voice together create religious and patriarchal power. Addison declares Milton a sublime poet in *An Account of the Greatest English Poets* (1694), not only because Milton's verse so neatly corresponds with Longinus's definition of rhetorical sublimity but because Addison emphasizes the epic genre in general as sublime. The primary link, then, between Milton and W. Wordsworth is through Longinus and the eighteenth-century co-optation of him as received and revised yet again by the romantics. In addition, Addison's popularizing of the ongoing discussion concerning the sublime turned the current interest from rhetoric to explorations of the limits of the imagination. To this point, beauty had been necessary to the aesthetic appreciation of the sublime, just as the pathetic was its emotional vehicle. The next evolution in theories of the sublime was to dissociate beauty and sublimity through the notion of pleasure. Vastness takes on a sense of lack, an insufficiency of harmony and proportion, which are to be found in the beautiful. Vastness, chaos, and the ugly are now relegated to the sublime as a space suddenly separate from and above the beautiful.

26. Naomi Schor discusses Freud's perturbation at realizing his case histories are more like short stories once written down (that is, detailed) than while still oral: "The problem posed by the written detail [is that] due to its apparent lack of seriousness it threatens the scientificity, not to say the veracity, of the text it invades" (69).

27. "Thoughts on my sick-bed," for instance, explores the conversation poem, and the cottage poems work with the locodescriptive meditation. These poems represent D. Wordsworth's feminine romanticism, for the "Thoughts" are entirely in response to William's earlier demands on the maiden; by completing the dialogic circle the poem preserves and nestles the intertextual exchange while circumventing the transcendent posture of the sublime poet. The cottage poems also dance at the edges of lyric but avoid transcendence through their evasion of mastery: D. Wordsworth reworked these incompleted poems several times but never finished them as a whole, so that they are not romantic fragments but merely unmastered lyric segments. Although each is a compelling meditative tale employing the visual tracking of the conversation poem, and the valuation of the scape to connote meaning in the speaker's life history, none gestures at sublime themes or calls on the muse.

28. In his study of iconology, W. J. T. Mitchell has analyzed these gender-specific concepts in Burke's language according to the patriarchal assumptions underlying notions of the sublime, with the beautiful as its feminine complement (116–49).

29. Burke's commentary on love in Part I of the *Enquiry* is instructive: "The violent effects produced by love, which has sometimes been even wrought up to madness is no objection to the rule which we seek to establish. When men have suffered their imaginations to be long affected with any idea, it so wholly engrosses them as to shut out by degrees almost every other" (41).

30. David Simpson, "Commentary: Updating the Sublime," *Studies in Romanticism* 26 (1987):245–55. The sublime is not unified and indivisible; there are multiple sublimes, or fragmented aspects of the sublime. As early as Addison, theorists had distinguished among rhetorical, theological, and aesthetic sublimity. There are also the natural sublime itself, what Samuel Johnson called the ethical sublime, Kant's mathematical sublime and humanistic sublime, Keats's egotistical sublime, as well as twentieth-century coinages such as the political sublime, the comic sublime, the urbane sublime, and the liminal sublime. See Weiskel, *Romantic Sublime.*

31. John Dennis left one of the earliest written accounts of the encounter with the Alps; Addison, Walpole, Gray, and Rousseau all wrote of their impressions of the sublime mountains as well. Neil Hertz's comment that "the self cannot simply think but must read the confirmation of its own integrity, which is only legible in a specular structure," reveals the specular act that commences engagement with the invisible sublime (54).

32. Writing of Demosthenes, Longinus describes the power of rhetoric: "observe what he effects by this single figure of conjuration, or 'apostrophe' as I call it here. He deifies his audience's ancestors. . . . He inspires the judges. . . . He transforms his demonstrations. . . . At the same time he injects into his heroes' minds. . . . In short, the figure enables him to run away with his audience" (16.2; quoted from Hertz, 13).

33. For an early and authoritative analysis of this cultural system, see Simone de Beauvoir, *The Second Sex* (New York: Alfred Knopf, 1953).

34. This is Ferguson's argument in her chapter on the Lucy cycle in *Wordsworth.*

35. Marlon Ross makes this point in "Naturalizing Gender."

➲ *Chapter 5. The Poetics of Negotiating Charts*

1. Gittings and Manton comment that while she was still at her grandparents' home it seemed to Dorothy "that only in her heart could she hold these scattered brothers together as a true family" (14).

2. "On *Gusto,*" in *Selected Writings,* 201.

3. See Froula's reading of this passage in "When Eve Reads Milton."

4. Wordsworth declared that holding a pen made him ill, and he often composed orally and dictated the results to Dorothy, Mary, or Sara. Revision for publication was even more disturbing, perhaps from the additional editorial perspective required (see Gill, *William Wordsworth,* 160, 186, 192).

5. Alan Liu reads this passage rather differently, assuming that Dorothy's emphasis of the beggar's red nose reflects her concern with dirt in her attempt to wash clean the world ("Autobiographical Present," 129), a notion with affinities to Homans's discussion of "tidiness" in Dorothy's Green narrative (Homans, *Women Writers and Poetic Identity*, 60).

6. D. Wordsworth refers several times in her journals to William's request that she keep them, and at times she overtly gestures toward his desire: "He asks me to set down the story of Barbara Wilkinson's turtle dove. Barbara is an old maid. She had two turtle doves. One of them died, the first year I think. The other bird . . . [etc]" (*Grasmere Journals*, 30 January 1802). William's subsequent poem, "The Poet and the caged Turtledove," makes eloquent Dorothy's uninspired passage; she has fulfilled his request here, but the short, pragmatic sentences thinly veil a resistance to the task. Her poetic passages occur when she is writing of her own initiative even though he is the intended audience. In similar fashion, Dorothy's journals are full of references to epitaphs, which her early editors had judiciously edited out as being too morbid, too preoccupied with death. Yet it is William who in his long "Essay upon Epitaphs" discusses the importance of gravestones and their words. And it is William's morbidity concerning the grave that so shocked Coleridge when together William and Dorothy lay in a trench and William fantasized the sensation of a living death (*Grasmere Journals*, 29 April 1802). It is also William's morbidity that sees beauty in a Lucy who is so intimately connected with death that she rolls around the diurnal earth as an insensible thing. Thus, again, William's obsession is reflected in Dorothy's data gathering.

7. While William is engaged in revising several of Chaucer's tales, Dorothy repeatedly records her own reading of Chaucer and the making of fair copies of William's versions.

8. William Beckford so detested the sentimental novels produced by his stepsister, Mrs. Elizabeth Hervey, that he wrote two parodies of the genre in 1796–97: *Modern Novel Writing; or, The Elegant Enthusiast* and *Azemia: A Descriptive and Sentimental Novel, Interspersed with Pieces of Poetry*. The second novel goes so far as to include its own responses to anticipated critical reviews. By the time Dorothy Wordsworth is experimenting with the form, more than twenty years after the sentimental novel reached its height, her concern is more with the stretching of genre than it is with the emotive pretensions Beckford has found laughable in the novels of "scribbling women."

9. This is Homans's formulation of W. Wordsworth's myth of self-origination (*Women Writers*, 71).

10. Liu points out that in the quattrocento landscape tradition Claude Lorrain drew on for defining picturesque paintings the narrative of the Virgin usually dominates the scape. Here, the Annunciation (*Humiliatio*) was conceived as the "submission" of the Virgin, while the *Conturbatio* depicts the moment of her "disquiet" (*Wordsworth*, 67), both moments of deep abjection. George Beaumont

prized his Claude, *Landscape with Hagar and the Angel* (purchased between 1792 and 1795), which the Wordsworths would have known.

11. Fry associates Burke's fear with the romantic introjection of the devil into the human soul, thereby accounting for the impulse toward the sublime in an age characterized by the lyric. Wordsworth cites the (Miltonic) story of Belial as "the most sensual spirit of the fallen Angels" (Owen and Smyser, 2:355) to further elucidate the link between the demonic and Woman.

12. Lacan, "God and the *Jouissance* of Woman," in *Feminine Sexuality*, 147; see esp. 137–48.

13. William's essay "The Sublime and the Beautiful" characterizes the beautiful as that which we see daily and so do not perceive until its presence gradually becomes absorbed; the sublime, in contrast, strikes or hits us immediately.

14. The differences appear to be less critical in William's notebooks, and Liu uses commonplace book and reading notebook interchangeably (*Wordsworth*, 192).

15. "A french Poste is from 5–6 English miles — Each horse is charged 1 1/2 Franc, For three horses 4 1/2, Postilian [*sic*] generally receives 1 1/2–6 Francs = 5ˢ–6 Francs per pound."

16. Thanks to Irene Tayler for this correction.

17. Mary Barker copied several of D. Wordsworth's early poems into her own notebook, and their strengths seemed to support each other as friends. M. Barker had a house built for her in an isolated vale, but the costs outran her savings and she had to retire to the French side of the Channel, a popular route for English bankrupts. However, Mary Barker's spirit can be traced in D. Wordsworth's "Excursion to Ullswater," reprinted as an appendix in W. Wordsworth's *Guide to the Lakes*.

Bibliography

Abrams, M. H. *The Mirror and the Lamp: Romantic Theory and the Critical Tradition.* 1953; New York: Oxford University Press, 1971.

Abrams, M. H. *Natural Supernaturalism: Tradition and Revolution in Romantic Literature.* New York: W. W. Norton, 1971.

Abrams, N. H. "Structure and Style in the Greater Romantic Lyric." In *From Sensibility to Romanticism,* ed. Frederick W. Hilles and Harold Bloom, pp. 527–60. New York: Oxford University Press, 1965.

Addison, Joseph, Richard Steele, et al. *The Spectator.* Edited by Donald F. Bond. Oxford: Clarendon Press, 1965.

Althusser, Louis. *Lenin and Philosophy.* New York: Monthly Review Press, 1971.

Andrews, Malcolm. *The Search for the Picturesque: Landscape Aesthetics and Tourism in Britain, 1760–1800.* Stanford: Stanford University Press, 1989.

Armstrong, Nancy. *Desire and Domestic Fiction: A Political History of the Novel.* New York: Oxford University Press, 1987.

Austen, Jane, *Pride and Prejudice.* Edited by James Kinsley and Frank Bradbrook. Oxford: Oxford University Press, 1984.

Bakhtin, Mikhail. *The Dialogic Imagination.* Translated by Caryl Emerson and Michael Holquist. Austin: University of Texas Press, 1981.

Bakhtin, Mikhail. *Problems of Dostoevsky's Poetics.* Translated and edited by Caryl Emerson. Minneapolis: University of Minnesota Press, 1984.

Barrell, John. *The Idea of Landscape and the Sense of Place, 1730–1840.* Cambridge: Cambridge University Press, 1972.

Bateson, F. W. *Wordsworth: A Reinterpretation.* London: Longman Group, 1954.

Bialostosky, Don H. *Making Tales: The Poetics of Wordsworth's Narrative Experiments.* Chicago: University of Chicago Press, 1984.

Bloom, Harold. *Anxiety of Influence.* New York: Oxford University Press, 1973.

Blythe, Ronald, ed. *William Hazlitt: Selected Writings.* New York: Penguin, 1970.

Burke, Edmund. *A Philosophical Enquiry into the Origin of Our Ideas of the Sublime and Beautiful.* Edited by James T. Boulton. Notre Dame: University of Notre Dame Press, 1968.

Burton, Mary E., ed. *The Letters of Mary Wordsworth, 1800–1855.* Oxford: Clarendon Press, 1958.

Butler, Marilyn. *Romantics, Rebels, and Reactionaries: English Literature and Its Background, 1760–1830.* Oxford: Oxford University Press, 1981.

Byron, George Gordon (Lord Byron). *Manfred.* In *Byron: Poetical Works,* ed. Frederick Page, rev. John Jump. Oxford: Oxford University Press, 1970.

Chandler, James K. *Wordsworth's Second Nature: A Study of the Poetry and Politics.* Chicago: University of Chicago Press, 1984.

Cixous, Hélène, and Catherine Clément. *The Newly Born Woman.* Translated by Betsy Wing. Minneapolis: University of Minnesota Press, 1986.

Cooke, Michael. *The Romantic Will.* New Haven: Yale University Press, 1976.

Curran, Stuart. *Poetic Form and British Romanticism.* New York: Oxford University Press, 1986.

Darlington, Beth, ed. *The Love Letters of William and Mary Wordsworth.* Ithaca: Cornell University Press, 1981.

Dekker, George. *Coleridge and the Literature of Sensibility.* New York: Barnes and Noble, 1978.

de Man, Paul. *Allegories of Reading: Figural Language in Rousseau, Nietzsche, Rilke, and Proust.* New Haven: Yale University Press, 1979.

de Man, Paul. "The Rhetoric of Temporality." In *Blindness and Insight: Essays in the Rhetoric of Contemporary Criticism,* pp. 187–228. Minneapolis: University of Minnesota Press, 1983.

De Quincey, Thomas, *Recollections of the Lakes and the Lake Poets.* London: Penguin, 1970.

Derrida, Jacques. *Writing and Difference.* Translated by Alan Bass. London: Routledge and Kegan Paul, 1978.

de Selincourt, Ernest. *Dorothy Wordsworth: A Biography.* 1933; Oxford: Clarendon Press, 1965.

de Selincourt, Ernest, ed. *The Early Letters of William and Dorothy Wordsworth (1787–1805)*. Oxford: Clarendon Press, 1935.

de Selincourt, Ernest, ed. *George and Sarah Green*. Oxford: Clarendon Press, 1936.

de Selincourt, Ernest, ed. *The Journals of Dorothy Wordsworth*. 2 vols. Oxford: Oxford University Press, 1941.

de Selincourt, Ernest, and Helen Darbyshire, eds. *The Poetical Works of William Wordsworth*. 5 vols. Oxford: Clarendon Press, 1940–49.

de Selincourt, Ernest, Mary Moorman, and Alan G. Hill, eds. *The Letters of William and Dorothy Wordsworth: The Middle Years*. Oxford: Clarendon Press, 1970.

Douglas, Mary. *Purity and Danger*. London: Routledge and Kegan Paul, 1966.

Easthope, Antony. *Poetry as Discourse*. London and New York: Methuen, 1983.

Easthope, Antony. *Poetry and Phantasy*. Cambridge: Cambridge University Press, 1989.

Empson, William. *Some Versions of Pastoral*. 1938; Norfolk, Conn.: New Directions, 1950.

Engell, James, and W. Jackson Bate. *Biographia Literaria: The Collected Works of Samuel Taylor Coleridge*. Vol. 7. Princeton: Princeton University Press, 1983.

Ferguson, Frances. *Wordsworth: Language as Counter-Spirit*. New Haven: Yale University Press, 1977.

Ferry, David. *The Limits of Mortality*. Middletown: Wesleyan University Press, 1959.

Foucault, Michel. *The History of Sexuality*. Vol. 1. Translated by Robert Hurley. New York: Vintage/Random House, 1980.

Friedman, Michael H. *The Making of a Tory Humanist: William Wordsworth and the Idea of Community*. New York: Columbia University Press, 1979.

Froula, Christine. "When Eve Reads Milton: Undoing the Canonical Economy." *Critical Inquiry* 10 (1983):321–47.

Fry, Paul. "The Possession of the Sublime." *Studies in Romanticism* 26 (1987):187–208.

Galperin, William. *Revision and Authority in Wordsworth: The Interpretation of a Career*. Philadelphia: University of Pennsylvania Press, 1989.

Gay, Peter. *The Bourgeois Experience*. Vol. 1. New York: Oxford University Press, 1984.

Gay, Peter. *The Enlightenment, an Interpretation: The Rise of Modern Paganism*. New York: W. W. Norton, 1966.

Gelpi, Barbara Charlesworth. *Shelley's Goddess: Maternity, Language, Subjectivity*. New York: Oxford University Press, 1992.

Gilbert, Sandra, and Susan Gubar. *The Madwoman in the Attic: The Woman Writer and the Nineteenth-Century Literary Imagination*. New Haven: Yale University Press, 1979.

Gill, Stephen. *William Wordsworth: A Life*. Oxford: Oxford University Press, 1989.

Gill, Stephen, ed. *The Oxford Authors: William Wordsworth*. Oxford: Oxford University Press, 1984.

Gilpin, William. *Observations relative chiefly to Picturesque Beauty, Made in the Year 1772, on Several Parts of England; particularly the Mountains, and Lakes of Cumberland, and Westmoreland*. London, 1786.

Gilpin, William. *Three Essays: — On Picturesque Beauty; — on Picturesque Travel; and, on Sketching Landscape: to which is added a Poem, on Landscape Painting*. London, 1792.

Gittings, Robert, ed. *Letters of John Keats: A Selection*. 1970; Oxford: Oxford University Press, 1985.

Gittings, Robert, and Jo Manton. *Dorothy Wordsworth*. Oxford: Clarendon Press, 1985.

Goethe, Johann Wolfgang von. *Faust*. Part I. Edited by Philip Wayne. London: Penguin, 1949.

Goethe, Johann Wolfgang von. *Faust*. Part II. Edited by Philip Wayne. London: Penguin, 1959.

Gosse, Edmund, ed. *The Works of Thomas Gray*. Vol. 1. London, 1884.

Hargreaves-Mawdsley, W. N. *The English Della Cruscans and Their Time, 1783–1828*. The Hague: Martinus Nijhoff, 1967.

Hartman, Geoffrey. *Wordsworth's Poetry, 1878–1814*. New Haven: Yale University Press, 1964.

Hayden, John O., ed. *William Wordsworth: The Poems*. 2 vols. New Haven: Yale University Press, 1981.

Heinzelman, Kurt. "The Cult of Domesticity: Dorothy and William Wordsworth at Grasmere." In *Romanticism and Feminism*, ed. Anne K. Mellor, pp. 52–78. Bloomington: Indiana University Press, 1988.

Herrick, Robert. *Poetical Works*. Edited by L. C. Martin. Oxford: Oxford University Press, 1956.

Hertz, Neil. *The End of the Line*. New York: Columbia University Press, 1985.

Holmes, Richard. *Coleridge: Early Visions*. New York: Viking/Penguin, 1989.

Homans, Margaret. *Bearing the Word: Language and Female Experience in Nineteenth-Century Women's Writing*. Chicago: University of Chicago Press, 1986.

Homans, Margaret. *Women Writers and Poetic Identity: Dorothy Wordsworth, Emily Brontë, and Emily Dickinson*. Princeton: Princeton University Press, 1980.

Hooker, Edward, ed. *The Critical Works of John Dennis*. Baltimore: Johns Hopkins University Press, 1939.

Hošek, Chaviva, and Patricia Parker, eds. *Lyric Poetry: Beyond the New Criticism*. Ithaca: Cornell University Press, 1985.

Hunt, Lynn. "The Unstable Boundaries of the French Revolution." In *A History of Private Life,* vol. 4, ed. Michelle Perrot, pp. 13–34. Cambridge, Mass.: Harvard University Press, 1990.

Hutchinson, Thomas, and Ernest de Selincourt, eds. *The Poetical Works of William Wordsworth.* London: Oxford University Press, 1956.

Jacobus, Mary. *Reading Woman: Essays in Feminist Criticism.* New York: Columbia University Press, 1986.

Jacobus, Mary. *Romanticism, Writing, and Sexual Difference: Essays on "The Prelude."* Oxford: Clarendon Press, 1989.

Jameson, Fredric. "Baudelaire as Modernist and Postmodernist: The Dissolution of the Referent and the Artificial 'Sublime.'" In *Lyric Poetry: Beyond the New Criticism,* ed. Chaviva Hošek and Patricia Parker, pp. 247–63.

Johnston, Kenneth R., Gilbert Chaitin, Karen Hanson, and Herbert Marks, eds. *Romantic Revolutions: Criticism and Theory.* Bloomington: Indiana University Press, 1990.

Kant, Immanuel. *Critique of Judgement.* Translated by J. H. Bernard. New York: Hafner/Macmillan, 1951.

Klancher, Jon. *The Making of English Reading Audiences, 1790–1832.* Madison: University of Wisconsin Press, 1987.

Knight, William, ed. *The Poetical Works of William Wordsworth.* 11 vols. Edinburgh: W. Paterson, 1882–89.

Kristeva, Julia. *Desire in Language: A Semiotic Approach to Literature and Art.* Translated by Thomas Gora, Alice Jardine, and Leon S. Roudiez. New York: Columbia University Press, 1980.

Kristeva, Julia. *Powers of Horror: An Essay on Abjection.* Translated by Leon S. Roudiez. New York: Columbia University Press, 1982.

Kristeva, Julia. *Revolution in Poetic Language.* Translated by Margaret Waller. New York: Columbia University Press, 1984.

Kristeva, Julia. *Strangers to Ourselves.* Translated by Leon S. Roudiez. New York: Columbia University Press, 1991.

Kristeva, Julia. *Tales of Love.* Translated by Leon S. Roudiez. New York: Columbia University Press, 1987.

Lacan, Jacques. *Ecrits.* Translated by Alan Sheridan. New York: W. W. Norton, 1977.

Lacan, Jacques. *Feminine Sexuality.* Edited by Juliet Mitchell and Jacqueline Rose. New York: W. W. Norton, 1982.

Lacoue-Labarthe, Philippe. "On the Sublime," including Jean-François Lyotard's "A Response" and "Philippe Lacoue-Labarthe Responds." Translated by Geoff Bennington. In *Postmodernism: ICA Documents,* ed. Lisa Appignanesi, pp. 11–18. London: Free Association Books, 1989.

Langbauer, Laurie. *Women and Romance: The Consolations of Gender in the English Novel.* Ithaca: Cornell University Press, 1990.

Lerner, Gerda. *The Creation of Patriarchy.* Oxford: Oxford University Press, 1986.

Levin, Susan M. *Dorothy Wordsworth and Romanticism.* New Brunswick: Rutgers State University Press, 1987.

Levin, Susan M. "Subtle Fire: Dorothy Wordsworth's Prose and Poetry." *Massachusetts Review* 21 (1980):345–63.

Levinson, Marjorie. *The Romantic Fragment Poem.* Chapel Hill: University of North Carolina Press, 1986.

Levinson, Marjorie. *Wordsworth's Great Period Poems.* Cambridge: Cambridge University Press, 1986.

Liu, Alan. "On the Autobiographical Present: Dorothy Wordsworth's *Grasmere Journals.*" *Criticism* 26 (1984):115–37.

Liu, Alan. *Wordsworth: The Sense of History.* Stanford: Stanford University Press, 1989.

Longinus. "On the Sublime." In *Aristotle, Horace, Longinus: Classical Literary Criticism.* 1965; Harmondsworth: Penguin, 1984.

Loughrey, Bryan. *The Pastoral Mode.* London: Macmillan, 1984.

Lovell, Terry. *Consuming Fiction.* London: Verso Press, 1987.

Lyotard, Jean-François. "Complexity and the Sublime." Translated by Geoff Bennington. In *Postmodernism: ICA Documents,* ed. Lisa Appignanesi, pp. 19–26. London: Free Association Books, 1989.

McGann, Jerome J. *The Beauty of Inflections: Literary Investigations in Historical Method and Theory.* Oxford: Clarendon Press, 1985.

McGann, Jerome J. "'My Brain Is Feminine': Byron and the Poetry of Deception." In *Byron: Augustan and Romantic,* ed. Andrew Rutherford, pp. 26–51. New York: St. Martin's Press, 1990.

McGann, Jerome J. *The Romantic Ideology: A Critical Investigation.* Chicago: University of Chicago Press, 1982.

Manning, Peter J. *Reading Romantics: Text and Context.* New York: Oxford University Press, 1990.

Mavor, Elizabeth. *The Ladies of Llangollen.* 1971; Harmondsworth: Penguin Books, 1983.

Matlak, Richard. "Classical Argument and Romantic Persuasion in 'Tintern Abbey.'" *Studies in Romanticism* 25 (Spring 1986): 97–129.

Mellor, Anne K. *English Romantic Irony.* Cambridge, Mass.: Harvard University Press, 1980.

Mellor, Anne K. *Romanticism and Gender.* New York: Routledge, 1993.

Mellor, Anne K., ed. *Romanticism and Feminism.* Bloomington: Indiana University Press, 1988.

Mitchell, L. G. *The Writings and Speeches of Edmund Burke.* Vol. 6. Oxford: Clarendon Press, 1989.

Mitchell, W. J. T. *Iconology: Image, Text, Ideology.* Chicago: University of Chicago Press, 1986.

Monk, Samuel. *The Sublime: A Study of Critical Theories in XVIII-Century England*. Ann Arbor: University of Michigan Press, 1960.

Moorman, Mary. *William Wordsworth: A Biography*. Oxford: Clarendon Press, 1957.

Moorman, Mary, ed. *Journals of Dorothy Wordsworth*. London: Oxford University Press, 1971.

Murdoch, John. *The Discovery of the Lake District: A Northern Arcadia and Its Uses*. London: Victoria and Albert Museum, 1984.

Murdoch, John. "The Landscape of Labor: Transformations of the Georgic." In *Romantic Revolutions: Criticism and Theory,* ed. Kenneth R. Johnston et al., pp. 176–93. Bloomington: Indiana University Press, 1990.

Nabholtz, John R. "Dorothy Wordsworth and the Picturesque." *Studies in Romanticism* 3 (1964):118–28.

Nye, Andrea. "Woman Clothed with the Sun: Julia Kristeva and the Escape from/to Language." *Signs* 12 (1987): 664–86.

Onorato, Richard J. *The Character of the Poet: Wordsworth in "The Prelude."* Princeton: Princeton University Press, 1971.

Ortner, Sherry B. "Is Female to Male as Nature Is to Culture?" In *Woman, Culture, and Society,* ed. Michelle Z. Rosaldo and Louise Lamphere, pp. 76–87. Stanford: Stanford University Press, 1974.

Ortner, Sherry B., and Harriet Whitehead. "Accounting for Sexual Meanings." In *Sexual Meanings: The Cultural Construction of Gender and Sexuality,* ed. Ortner and Whitehead, pp. 1–28. Cambridge: Cambridge University Press, 1981.

Owen, W. J. B., and Jane Worthington Smyser, eds. *The Prose Works of William Wordsworth*. 3 vols. Oxford: Clarendon Press, 1974.

Poovey, Mary. *The Proper Lady and the Woman Writer: Ideology as Style in the Works of Mary Wollstonecraft, Mary Shelley, and Jane Austen*. Chicago: University of Chicago Press, 1984.

Price, Uvedale. *An Essay on the Picturesque as Compared to the Sublime and the Beautiful*. London, 1794.

Reed, Arden, ed. *Romanticism and Language*. Ithaca: Cornell University Press, 1984.

Rose, Phyllis. *Parallel Lives: Five Victorian Marriages*. New York: Vintage Books, 1983.

Ross, Marlon B. *The Contours of Masculine Desire: Romanticism and the Rise of Women's Poetry*. New York: Oxford University Press, 1989.

Ross, Marlon B. "Naturalizing Gender: Woman's Place in Wordsworth's Ideological Landscape." *ELH* 53 (1986):391–410.

Rousseau, Jean-Jacques. *Emile; or, On Education*. London: J. M. Dent, 1974.

Rousseau, Jean-Jacques. *The Reveries of the Solitary Walker*. Translated by Charles Butterworth. New York: New York University Press, 1979.

Saint-Pierre, Jacques Henri Bernardin de. *Paul et Virginie.* Translated by Raymond Hein. Mauritius: Editions de l'Ocean Indien, Moka, 1788.

Schapiro, Barbara. *The Romantic Mother: Narcissistic Patterns in Romantic Poetry.* Baltimore: Johns Hopkins University Press, 1983.

Schor, Naomi. *Reading in Detail: Aesthetics and the Feminine.* New York: Methuen, 1987.

Sedgwick, Eve Kosofsky. *Epistemology of the Closet.* Berkeley: University of California Press, 1990.

Shaver, Chester L., Mary Moorman, and Alan G. Hill, eds. *The Letters of William and Dorothy Wordsworth.* Vol. 1, *The Early Years, 1787–1805;* vol. 2, *The Middle Years, 1806–1820.* Rev. ed. 6 vols. Oxford: Clarendon Press, 1967–82.

Shaver, Chester L., and Alice C. Shaver. *Wordsworth's Library: A Catalogue.* New York: Garland, 1979.

Smith, Charlotte. *Ethelinde; or, The Recluse of the Lake.* 3 vols. Dublin: printed for H. Chamberlaine et al., 1790.

Spivak, Gayatri Chakrovorty. *In Other Worlds: Essays in Cultural Politics.* New York: Methuen, 1987.

Spivak, Gayatri Chakrovorty. *The Post-Colonial Critic: Interviews, Strategies, Dialogues.* Edited by Sarah Harasym. New York: Routledge, 1990.

Squiers, Michael. *The Pastoral Novel: Studies in George Eliot, Thomas Hardy, and D. H. Lawrence.* Charlottesville: University Press of Virginia, 1975.

Stocking, Marion Kingston, ed. *The Journals of Claire Clairmont.* Cambridge, Mass.: Harvard University Press, 1968.

Thorburn, David, and Geoffrey Hartman, eds. *Romanticism: Vistas, Instances, Continuities.* Ithaca: Cornell University Press, 1973.

Todd, Janet. *The Sign of Angellica: Women, Writing, and Fiction, 1660–1800.* New York: Columbia University Press, 1989.

Vološinov, V. N. *Freudianism: A Critical Sketch.* Translated by I. R. Titunik; edited by Titunik and Neal Bruss. Bloomington: Indiana University Press, 1987.

Wasserman, Earl. "The English Romantics: The Grounds of Knowledge." In *Romanticism: Points of View,* ed. Robert F. Gleckner and Gerald E. Enscoe, pp. 331–46. 1962; Detroit: Wayne State University Press, 1979.

Weiskel, Thomas. *The Romantic Sublime: Studies in the Structure and Psychology of Transcendence.* Baltimore: Johns Hopkins University Press, 1976.

West, Thomas. *A Guide to the Lakes in Cumberland, Westmorland, and Lancashire.* London, 1778.

Williams, Anne. *Prophetic Strain: The Greater Lyric in the Eighteenth Century.* Chicago: University of Chicago Press, 1984.

Williams, Raymond. *The Country and the City.* New York: Oxford University Press, 1982.

Wolfson, Susan J. "Individual in Community: Dorothy Wordsworth in Conversation with William." In *Romanticism and Feminism,* ed. Anne K. Mellor, pp. 139–66. Bloomington: Indiana University Press, 1988.

Wollheim, Richard. "What the Spectator Sees." In *Visual Theory: Painting and Interpretation,* ed. Norman Bryson, Michael Ann Holly, and Keith Moxey, pp. 101–50. New York: Polity Press/Harper Collins, 1991.

Woof, Pamela. "Dorothy Wordsworth, Writer." *Wordsworth Circle* 17 (1986): 95–110.

Woof, Pamela, ed. *The Grasmere Journals.* Oxford: Clarendon Press, 1991.

Wordsworth, Dorothy. DCMS 120. Commonplace Book. Notebooks held in the Dove Cottage Library, Wordsworth Trust, Grasmere.

Wordsworth, Jonathan, M. H. Abrams, and Stephen Gill, eds. *The Prelude: 1799, 1805, 1850.* New York: W. W. Norton, 1979.

Index